Raising Capital:
How To Write A Financing Proposal

By Lawrence Flanagan

Published by The Oasis Press
Grants Pass, Oregon

Published by The Oasis Press®
300 North Valley Drive
Grants Pass, OR 97526

Copyright 1993 by Lawrence Flanagan

All rights reserved.

No part of this work may be reproduced or used in any form or by any means, graphic, electronic or mechanical, including photocopying, recording, taping, or information storage and retrieval systems without written permission of the publishers.

This publication is designed to provide accurate and authoritative information in regard to the subject matter covered. It is sold with the understanding that the publisher is not engaged in rendering legal, accounting, or other professional service. If legal advice or other expert assistance is required, the services of a competent professional person should be sought.
— *from a declaration of principles jointly adopted by a committee of the American Bar Association and a committee of publishers.*

The names of companies, individuals, and events presented in this book are fictitious and any resemblance to actual persons, businesses, or events is purely coincidental.

Please direct any comments, questions, or suggestions regarding this book to:

The Oasis Press/PSI Research
300 North Valley Drive
Grants Pass, OR 97526
(503) 479-9464
(800) 228-2275

The Oasis Press is a Registered Trademark of Publishing Services, Inc., an Oregon corporation doing business as PSI Research.

ISBN: 1-55571-305-X (paperback)
       1-55571-306-8 (3-ring binder)

Printed in the United States of America

First edition   10 9 8 7 6 5 4 3 2 1   Revision Code: 93AA

 Printed on recycled paper when available.

Table of Contents

Introduction		vii
Chapter 1	There Is A Plan to Meet Your Financing Needs	1
Chapter 2	How To Present Your Proposal	5
Chapter 3	Some Additional Suggestions to Help You	11
Chapter 4	A Business Plan Guide	13

Appendices

Appendix A	The Private Placement Circular For New Life Publications, Inc.	15
Appendix B	Prospectus For A Small Public Offering — Earth Stabilizers, Inc.	53
Appendix C	A Limited Partnership Circular — VBF American Ginseng Crop 1991	89
Appendix D	A Private Placement Circular — Shorewood Press, Inc.	127
Appendix E	Prospectus For A Large Public Offering — American Pipeline Services, Inc.	161
Appendix F	Bank Or Private Loan Proposal — The Birchwood Logging Company, Inc.	199
Index		221

Dedication

To Tara, Kelly, Cindi and Chari

About The Author

Lawrence Flanagan's background spans over 35 years in business management and he has worn virtually all of the hats in the corporate world. A few years ago, he elected to pursue his hobby as a writer, but continues to enjoy helping entrepreneurs grow their businesses as a consultant in the Minneapolis/St. Paul metropolitan area. His specialties include reorganization, financial counseling and the development of marketing strategies for his clients.

He is also the author of *What Every Executive Should Know About Preparing and Using A Cash Flow Forecast*, published by Dartnell; has recently completed the latest annual edition of *The Money Connection: Where and How to Apply for Business Loans and Venture Capital*, and is currently writing a new book about marketing strategies for small businesses.

His other hobbies include botanical farming at the family's wilderness retreat in Northern Minnesota, minerals prospecting and fishing. He and his wife, Lindi, have four grown children and four grandchildren.

Introduction

The purpose of this book is to help the entrepreneur who wishes to secure a business loan or raise venture capital to finance a new enterprise or expand an existing one.

Chapters 1-4 describe the types of documents used to secure loans and investment capital; discuss the components needed to develop a comprehensive financing proposal; offer several suggestions that will help you write it, and explain how to present your case.

Appendices A-F provides six examples of various financing proposals that will help you understand how they are written and what information should be included for the type of financing required. The proposals presented are:

(1) A Private Placement Circular for New Life Publications, Inc., a company in formation that is seeking either a business loan or equity investment;

(2) A Public Offering Prospectus for Earth Stabilizers, Inc., a newly formed company seeking public investors to begin operations;

(3) A Limited Partnership Circular for VBF American Ginseng Crop 1992, a botanical farming corporation seeking limited partners to invest in a specific crop;

(4) A Private Placement Circular for Shorewood Press, Inc., a currently operating publishing company seeking investors to finance its expansion plans;

(5) A Public Offering Prospectus for American Pipeline Services, Inc., a new company in formation that needs public investors to commence its national and international operations; and

(6) A Bank Financing Proposal for The Birchwood Logging Company, Inc., a new company requiring a bank or private business loan to finance its proposed logging and firewood inventories for resale.

Deciding which financing approach to take depends on the capital needs of your company or proposed business, its current assets or the investment you and others are willing to commit to it, the personal collateral you and others can pledge if you are seeking a loan, and whether or not you are willing to give up a portion of the company's equity to raise funds through a public or private offering of its shares.

Very often, it is difficult for an entrepreneur to accept the fact that when searching for public or private funds to capitalize a business, a certain portion of the equity ownership must be sold to secure venture capital. And, depending upon the amount of the financing one needs, the stock equity to be given up hinges on the type of business involved, the level of risk, the competition, its growth potential and how much capital the owner, entrepreneur and others have invested or are willing to invest in the enterprise.

Regardless of the strategy one chooses to raise financing capital, the first step is to prepare a proposal that fully explains the business, its objectives, and how the loan or investment proceeds will be used. If you are searching for investors to purchase stock in your company or in a limited partnership, be sure to discuss the legal requirements with your attorney and the securities commission or department in your state before attempting such an offering. There are many federal and state regulations that govern partnerships, public and private sales of stock, and retaining an experienced lawyer who specializes in corporate law, plus the guidance of a qualified accountant is absolutely essential. This book is not intended to replace that kind of professional assistance.

Having said that, and by thinking through and writing your own proposal, private placement circular or prospectus, you can literally save thousands of dollars in fees that would otherwise have to be spent for an *expert* to prepare it from scratch.

Once the first acceptable draft has been completed, present a copy of it to your attorney and accountant for their comments for review. After receiving their recommendations, the revised plan can then be submitted to your state securities authorities and to a prospective underwriter, if underwriting services are needed to raise the funds.

While legal advice is generally not required when preparing a proposal to secure a business loan, you may want your attorney and accountant to *look over* the document and the financial statements before commencing a search for prospective lenders. Their suggestions could prove extremely valuable.

Securing capital to finance or expand a business today definitely requires a well documented plan or proposal, a strong personal commitment and perseverance.

Certainly the creation of a loan proposal, circular or prospectus takes time and patience, but the great majority of entrepreneurs who have written their own are quick to say "it saved them money and was worth the trouble." And, if a prospective lender or investor knows that you personally prepared the plan, it will demonstrate that you have given the project careful thought and have the management ability to carry it out.

If you are experiencing difficulty in finding good sources for startup or expansion capital, and need a comprehensive listing to contact, you might want to consider my book *The Money Connection: Where and How to Apply for Business Loans and Venture Capital.* Updated annually, it offers hundreds of excellent financing sources located throughout the United States and includes detailed information about the most current federal, state, county and community loan and investment programs available. Call The Oasis Press at 1-800-228-2275 for more information.

I sincerely hope the information presented in the following pages will serve as a useful guide when writing your plan and that it makes your financing quest an easier one.

Lawrence Flanagan

Chapter 1
There Is A Plan To Meet Your Financing Needs

This book covers four of the most common types of proposals one can use to raise venture capital and loans. The first is the *Financing Proposal*, which is generally used by a new or existing business to secure a loan from an individual, bank or other lending institution.

The second is a *Private Placement Circular*, sometimes called a *Private Placement Memorandum* or a *Private Placement Offering*, which is often utilized to raise funds for a business in the form of a loan and the sale of stock. When used to obtain investment capital for a business, this type of *offering* is limited to a small number of private investors — as regulated by the SEC and each state's securities department. Usually, the intended purpose is to raise funds in exchange for a equity position in a company's stock, but it can be used to secure a loan or a combination of the two.

The third type of financing proposal is a *Prospectus* or *Public Offering Circular* which is used to raise capital from the general public. A specific number of shares are offered at a predetermined price and the *proceeds*, less the expenses of the offering, are used by a company for its specified operating needs and working capital. A public offering can be small or very large, but all are regulated by the Securities and Exchange Commission and by each state's securities department. Generally, a public offering is underwritten by a underwriter or brokerage house who conducts and manages the sale of shares.

The fourth type is the *Limited Partnership Offering* — which is used to solicit a limited number of investors to participate in a business enterprise that is managed by a general partner. The limited partnership described in **Appendix C** focuses on selling limited shares in a specific botanical crop, but a similar proposal could be written to sell equity shares in an apartment building, shopping center, business or anything of value that will generate income. The funds raised through the sale of a limited partnership's shares are used by the general partner to finance and manage the affairs of the partnership, and as with a private or public offering, the investment usually involves a moderate to high degree of risk. In some instances, the law requires that the personal net worth of a subscribing limited partner must be sufficient to sustain the possible loss of his or her investment should the business of the partnership fail.

After you have reviewed the six proposals presented in the appendices, you should be able to decide which financing strategy will best meet your personal preference and your company's needs. Once this decision has been made, you can begin drafting the outline for your proposal. The next chapter discusses this process in detail, but before going into it, there are some important things you should know before you begin.

Be Brief But Informative

It is vital that your proposal tells the prospective lender or investor the *Who, What, Why* and *Where* about your business, but it should also be written with brevity and without exaggeration. There is nothing worse than a proposal that rambles on for a hundred pages, when the *important* information could have been presented in fifty pages or less.

In some cases, especially when writing a public or private offering circular or a limited partnership prospectus, certain information is required by law and must be included. While some of this information is *boiler plate legalese* and may seem repetitious and even *boring* to you, the styles in which I have presented it will help your circular conform to the accepted criteria established by the SEC, your state's securities department and the underwriter. If you are in doubt about writing any particular segment of the circular or proposal, leave it blank until you have discussed it with your attorney and accountant, and of course the underwriter if one is participating in the offering.

Write In The Third Person

With the possible exception of a loan proposal, always present your information in the *third person*. This means leaving out all of the first and second person references such a *I, we, our, ourselves, us* and so on. Refer to the company as a separate entity by using it's full name, abbreviated name, "the Company" or as "it." After all, a corporation is an entity in its own right and "it" is the enterprise seeking financing, not you. This arms-length approach to writing the proposal will help you avoid any personal financial repercussions should the business fall on hard times or fail. Likewise, even though you probably intend to manage the company, always refer to yourself and those associated with it as the *management, directors and employees*. In other words, even if you and others own the business, you are, in essence, working for the entity, not visa versa. There are some sections of all proposals that do require the names of the current owners, shareholders, directors and officers and key employees of a business and they should be included when it is appropriate to do so.

Include The Risk Factors

With the exception of a proposal written to secure a business loan (usually granted only if the borrower has the necessary collateral, some assets to pledge or a co-signer), all other circulars should include the *risk factors* associated with the investment being solicited. The reason is simple. If something does go wrong with the business, at least the investors were warned that their investment might be lost, and if the funds raised were properly used by management, they generally cannot make a claim against the company other than for their possible share of the assets, if any, should the company enter a Chapter 7 bankruptcy, be liquidated or dissolved. Disclosing the risk factors is required in a public or private stock offering and in limited partnership investment circulars. If the idea of discussing the weaknesses of your company makes you uneasy, remember that most experienced investors are *used to* seeing the risk factors mentioned in prospectuses and will hardly give them a second thought if they like what they read in the rest of the document and the investment, albeit a risk, appeals to them.

Credible Financial Statements

While unaudited financial statements may be acceptable to some lenders if they match your tax returns and have been prepared by an outside accounting firm, most want an independent certified public accountant's view of your business. Audited financials are required for public stock offerings and limited partnership solicitations, and should be included with private placement proposals as well. Audits do cost money and before you decide to have one done by a CPA firm, contact your attorney, accountant and the underwriter, when necessary, to discuss the feasibility of raising the funds you need. Armed with their assessment for a successful offering, you will know whether or not to call in the number crunchers.

It is also important to realize that any CPA firm can perform the audit and that the cost can vary considerably depending on the firm you hire. A new business with no history requires very little auditing work, but one with a history and no previous audits can be an expensive proposition. I recommend requesting a firm quote before contracting this work to be done. And, be sure that the auditor's report you receive includes the *auditor's opinion letter* — sometimes called a *comfort letter* in accounting circles — since it and the audited statements must be exhibited in the prospectus or circular.

Most lenders requesting a personal financial statement from you or a co-signer, will accept an unaudited statement of your assets less liabilities, but may also want to see your personal tax returns for the past three years. It is therefore a good idea to gather this information together *before* applying for a loan in order to speed up the process. When a private placement circular is used to secure a loan and an equity investment, most private investors and institutions that make investments, will routinely request copies of your business tax returns for the past three years, and a few may want to see your personal returns as well — especially if the company is an *S Corporation* or a *Sole Proprietorship*.

These requests are not an assault on your personal integrity, character or honesty. They are nothing more than sound business practices that enable the lender or investor to make a financing decision. Rest assured that all of the information you provide will be kept confidential.

Chapter 2
How To Present Your Proposal

The Financing Proposal

Used primarily to secure a loan from a individual, bank or other lending institution, the *Financing Proposal* must include complete information about your business, current financial statements and detailed proforma (projected) financial statements that demonstrate that the loan will adequately meet the needs of the company and that it will be able to repay the debt with interest over a specified period of time. Please see the proposal for The Birchwood Logging Company, Inc. in **Appendix F**.

The Financing Proposal should include:

1. Cover Page

2. Table of Contents

3. A Summary
   A concise summary of the proposal which can be read quickly.

4. The Company
   A brief history of the company, its type of organization, management, stock ownership, the loan needed, how the proceeds will be used, collateral offered and the terms desired.

5. Business of the Company
   Fully describe your business, current ownership, products and services, markets, competition, management's background and compensation, employees, equipment owned, patents and other intangible assets and property owned, mortgaged or leased.

6. Financial Statements (Exhibits)
   Provide a personal financial statement (if requested); a current balance sheet and income statement; proforma balance sheets, profit and loss statements, sales forecasts and cash flow forecasts for at least three years into the future. If the business is small, include your business and personal income tax returns for the past three years and indicate whether or not the current business financial statements are audited or unaudited. If audited, include the auditor's opinion letter.

7. Other Exhibits
   These could include letters of support, testimonials, product or service literature, letters from suppliers, copies of contracts, equipment purchase quotes from vendors, photographs, drawings, patent abstracts, etc.

The Private Placement Circular

Also referred to as a *Private Placement Memorandum* or a *Private Placement Offering*, this proposal is generally used when a company is seeking a limited number of private investors to provide financing in exchange for a equity position in the company's stock. It can also be worded more broadly to include a possible loan, the sale of shares or a combination of both in order to raise the proceeds required.

The Private Placement Circular also has the flexibility of being able to offer business projections in the form of proforma statements, however, it should be written in a more formal style and include the *risk factors* previously mentioned. The proposals for New Life Publications, Inc. (**Appendix A**) and Shorewood Press, Inc. (**Appendix D**) demonstrate the methods one can use to prepare this type of presentation.

The Private Placement Circular should include:

1. Cover Page of the circular announcement
2. Table of Contents
3. A Summary of the Private Placement Circular or Memorandum
4. A Description of the Company
5. Risk Factors
6. Business of the Company
   Include details about your products/services, production costs, markets, competition, employees, property, patents, copyrights and intangible assets.
7. Dilution of Stock
8. Use of Proceeds
9. Background of Management
   Include details about employees.
10. Controlling Shareholders
11. Capitalization
12. Remuneration of Officers and Directors
13. Description of Stock and Other Information
    Include detailed information about the company's stock, dividend policy, rights and provisions of the stockholders, litigation pending, name and addresses of legal counsel and the auditing firm preparing the financial statements as well as the procedures for purchasing the shares offered.
14. Financial Statements
    Include a current balance sheet and income statement and proforma statements for three years into the future (i.e., balance sheets, profit and loss statements, cash flow forecasts, sales forecasts, payroll and inventory schedules). The more financial information presented, the better. Be sure to state on the current balance sheet and income statement if they are audited or unaudited. If audited, include the auditor's opinion letter. Do not include your business or personal income tax returns unless they have been requested.
15. Exhibits
    Provide any supporting documents that will help the investor understand your business. These might include brochures, product/service catalogs, supporting letters, testimonials, vendor letters confirming prices or quotations, photographs, patent abstracts, copyrights, drawings and photographs.

The Public Offering Circular

Used exclusively to sell stock in a company, the Public Offering Circular or Prospectus is a formal, binding and legal document. Depending on the amount of money a company needs to raise, a public offering of its shares may be the only option available to secure financing. Public offerings are regulated by the Securities and Exchange Commission and each state's securities commission or department.

In addition to preparing the circular, a company must also file a Registration Statement with the SEC and provide audited financial statements in its circular. Generally, the services of an underwriter (brokerage house) are required to manage the sale of shares to be offered. The underwriter's fees and unaccountable expenses must be negotiated prior to printing the circular because the details of these negotiations are included in it.

There are thousands of small companies that have successfully conducted a public offering without the services of an underwriter, but unless you have experience in selling securities and the investor contacts, the attempt could meet with failure.

The first step is to write the initial draft of the circular and have your attorney review it. After the revised document has been completed, you can begin shopping for a underwriter to represent the company. Once you have overcome this hurdle, the formal prospectus or circular is finalized and submitted to the SEC together with the Registration Statement and audited financials for their review and comments. While the SEC does not approve or disapprove an offering, they can require you to present additional information in the circular or delete certain misleading and inappropriate statements.

The entire process for a public offering — from the date a decision is made to attempt it, to the final closing of the sale of shares — can take between four and twelve months to complete. Since there is seldom a guarantee that all of the shares offered will be sold, one must be aware that the up-front expenses such as legal, auditing, filing fees, printing and the underwriter's unaccountable expenses will be lost if the offering is not successful. Therefore, and before choosing this financing option, discuss it thoroughly with your lawyer, auditor and a experienced underwriter who has managed several Initial Public Offerings (IPOs) in the past.

For a small public offering, see the prospectus for Earth Stabilizers, Inc. and for a larger one, see the circular for American Pipeline Services, Inc. in **Appendix E**.

The Public Offering Circular must include:

1. The Cover or The Offering Announcement
2. Referral Notes to the information presented on the cover
3. Table of Contents
4. Prospectus Summary
5. The Company
6. Special Considerations (if any)
7. Risk Factors
8. Dilution and Other Comparative
   Show the dilution values of shares purchased by the public investors.
9. Use of Proceeds
10. Business of the Company
11. Equipment and Services
12. Marketing
13. Competition
14. Property
15. Intangible Assets
16. Management and Controlling Shareholders
17. Capitalization
18. Transactions With Management & Management Compensation
19. Special Agreements
    An example of a special agreement might be that some of the proceeds will be used to buy the assets of another company.
20. Description of Common and Preferred Stock
21. Underwriting
    This information is provided by the underwriter.
22. Underwriter's Warrants
    It is not uncommon for a company to offer warrants to an underwriter to purchase a certain number of the company's shares within a specified period of time, at a predetermined price. Usually, this arrangement is offered to the underwriter as an inducement to represent the company or is considered to be a partial payment for services rendered. A good description can be found in the

prospectus for American Pipeline Services, Inc. in **Appendix E**.

23. Legal Matters
24. Litigation
25. Experts and Escrow Agent
26. For Further Information
27. Financial Statements
    Financial Statements must include the auditor's opinion letter, a audited balance sheet, statement of operations for the current and preceding three years, a statement of the current stockholders' equity and the auditor's notes to the financial statements. Other statements can include a current cash flow statement, a statement of changes in the company's financial position, a statement of increase or decrease in working capital and certain changes in the components of working capital. They CANNOT include projections of future revenues and expenses.
28. Exhibits
    The types of exhibits that can be presented in a public offering prospectus are limited, but many companies do provide photographs of specialized equipment, products, business facilities, drawings and patent abstracts when appropriate. The underwriter can tell you what is and is not acceptable by the SEC.

The Limited Partnership Circular

Similar in some ways to the Private Placement Circular, the Limited Partnership Prospectus is geared to a specific number of investors who invest capital for shares of ownership as limited partners in a partnership managed and controlled by a general partner. To better understand how such a partnership works, review the Limited Partnership Circular presented for VBF American Ginseng Crop 1991 in **Appendix C**.

All partnership offerings must conform to certain state and federal regulations and it is strongly recommended that the services of legal counsel be retained to provide the advice and guidance needed prior to making such a offering to the general public.

The Limited Partnership Circular must include:

1. The Cover or Announcement Page
2. The Circular's Purpose
3. A Brief Statement About Investment Suitability
4. A Brief Statement About Subscription Procedures
5. Table of Contents
6. Photographs or Drawings (optional)
7. Summary of the Partnership and the Offering
8. Risk Factors
9. Fiduciary Responsibilities of the General Partner
10. No Future Contributions
11. Accounting
12. Summary of Estimated Cash Proceeds
13. Potential Return for Investors (Not Guaranteed)
14. The Partnership (a complete description)
15. The General Partner (a complete description)
16. The Business of the Partnership
17. Marketing
18. Competition
19. Directors and Officers of the General Partner

20. Shareholders of the General Partner
21. Balance Sheet of the General Partner
22. Exhibit A — Partnership Agreement/Certificate of Limited Partnership
23. Schedule A to the Partnership Agreement/Certificate of Limited Partnership
24. Exhibit B — Subscription Agreement
25. Exhibit C — Investment Letter to the Partnership
26. Exhibit D — Estimated Expenses of the General Partner

Note: Depending on the state in which you live, more detailed financial information may be required about the General Partner.

Chapter 3
Some Additional Suggestions To Help You

Other than a public offering prospectus, which should be printed, a proposal to raise venture capital or a business loan must be typed or prepared on a letter quality computer printer. I personally believe that double spacing the text makes it easier to read, but single spacing is acceptable by most lenders and investors. Do not double space the information presented in the financial section or the exhibits, and be sure to number each page and include a table of contents.

If you intend to bind the proposal in a cover that requires holes to be punched or a binder on the left side of the document, allow a minimum margin on all pages of one and a half to two inches on that side. Although a fancy cover or jacket is not required, an inexpensive cover will *dress up* your proposal and give it a professional appearance.

Make several copies of the proposal for submission to prospective lenders, venture capital firms and individual investors, and keep the original in a safe place so that more copies can be made if necessary. Always include a brief cover letter with each proposal you mail or hand out, and if you mail them, use first class postage to ensure prompt and safe delivery.

Searching for Financing Sources?

If finding prospective financing sources has been a problem, my book *The Money Connection: Where and How to Apply for Business Loans and Venture Capital* can help you. It offers a number of tips for entrepreneurs and small businesses seeking capital and provides hundreds of excellent, nationally recognized sources to contact. *The Money Connection* is updated annually and if your bookstore does not have it in stock, you can order a copy from the publisher as mentioned in the Introduction to this book.

How to Save Some Money

While preparing a good financing proposal does involve advance planning, some accounting knowledge, patience and writing ability, the six circulars detailed in **Appendix A-F** will give you a better understanding of how the information should be presented. By taking the time to write your own, you will gain a unique insight into the strengths and weaknesses of your business, and by addressing these issues honestly, your proposal will be far more credible to a prospective lender or investor. After all, no one knows your business better than you do and even if the decision is made to hire an attorney, accountant or consultant to write the first draft, they will not be able to accomplish the task without requiring a great deal of your time, assistance and cooperation. And, their services could cost you several thousands of dollars.

If instead, you write the initial draft yourself and *then* present it to your lawyer, accountant and a underwriter (if one is participating) for their comments, additions, corrections and modifications, you will reduce the costs significantly. To give you an idea of the savings involved, it is not uncommon for a good business lawyer to charge a minimum fee of $10,000 to $20,000 plus expenses to write a brief prospectus or financing proposal. At first blush, this may seem fairly reasonable considering the number of hours entailed to write one, but more often than not, once a lawyer or a consultant has completed the document, the business owner or entrepreneur may find that major portions of it have to be *rewritten* because the *expert* obviously didn't have a good understanding about the business or the products and services it provides or intends to offer.

This is not to suggest that the professional services of an experienced business attorney are unnecessary. One is most definitely needed for his or her *legal expertise* and to be certain that your prospectus, circular or proposal conforms with the laws and regulations of the state in which you live, the federal government and when appropriate, the Securities and Exchange Commission.

When hiring a Certified Pubic Accountant to audit your company's financials, always obtain a firm quote for the services to be provided. If you are starting a new business, the fee to provide you with an audited balance sheet and an opinion letter should be modest. If, on the other hand, the business has a lengthy history and has never been audited, you could be required to furnish audited statements for the past three years of operation. And, depending upon the size of the business, the expense could be significant. In this event, the best approach is to solicit quotes from at least three reputable CPA firms in your community and then select the most reasonable offer based on your needs. The savings could prove to be worth the extra effort involved.

Chapter 4
A Business Plan Guide

Although a proposal to raise financing and a business plan are similar in many respects, a financing proposal is actually a brief, tightly written summary of a more comprehensive business strategy plan.

Some private investors may request a copy of your business plan before making a commitment and the following guideline will help you write one.

Components Of A Business Plan

1. **The Summary**
    - A. Business Description
        - — name of enterprise
        - — location and plant description
        - — products and services
        - — markets and competition
        - — management
        - — key employees
    - B. Business Goals

2. **Market Analysis**
    - A. Description of Markets
    - B. Industry Trends
    - C. Special or Target Markets
    - D. Competition
    - E. Potential New Markets
    - F. Test Marketing Projects

3. **Products and Services**
    - A. Description of Products/Services
    - B. Proprietary Assets
        - — patents
        - — copyrights
        - — technologies
    - B. Proprietary Assets (continued)
        - — technical capabilities
        - — new product/service development
    - C. Comparisons of Products/Services to Those of the Competition

4. **Manufacturing or Assembly Process**
    - A. Inventory Materials/Turnover Ratios
    - B. Vendors/Sources of Supply
    - C. Production Methods and Improvements
    - D. Work in Process
    - E. Equipment/New Equipment Purchases Planned

5. **Marketing Strategy**
    - A. General Strategies
    - B. New Strategies Under Development
    - C. Pricing Policies
    - D. Sales Terms
    - E. Methods of Selling, Distribution and Servicing

6. **Management Plan**
    - A. Form of Business Organization
    - B. Board of Directors
    - C. Officers
        - — organization chart
        - — responsibilities
    - D. Resumes of Key Personnel
    - E. Staffing Plan
        - — number of employees
        - — job functions

E. Staffing Plan (continued)
   - compensation plan
   - employee benefits program
   - employee training programs
   - new hires planned

F. Facilities
   - plant/office diagram/drawings
   - capital improvements planned
   - plant safety program

G. Operating Plan
   - schedule of upcoming work for next year
   - foreseeable changes in business operation

7. **Financial Information**

   A. Financial History
      - past five years

   B. Three Year Financial Projections
      - proforma profit and loss statements
      - proforma balance sheets
      - proforma cash flow statements
      - capital expenditures estimates

   C. Explanation of Projections

   D. Key Business Ratios
      - changes in financial condition
      - changes in working capital
      - ratios of accounts receivable, accounts payable and inventory turnover

8. **Exhibits**

   A. Product/Service Catalogs

   B. Product/Service Brochures

   C. Personnel Policy Manual

   D. Most Recent Annual Report

Certainly, a business plan can contain even more than I have mentioned here, but perhaps the most important things to remember are — to include all activities of the business that are essential to its operation and to *build in* bench marks that will help you and others monitor its progress closely. If your company's goals are not materializing, a good plan will at least indicate where the problem areas are if management routinely compares it with internal status reports (hopefully frequent), and the monthly financial statements. When a business is exceeding its original objectives and management believes the trend will continue, the plan is probably obsolete and it's time to think about new goals, how to attain them and happily write another one.

If you would like detailed help in preparing a business plan, I recommend *The Successful Business Plan*, by Rhonda Abrams, and also available from The Oasis Press. *The Successful Business Plan* also contains many helpful hints about raising venture capital as well as help in writing your business plan.

Appendix A
The Private Placement Circular for New Life Publications, Inc.

Highlights of the Circular Presented

1. Business of the Company

2. Products and Pricing

3. Marketing Plan

4. Management's Background

5. Proforma Financials
   (2 years have been presented but 3 years is recommended)

==

Private Placement Circular
for
New Life Publications, Inc.

==

Table of Contents

	Page
Summary of Circular	3
The Company	6
Risk Factors	8
Financing	9
Business Location	10
Remuneration of CEO/CFO	10
Employees and Bonuses	11
Employee Stock Option Plan	11
Bargaining Agreements	11
Use of Proceeds	12
Products of the Company	13
Pamphlet Publishing	13
Poster Publishing	14
Booklet Publishing	15
Curriculum Development	15
Audio and Video Productions	16
Development Costs	16
Marketing	17
Catalog	17
Catalog Costs	17
Direct Mail Flyers	17
Print Advertising	18
Trade Shows	18
800 Telephone Number	18
Film/Video Preview and Rental Library Service	18
Domestic Markets	18
Foreign Markets	19
Sales Projections	19
Customer Lists	19
Shipping and Handling Charges	20
Credit Policy	20
Competition	20
Copyrights	20
Property	21
Startup Inventory/Equipment Purchases	22
Background of Management	23
Financial Statements:	
Proforma Balance Sheet (two year projection)	24
Proforma Profit and Loss Statements (two year projection)	25
Proforma Cash Flow Forecasts (1st and 2nd year of Operation)	26 & 31
Supporting Schedules:	
Sales, Accounts Receivable Forecasts & Inventory Costs (1st and 2nd year)	27 & 32
Marketing Expenses and Advertising Schedules (1st and 2nd year)	28 & 33
Payroll Forecasts (1st and 2nd year)	29 & 34
Administrative Overhead Forecasts (1st and 2nd year)	30 & 35

Contact:
John D. Smith
12 Oakridge Avenue
Edina, Minnesota 55343
Residence: (612) 333-0000

===

Summary of Private Placement Circular

The following is a brief synopsis of the more detailed information and financial statements appearing elsewhere in this circular which prospective investors or lenders should read in its entirety.

Introduction

The purpose of this Private Placement Circular is to raise $300,000 in additional working capital to finance the formation of a new company to be called **New Life Publications, Inc.**, hereafter called the "Company." See "Financing."

John D. Smith, age 48, is the founder, promoter and proposed chief executive officer/chief financial officer for the Company — hereafter referred to as "Management." He directed the publishing, film/video production and marketing startups of two adolescent and adult chemical dependency training and consulting organizations from 1976-81 and 1981-92. He is the former publisher of *The Chemical Dependency Digest* and has 25 years experience in publishing, administration and marketing management. See "Background of Management."

The Company

New Life Publications, Inc. is a non-incorporated, non-operating business enterprise that is in the organizational stage of development. Mr. Smith has $200,000 in cash, to invest in the business and seeks an additional $300,000 in the form of a investment for stock, a business loan or a combination of both.

The proposed business of the Company will be to publish, produce and market books, booklets, pamphlets, films, audio and video training programs, classroom curriculum, teaching aids, visual arts and other educational information that focus on a wide range of adolescent and adult problems and concerns.

In its capacity as a publisher, some of the areas where the Company's products can play an important role include: the prevention, intervention and treatment of adolescent/adult alcohol and drug dependencies; child abuse; teen pregnancy; suicide; sexual abuse; peer pressure; divorce; parenting; family relationships; domestic violence; preventive health care; alternative "highs" for kids; and the development of teaching curriculum, counseling and educational programs.

Marketing

Utilizing a national catalog and direct mail marketing program, the Company will also promote and sell selected publications, films, video, audio productions and selected educational products produced by other publishers, film makers and professional organizations.

Markets to be served will include public, private and parochial schools and colleges; teaching and counseling professionals; hospital and other health care providers; social service agencies; libraries; churches; parent/teacher organizations; law enforcement agencies; the judicial system; state and federal agencies; and, self-help organizations and their memberships. See "The Company," "Products," and "Marketing."

Company Location

Management is willing to locate the Company in a community (any State except Alaska or Hawaii) where its required capitalization can be arranged. The community to be selected must offer adequate postal services for bulk mail distribution; United Parcel Service pickup and delivery; easy access to 4-color catalog, booklet, brochure printing and graphic arts service companies; business rental property that is heated, air conditioned, in good repair and reasonably priced; available housing for the chief executive officer and his family; and, a reasonably well educated labor force that can be trained to conduct the Company's business.

Management projects the Company's labor needs as follows:

Year:	Employees:	Estimated Payroll:
1st	10 to 12	$248,000 to $288,000
2nd	18 to 24	$518,000 to $620,000
3rd	35 to 40	$850,000 to $925,000

The Company plans to offer competitive salaries, hospital, medical and life insurance, vacation and sick pay benefits to its employees. See "Payroll." If the community can provide some of the local services the Company will require, expenditures (excluding payroll) are estimated to be as follows:

Year:	Est. Local Goods & Services Purchased:
1st	$ 900,000
2nd	$ 1,275,000
3rd	$ 2,000,000

Financing and Use of Proceeds

To commence operations, the Company will required a total of $500,000 in working capital for the purchase of inventories, product development, marketing, office/warehouse equipment, the payment of salaries and for general operating purposes. See "Use of Proceeds" and "Start-Up Inventory."

Mr. Smith is open to alternative methods of financing (equity investment, loans or a combination of both). He is willing to negotiate percentages of equity ownership in the Company and is interested in discussing the Company's needs, plans and objectives with a serious investor, lender or community representative. To demonstrate his good faith in this project, he will pledge a personal investment of $200,000 in cash in exchange for common stock in the Company once it is incorporated. These funds will be considered an investment and not a loan to the business. See "Financing" for details.

Certain Risk Factors

The Company does not have a operating history; the business will be dependent upon the chief executive officer; there can be no assurance that the Company will be able to operate profitably; and, although management believes the initial financing required will adequately meet the Company's cash needs, additional working capital may be required in the future. See "Risk Factors."

Financial Statements

This circular contains proforma financial statements for a two year operating period and includes: Balance Sheets, P & L Statements; Cash Flow Projections; Sales, Inventory and Accounts Receivable Forecasts; Marketing and Advertising Budget Schedules; Payroll, General Overhead and New Product Development Forecasts. Please see the "Table of Contents" for the appropriate page numbers.

For additional information about the Company, please contact Mr. Smith at (612) 333-0000. His mailing address is: 12 Oakridge Avenue, Edina, Minnesota 55434.

***

The Company

New Life Publications, Inc., the "Company," is a non-incorporated, non-operating business enterprise that is in the organizational stage of development and has no assets or liabilities.

The proposed business of the Company will be to publish, produce and market books, booklets, pamphlets, films, audio and video training programs, classroom curriculum, teaching aids, visual arts and other educational information that focus on a wide range of adolescent and adult concerns and problems. The products of the Company will be topical in nature and follow national trends and issues.

Some of the areas where the Company's products can have the greatest impact include: alcohol and drug dependencies (prevention, intervention, counseling and treatment); child abuse; teen pregnancy; suicide; sexual abuse; peer pressure; divorce; parenting, family relationships, domestic violence; preventive health care; alternative "highs" for kids; and the development of classroom curriculum, teaching aids, counseling strategies and other educational programs.

Since producing its own line of products is expected to take time and because management wants to generate immediate revenues and national visibility, the Company will market selected books, publications, films, videos, audios and curriculum programs produced by other publishers, film makers and organizations located throughout the United States. This will be achieved by establishing favorable wholesale agreements to market their products. Management's experience has been that most of these companies do not have the sales expertise to reach many of the markets the Company will serve and they are eager to enter into such agreements. Discounts offered to the Company will range from 40% to 60% off retail which will produce a good gross profit margin on the these products.

To generate sales within 120 and 150 days after operations commence, the Company will prepare and mail 125,000 attractively illustrated catalogs promoting 180-200 products of other publishers, producers, and vendors. Subsequent catalog promotions of 125,000 pieces each — scheduled for mailing the 8th and 10th month of operation — will begin to advertise products developed by the Company. Management's goal is to build the company's product line to a level where 50% of all items offered for sale are its own. A total of 375,000 catalogs will be mailed the first year of operation and up to 575,000 the second year to selected prospective customers.

During the first year, the Company will also mail 400,000 4-page illustrated flyers designed to introduce new products as they are developed. Current plans are to mail 100,000 in the 5th month, 200,000 the 8th and 100,000 the 11th month. Up to 500,000 flyers will be mailed in the second year. See "Products" and "Marketing."

Markets to be served will include public, private and parochial elementary, middle, junior and senior high schools and colleges; teaching and counseling professionals; hospitals and other health care and treatment providers; social service agencies; public and private libraries; churches; parent/teacher organizations; law enforcement agencies and a number of self-help organizations and their memberships. It is believed that some of the Company's products will be suitable for sale in retail store establishments, but management has not included these potential sales in the first two years of operation. See "Marketing."

Management's previous experience in directing two similar publishing and catalog sales operations in Minneapolis has demonstrated a rapidly growing demand for products the Company plans to develop and market because:

1. The public awareness regarding alcohol, drugs and many other social issues has never been stronger. Especially issues affecting America's children. At this time, the major focus has been on the nation's drug problem, but equally sensitive areas such as child abuse, teen pregnancy, sexual abuse of children and domestic violence are steadily gaining national attention.

2. For F/Y 199-, the federal government allocated $7.9 billion dollars to fight the war on drugs with approximately $2.0 billion targeted for drug prevention, education, intervention, counseling and treatment. Funding for F/Y 199-, is expected to increase substantially for student education, treatment programs and law enforcement. Many cities and states are also appropriating more funding for drug education and community awareness programs.

Management's philosophy on this issue is: "Even if we can stop the flow of cocaine, heroin and marijuana from outside sources — which is extremely doubtful — the real threat of the nineties and beyond will be the deadly, home-made designer drugs now surfacing throughout the country. The only way we will significantly reduce this problem to a manageable level is to direct our talents and resources toward a serious national drug awareness program, parent/teacher involvement, preventive education for kids, intervention in our homes, businesses and schools, and by providing treatment and counseling to those who need it."

3. Thousands of schools across the country have recently started Student Assistance Programs (SAPs) that not only address alcohol and drug abuse, but help kids with a wide spectrum of other personal and family problems. These programs are growing in popularity and although financed primarily with state educational monies at this time, some funding is becoming available at the federal level. Management believes that America's schools will become increasingly more involved in providing these important services to students in the years ahead.

As a national supplier of educational materials, the Company will be in a position to help thousands of professionals in their work and millions of children and their families deal more effectively with their personal problems. By marketing its own products and the best from others, the Company believes it has a excellent opportunity to become a leading source for the most up-to-date and reliable materials and products available.

Employees will be recruited and hired who have the necessary backgrounds and expertise to conduct the Company's business activities. The actual writing, editing, typesetting, layout, design, photography, graphic arts, printing of manuscripts and advertising pieces, and the creation of all visual art products will be contracted with individuals and firms specializing in such services. In the future, it is possible that employees may be hired to perform these tasks if it proves cost effective to do so. See "Products" and "Employees."

Following the capitalization of the Company, management will establish the business in the community selected. Office and warehouse space of approximately 4,000 square feet will be leased and furniture, office and warehouse equipment purchased. Wholesale purchasing and distribution agreements will be negotiated with other publishers, film producers and organizations to represent their products, and the initial inventories will be purchased from them.

Simultaneously to the above, key managers and employees will be recruited as required; the first catalog will be produced and mailed, and writers/artists retained to begin the work of writing and preparing the Company's own educational materials for publication and marketing.

A substantial portion of the Company's capital will be invested in inventories, marketing and new product development. The balance of the funds will be used for salaries and general operating expenses. Please see "Use of Proceeds," "Startup Inventory," "Products," "Marketing," and the proforma financial information provided in this Circular.

Risk Factors

Management believes that the proceeds received as a result of this Private Placement Circular will be sufficient to satisfy the Company's cash requirements, however, the investment should be considered speculative, involves risk and should only be considered by investors who can afford to lose their entire investment. Prospective investors should therefore consider the following risks associated with the Company as well as the other information presented herein.

1. The Company does not have a operating history as a viable entity.

2. There can be no assurance that the Company will be able to operated profitably.

3. The business of the Company is directly dependent upon the leadership and full-time participation of its Chief Executive Officer. Loss of his services could adversely affect the conduct of the Company's business.

4. Additional financing may be required. Although management believes that the funds raised through this Circular will be sufficient for the Company's growth needs, the conduct of the Company's business and unforeseeable circumstances may require the raising of additional funds in the future.

5. Management assumes that the Company would be incorporated as a Subchapter "S" Corporation with the profits, if any, passing directly to the shareholders as ordinary income. Since profits cannot be guaranteed, investors who anticipate the need for immediate income from their investment should refrain from purchasing equity in the business.

6. The Company will be in competition with other publishers, film producers and organizations who serve part or all of the markets where it plans to promote and sell its products. Some of these competitors are larger and have more resources at their disposal.

7. Once the shares of its common stock are issued to investors, there can be no assurance that a market for the Company's outstanding shares will ever develop or that such shares may be resold after purchase or resold without incurring a loss.

Financing

To commence operations, the Company requires a additional investment or loan of $300,000 for the purchase of inventories, product development, marketing, office and warehouse equipment, furniture, the payment of salaries and for general operating purposes. See "Use of Proceeds" and "Startup Inventory."

Although the first year's projected cash flow does indicate that the Company may be able to start operations will less capital, much would depend on its sales performance and accounts receivable collection rate during the initial twelve month period. Therefore, $500,000 is considered to be a realistic assessment of the Company's startup **capitalization needs.**

Mr. Smith, the Company's proposed CEO/CFO, is willing to negotiate the type of financing (investment for shares, a loan or a combination of both), the type of corporation to be formed (Subchapter "S" or "C"—the financials assume a Subchapter "S"), the State of incorporation, percentages of equity ownership to be owned by the investor(s) and himself, and the community site for the Company's location.

To demonstrate his good faith, Mr. Smith will invest the sum of $200,000 in cash in the business upon a pledge of $300,000 by the investors or a lender.

In the event the Company's total capitalization is in the form of investment in exchange for its common stock shares, it is proposed that his total equity ownership be based on his asset contribution and his service as the founder, promoter and proposed chief executive officer and financial officer of the business. At this time, he is willing to negotiate the exact percentages to be held by himself and by those investing in the business.

Business Location

Management is willing to locate the Company in a community (any State except Alaska or Hawaii), where its required capitalization can be arranged satisfactorily. The community must offer adequate postal services for bulk mailing; United Parcel Service (UPS) pickup and delivery; easy access to 4-color catalog, booklet, brochure printing and graphics arts service companies; business rental property that is heated, air conditioned, in good repair and reasonably priced; available housing for the Smith family and a reasonably well educated labor force that can be trained to conduct the Company's business operations.

Remuneration of the CEO/CFO

As the CEO/CFO, Mr. Smith would receive a first year salary of $60,000, reimbursement for his relocation expenses up to $10,000, paid hospital, medical and life insurance up to a maximum annual premium of $2,400. His future salary increases would be determined by the Company's sales performance, financial condition and by the Board of Directors.

Remuneration of Managers

The Company will recruit and hire key managers for the positions of Publishing Manager and Accountant. The Publishing Manager would receive a salary up to $36,000 and the Accountant a salary up to $34,200 during the first year of operation. Each would receive hospital, medical and life insurance benefits up to a total annual premium cost of $1,800. All managers and employees would receive future salary or wage increases based on their personal performance and the Company's sales and financial condition. The hiring of all managers and employees would be the responsibility of the CEO and the management staff as directed.

Employees

The Company will employ up to 7 full-time and 3 part-time employees the first year. They will include the: CEO/CFO, Publishing Manager, Accountant, (1) Warehouse/Shipping Manager, (1) Administrative Assistant, (1) Accounting Clerk, (2) Sales/Order Entry Representatives and (2) Shipping Clerks. If sales warrant, two additional employees will be added. During the second year, up to 18 employees will be required and up to 40 in the third year of operation.

All full-time employees (with the exception of the CEO/CFO), will receive hospital, medical and life insurance benefits up to a maximum annual premium cost of $1,800/each per year, two weeks of paid vacation, one week of sick leave and paid holidays as observed by the Company. Part-time employees will receive one week paid vacation, 3 days paid sick leave and all paid holidays granted to full-time employees each year.

The Company plans to recruit employees who are living in the community where it is located and intends to promote them from "within" whenever possible.

Bonuses

Annual bonuses may be paid to officers, managers and key employees based on the profits earned by the Company, however, no bonus plan has been developed.

Employee Stock Option Plan

Management would like to set aside up to 300,000 shares of the Company's common stock to establish a Employee Stock Option Plan. Options to purchase shares would be issued from time to time to directors, officers, managers and certain key employees as determined by the Board of Directors. The details of this plan would be drafted and adopted by the Board of Directors at the earliest possible date.

Bargaining Agreements

The Company does not plan to become a party to any union or collective bargaining agreement affecting its employees.

28 *Raising Capital: How To Write A Financing Proposal*

Board of Directors

Mr. Smith and the investor(s)/lender will appoint a Board of Directors to supervise the operations of the Company. Members would receive a $125 fee for attending all meetings and reimbursement for their out-of-pocket expenses when representing the Company in its behalf and at the direction of the Board.

Use of Proceeds

The net cash proceeds to the Company in the amount of $500,000 will be allocated and applied in the order of their priority as follows:

Book, booklet, pamphlet, film, video and audio inventories purchased from other publishers, producers and organizations for resale. See "Startup Inventory"	$ 90,000
Pamphlet, booklet and poster development costs	40,000
Pamphlet, booklet and poster printing costs	35,000
Catalog and flyer development costs, printing, mailing lists, preparation and postage	160,000
Office computer network system, hardware, software, equipment and furniture	25,000
Warehouse fixtures and equipment	5,250
Total	$ 355,250

The balance of the proceeds ($144,750) will be utilized for general operating purposes including working capital and the payment of personnel salaries.

The Company will further seek to establish lines of credit with its suppliers and other institutions to insure that sufficient working capital is available in the future. The Company does not have any intention to borrow funds except as may be necessary for its business development. Accordingly, and because unforeseen circumstances could cause some variation in the allocation of the proceeds received as a result of this Private Placement Circular, the Company reserves the right to make such variations as the circumstances may warrant.

To the extent that the foregoing proceeds are not immediately used, they will be invested in short term financial instruments such as government securities, certificates of deposit, money market or savings accounts.

Products of the Company

After the successful capitalization of the Company, management will establish wholesale buying agreements with a large number of book publishers, film video/audio production companies and other professional organizations to purchase selected products for marketing to its catalog customers. The Company's cost for these products will range from 40% to 60% off the retail selling prices. Management intends to allocate up to $90,000 for the purchase of these inventories which will have a retail catalog value of approximately $180,000.

The great majority of these products will focus on adolescent problems, but will include publications for teachers, counselors, social service and health care providers which are designed to help them in their respective fields of work.

Management's experience has demonstrated that publishers and producers are very interested in establishing wholesale agreements with catalog retailers and merchandisers because it helps them to reach certain markets that might otherwise be uneconomical to approach and improves their sales.

Since the available promotional space in each catalog is limited, the Company can be selective regarding the products it wants to promote and demand the best possible pricing from its suppliers.

The goal of management is to eventually reach the point where 50% or more of the products the Company sells are self produced.

Pamphlet Publishing

The Company will initially publish a series of low-cost student handout pamphlets that address many of the subjects previously mentioned. Each series will focus on a particular problem or concern. For example: the "Drug Series" might include 2 or 3 pamphlets that provide the reader with factual and interesting information about various drugs, their affects on people and how to get help if the reader or a friend is using them. Each subject addressed will be written for various age levels of children (K to 12) to ensure that they are easy to read and understand.

By offering these pamphlets at reasonable, yet profitable volume prices, management believes thousands of schools and other agencies will purchase them because of their educational value in the classroom and as a discussion piece among students and their families.

All pamphlets will be written by professionals who hold credentials in the fields and subjects selected for publication. These contributing writers will receive flat fees of $200 to $400 for each work accepted for publishing.

The costs to publish a pamphlet (typeset/art work, 2-color printing and folding) can cost about $750 (or $.075/each) for a first run of 10,000 pieces. If the volume price established was $.15, the gross profit margin would be $.075 or 50%. The second printing costs would drop to about $.04/each and the gross profit margin would then increase to $.11 or 73%. Management believes that because these pamphlets will be purchased in volume, the actual printing costs would be reduced even further and the selling prices could be lowered accordingly and still maintain the profit levels desired.

Although the Company cannot guarantee the sale of these pamphlets, the potential revenues are indeed interesting. For example: There are 15,000 public school districts in the United States representing approximately 120,000 (K through 12) schools. If each district office purchased an average of 2,000 pamphlets per year (of the several subjects available) at $.15/each, the Company's annual sales volume for this line would be $4,500,000.

Poster Publishing

Another area that management believes the Company can quickly develop is its visual arts publishing capability. The Company plans to recruit artists and photographers to develop a series of posters that depict a number of adolescent issues. Some will be self explanatory and others will be captioned. The artist/photographers will be paid a fee ranging from $250 to $500 or offered a royalty contract for each original work accepted for publishing.

Management believes there would be a wide acceptance of these posters in several of the markets it intends to serve and that they could prove popular with retail outlets as well. Selling prices will be determined by the costs to produce each work, the associated packaging costs and the volume purchased by a single source. Profit margins of 100% are anticipated from sales generated through the Company's retail catalogs and flyer promotions and 50% to 60% on sales to retail outlets.

The Company plans to produce between 16 and 20 posters during its first year of operation. Although sales cannot be guaranteed, management believes that up to 750,000 posters could be sold annually (not including those sold to retail outlets for resale). At a average selling price of $3.00 each, sales of $2,250,000 could be generated for the line.

Booklet Publishing

The Company intends to solicit booklet length manuscripts (up to 8,000 words) on a variety of topics of interest to adolescents and adults. These manuscripts will be purchased from their authors for flat fees of $350 to $750 each. Management plans to utilize the services of professional individuals and firms to edit, typeset, design the covers for these manuscripts and prepare them for printing. Printing bids would be requested and inventories produced.

The costs to publish a 24 page booklet can vary considerably. Assuming the Company elects to publish a first run of 3,000 copies of a work in a 5" x 7.5" format with a 4-color cover, the total cost can amount to $2,500 or $.83/each.

If the retail price for such a booklet was established at $2.25 — the gross profit margin would be $1.42 or 63%. After the first edition was sold out, the reprint costs would drop dramatically to about $.45/each. In this event, the gross profit margin would then increase to $1.80 or 80%.

Depending upon the financial condition of the Company, up to 6 booklets would be published the first year and perhaps 10 to 12 per year thereafter. These works would be authored by professionals with credentials in their respective fields and written in easy-to-understand formats. Most of the Company's booklets would be sold to schools, libraries, social service agencies and other health care providers. All pamphlets, posters and booklets would be copyrighted.

The Company will consider publishing full length books that are topical, but does not plan to do so during the first year of operation.

Curriculum Development

The Company plans to recruit educators, instructors and other professionals to develop classroom curriculum programs, teaching guides and student aids that can be utilized in multiple educational environments. The Company would give preference to programs that have become successful models, but would also consider new approaches and methods. Initially, the Company intends to develop curriculum programs suitable for schools, hospitals, treatment centers and social service agencies. Subjects for development might include: adolescent chemical dependency, prevention, intervention techniques, child abuse, sexual abuse, adolescent suicide, peer pressure, overeating, preventive teen pregnancy and domestic violence issues.

Since the development of curriculum program consumes a considerable amount of time and effort, the Company does not believe it would have any programs to market for at least 18 months. A fee of up to $5,000 and/or royalties would be paid by the

Company for a curriculum package ready for publishing. Depending upon the content, such packages could be sold at prices of $50 to $500 each. If teaching aids, student guides or workbooks were to be included with a program, they would be sold separately in quantity.

Audio and Video Productions

During the first year of operation, the Company plans to market films, videos and audio programs developed by other companies and organizations. As its financial capabilities strengthen, there are a number of opportunities in the A/V field where the development of professional "training productions" could enhance the Company's future growth.

Management's previous experience has demonstrated that A/V production costs need not be expensive to be effective. Using the current technology, a good "talking head" — 30 minute video presentation can be produced for as little as $2,250 — which includes the presenter's fee. Video duplication is equally inexpensive as current costs to duplicate a 30 minute master in small quantities (25 units with boxes) is about $4.50/each.

Selling prices for a 30 minute training video can range from $14.95 to $49.95 each depending on the content. Very often, training "talks" are presented in a series and are sold individually or at a discount for the entire package.

Flat fees of between $600 and $1,250 would be paid to a video Presenter for each 30 minute segment made, or if he or she preferred, the Company would negotiate a royalty contract for the work.

Audio training talks are generally taped during an actual presentation by a speaker. A flat fee up to $350 would be paid for each talk recorded for duplication and marketing. Audio duplication runs about $.90/per tape (depending upon length), and would sell for $6 each and up.

There are several "training presentations" the Company would consider for marketing when it is financially able to begin its own A/V production program.

Development Costs

In total, the Company plans to invest $40,000 in product develop (author/artist fees, editing, graphic arts and production layouts) the first year and up to $100,000 the second. These expenditures do not include actual inventory printing costs.

Authors, Artists and Curriculum Writers

The Company plans to recruit its authors, artists and curriculum writers through professional associations, trade magazines and newspaper advertising, its own catalogs, trade shows and through direct contact.

Marketing

The Company's marketing strategy would be to promote and sell its products and those of its suppliers through catalogs and direct mail flyers supported by small display advertisements in trade association and general interest publications. As the Company develops its own product line, it may also attend selected trade shows.

Catalog Specifications

The first catalog will be a 36 to 40 page unit offering up to 200 products. It will be a 8.5" x 11" piece with a four color cover and 2-color printing internally with photographs and descriptions of all items presented. The catalog would provide two order forms, a return envelope, shipping information and a toll-free telephone number that customers can use to place credit card or business purchase orders. Management estimates that it may take 12 to 16 weeks to prepare the first catalog, but plans to mail 125,000 pieces by the fourth month of operation. Please see "Marketing Expenses and Advertising Schedule" in the attached proforma financial statements for details regarding the scheduled promotions.

Catalog Costs

The current cost to prepare, publish and mail a 40 page catalog as previously described — printed in quantities of at least 125,000 units, would be approximately $.65/each. Reprint costs of the same catalog would be reduced by about five cents and the Company plans to mail "reprints" to additional prospect lists at various times of the year. All catalogs to be mailed would be labeled and prepared for bulk rate mailing at the Company.

Direct Mail Flyers

A four page 8.5" x 11" direct mail flyer would also be used to promote and sell the Company's pamphlets, posters and booklets to prospective customers. The cost to prepare, publish and mail these flyers would be about $.28/each in quantities of 100,000 pieces. Management plans to mail 100,000 flyers by the fifth month of operation. During the first year, 375,000 catalogs and up to 400,000 flyers would be scheduled for mailing and up to 575,000 catalogs and 500,000 flyers during the second year. Additional quantities of these promotional pieces would be printed for responding to inquiries received from the Company's display advertisements in various magazines and publications.

Print Advertising

Small 2 and 3 inch display ads would be placed in association, trade and general interest magazines and other publications to promote the Company's free catalog or specific products. A budget of $12,500 will be allocated for these advertisements the first year and $24,000 the second.

Trade Shows

Until the Company has developed a number of its own products, management does not believe attending trade shows would be profitable. The great majority of those who do attend these events will have received promotional materials from the Company or know of it. After the business has a operating history and has produced several publications, it may be beneficial to attend selected shows where its products can be featured.

800 Telephone Number

The Company will provide a toll-free 800 telephone number for its customers to order products. Telephone orders will be taken by Sales/Order Entry personnel who will enter them on the Company's computer network system. This system will automatically generate a shipping order, invoice, accounting detail, mailing lists, and inventory control records.

Film/Video Preview and Rental Library Service

The company will establish a film/video preview and rental library service and promote this service in its catalogs. Previews will be made available only to schools and public institutions to facilitate their film/video buying decisions. Rentals will be made available for a 3 day period at a cost of $35 plus shipping and handling charges. Film and video rentals would only be offered to schools, institutions and businesses and not to individuals.

Domestic Markets

Domestic markets include public, private and parochial elementary, middle, junior and senior high school principals, counselors and librarians; superintendents of schools and school district purchasing agents; college bookstores, public and private libraries; hospitals; social service and other health care providers and agencies; alcohol and drug training and treatment organizations; counselors, therapists and treatment center directors; large family oriented physician groups; parent/teacher associations; municipal, county, state and federal agencies; law enforcement agencies and judicial systems to name only a few. These markets total approximately 600,000 prospects and do not include potential retail outlets or a number of other organizations, churches and self-help groups around the country.

Foreign Markets

Management believes that a marketing opportunity exists for the Company's products in Canada. Although this market is smaller, the demand for information and educational materials on the subjects to be addressed by the Company is equal to that of the United States. Since the cost to mail catalogs into Canada is much higher (first class mail vs. bulk rate), the Company will test a prospect list of Canadian school principals and superintendents the first year. If this test is successful, additional markets in Canada will be pursued the second year.

After the Company develops its own line of publications and other products, and applies the appropriate translations to some of them, there are a number of foreign sales opportunities it will be able to develop in the future.

Sales Projections

Although the Company cannot guarantee its sales, management's experience selling similar products through catalog marketing programs generated sales of at least $3.00 plus shipping and handling charges per piece mailed when only 125 products were offered to an average mailing list of 100,000 prospects.

Because the Company is planning to offer up to 200 products in its first catalog, management is confident that at least $4 in sales plus shipping and handling charges will be generated from each piece mailed during the first year or sales of about $1,500,000. The direct mail 4-page flyers are expected to generate at least $2.00 in sales per piece mailed or $800,000 in revenues.

As new products are added to the Company's line, catalog sales are expected to increase to at least $5.00 per piece mailed and $2.50 per flyer mailed. These are considered to be conservative sales estimates because they do not include sales generated from the poster line to retail outlets.

Customer Lists

The Company plans to compile a mailing list of its customers and the products they purchase for marketing research, analysis and future promotions. It will also purchase lists from reputable sources that management has worked with in the past, and at prices below those normally paid for such lists.

Shipping and Handling Charges

All orders received would be subject to shipping and handling charges. These charges will be based on the dollar value of an order and calculated to defray all packaging and shipping expenses.

Credit Policy

The Company will offer "open-account" terms to schools, public institutions and credit approved businesses only. Terms will be Net 30 Days. The minimum order to establish an open account will be $50. All other customers will be required to send a check, money order or use a Visa, MasterCard or American Express card when placing an order.

Competition

There are hundreds of publishers and film makers in the United States, but most of them do not actively promote their products in the markets to be served by the Company. For many, it is not economical to promote a single film, video, or one or two books they have published, even though the customers in these markets might find them interesting. Instead, they prefer to market their works through catalog merchandisers and retailers, book and film distributors, bookstores, and other retail outlets.

By representing these publishers and producers as a catalog retailer, the Company's pricing structure would be competitive. The selling prices established for its own publications and products would be equally competitive in the marketplace.

Management believes the Company would enjoy two major advantages over its competition. First, it will not have the traditionally high overhead expenses experienced by many large publishers and producers since most of the development and publishing work will be "farmed out" on a fee-for-hire-basis. Second, by providing a wide selection of educational materials and products from several sources, and at competitive prices, the Company would be able to establish itself as a reliable, single source vendor.

Copyrights

The Company's policy will always be to copyright all books, booklets, pamphlets, posters, curriculum programs, video/audio presentations and training programs that it develops, publishes or produces.

Property

After the financing described in this Private Placement Circular is received, the Company will lease a 4,000 square foot facility in the community selected to headquarter its offices and warehouse. The maximum expenditure for this space is projected to be $3,500/per month and the facility should serve the needs of the business for at least three years.

Startup Inventory, Office/Warehouse Equipment Purchases

Product Inventories:

Quantity	Item	Copies	Retail Value	Discount	Cost
120	Ass't Books	50/ea	$ 60,000	50%	$ 30,000
10	Ass't Booklets	200/ea	5,900	50%	2,950
10	Curriculum Pkgs	25/ea	12,500	50%	6,250
10	VHS Training Videos	20/ea	18,000	50%	9,000
15	16MM Educational Films	2/ea	10,500	40%	6,300
15	VHS Educational Films	6/ea	31,500	40%	18,900
12	Posters	1M/ea	36,000	70%*	10,800
5	Pamphlet Series with 3 Publications ea.	10M/ea	22,500	50%*	11,250
-	Film/Video Preview/Rental Libr.		2,350	(at cost)	2,350
-	Reserve for Add'l Posters/Pamphlets & Other Inventory		68,000	60%*	27,200

Total Startup Inventory (Resale Value) $267,250 (Cost of Inv) $125,000

* Poster/Pamphlet costs are expected to decrease after the second printing. Development cost are not included. See "Use of Proceeds." Inventories from other suppliers can be reordered to replenish stocks as needed.

Office and Warehouse Equipment Purchases:

Computer Network System with 5 stations	$ 14,000
Accounting, Inventory Control, Word Processing Software	1,400
2 Typewriters — Used	600
Office Furniture — New	6,500
Copier — New	2,500
Lumber for building shelving; scales, postage meter, furniture, etc.	5,250
Total	**$ 30,250**

Background of Management

John D. Smith, age 48, is the founder, promoter and proposed chief executive officer/chief financial officer of the Company.

He is currently self-employed as a consultant to not-for-profit agencies specializing in chemical dependency services in the Minneapolis area. From 1981-87, he was the executive director for the Avery Home, a non-profit, adolescent chemical dependency counseling, consulting and publishing organization in St. Paul and from 1976-81, served as the executive director for the Lincoln Institute in Albany, New York, a adult and adolescent chemical dependency counseling, treatment, training and publishing organization with treatment facilities in six states. In addition to his administrative duties, he directed the startup publishing and video production operations for both organizations and served as LI's consultant to the U. S. Navy and Air Force at the Pentagon in Washington, DC.

From 1972-76, he was the executive vice president for Rocklund Manufacturing Corp. in Cincinnati, OH and directly supervised the marketing and sales activities of this auto parts manufacturer with annual sales of $550 million dollars. From 1966-72, he was employed as their national marketing director and participated in building the company's revenues from $50 million to $400 million per year.

Mr. Smith is a graduate of the University of Minnesota where he received his BA degree in Marketing in 1964 and his MBA in 1966.

New Life Publications, Inc.
Proforma Balance Sheet
Two Year Projection

End of Year(s)	One	Two
Current Assets:		
Cash/Savings	$ 389,780	$ 812,307
Accounts Receivable	557,000	621,875
Total Current Assets	$ 946,780	$1,434,182
Other Assets:		
Inventories @ Cost	$ 125,000	$ 125,000
Equipment & Furniture	30,250	50,250
Less: 3 Yr. Deprec. E & F	(10,983)	(27,733)
Total Other Assets	$ 144,267	$ 147,517
Total Assets	$1,091,047	$1,581,699

Liabilities and Stockholders' Equity:

	One	Two
Current Liabilities:		
Accounts Payable	$ 298,000	$ 309,375
Total Current Liabilities	$ 298,000	$ 309,375
Stockholders' Equity:		
Amount Paid In *	$ 500,000	$ 500,000
Profit or (Loss) for period for Stockholders' Distribution	293,047	772,324
Total Stockholders' Equity*	$ 793,047	$1,272,324
Total Liabilities and Stockholders' Equity*	$1,091,047	$1,581,699

* Assumes Capitalization by investment for shares. Distribution to Investors (Sub "S") Taxable Income $ 293,047 $ 772,324

| ROI Per Year | 58.6% | 154.5% |

New Life Publications, Inc.
Proforma Profit and (Loss) Statement
Two Year Projection

End of Year(s)	One		Two	
Sales	$1,990,000	100.0%	$3,960,000	100.0%
Less Operating Expenses:				
Cost of Goods Sold	867,000	43.6%	1,748,000	44.2%
Marketing	378,040	19.0%	595,000	15.0%
Payroll and Fringes	248,230	12.5%	517,860	13.1%
Admin. Overhead	152,700	7.6%	210,100	5.3%
New Product Development	40,000	2.0%	100,000	2.5%
Total Operating Expenses	$1,685,970	84.7%	$3,170,960	80.1%
Profit or (Loss)	$ 304,030	15.3%	$ 789,040	19.9%

Notes:

(1) Sales do not include interest earned on cash balances.
(2) Expenses do not include interest or principal payments if capitalization is in the form of loans.
(3) Expenses do not include furniture and equipment depreciation. See "Balance Sheets."
(4) Expenses do not reflect any bonuses that may be paid to officers, managers or key employees.

42 Raising Capital: How To Write A Financing Proposal

New Life Publications, Inc.
Proforma Cash Flow Statement - 1st Year of Operation

Month	One	Two	Three	Four	Five	Six	Seven	Eight	Nine	Ten	Eleven	Twelve
Cash Bal Fwd	0	465960	412685	381200	167085	66075	61590	135505	73620	108485	98450	233115
A/R's Collected	0	0	0	0	0	40000	166000	255000	178000	127000	276000	391000
Investment/Loan	500000	0	0	0	0	0	0	0	0	0	0	0
Cash Available	500000	465960	412685	381200	167085	106075	227590	390505	251620	235485	374450	624115
Less Operating Expenses:												
Payroll & Fringes	10190	14675	17135	19075	21010	23735	23735	23735	23735	23735	23735	23735
Admin Overhead	23850	8350	8350	11650	10000	11250	11350	11200	11400	12600	12600	20100
Marketing	0	0	0	87390	29000	3500	1000	142950	1000	80700	29000	3500
Inventories	0	0	0	90000	35000	0	50000	137000	105000	18000	74000	185000
New Prod Dev	0	0	6000	6000	6000	6000	6000	2000	2000	2000	2000	2000
Equipment	0	30250	0	0	0	0	0	0	0	0	0	0
Total Expenses	34040	53275	31485	214115	101010	44485	92085	316885	143135	137035	141335	234335
Cash Balance	465960	412685	381200	167085	66075	61590	135505	73620	108485	98450	233115	389780

Notes:
1. Operating expenses assume capitalization is an investment rather than a loan. If the $300,000 required is a loan, the interest would be paid monthly with a principal payment in the 12th month.
2. Cash balances do not reflect interest earnings.

New Life Publications, Inc.
Sales, Accounts Receivable Collection Forecast and Inventory Costs - 1st Year of Operation

Month	One	Two	Three	Four	Five	Six	Seven	Eight	Nine	Ten	Eleven	Twelve	TOTALS
SALES													
Catalog Sales @ $4	0	0	0	0	100000	250000	150000	0	100000	250000	250000	250000	1350000
Ea. Average Return													
Product Flyer Sales @ $2 Ea. Avg. Return	0	0	0	0	0	40000	100000	60000	80000	200000	120000	40000	640000
TOTAL SALES	0	0	0	0	100000	290000	250000	60000	180000	450000	370000	290000	1990000

A/R's AS COLLECTED (40% in 30 Days; 50% in 60 Days and 10% in 90 Days)

Month	Sales	One	Two	Three	Four	Five	Six	Seven	Eight	Nine	Ten	Eleven	Twelve	TOTALS
5	100000	0	0	0	0	0	40000	50000	10000	0	0	0	0	100000
6	290000	0	0	0	0	0	0	116000	145000	29000	0	0	0	290000
7	250000	0	0	0	0	0	0	0	100000	125000	25000	0	0	250000
8	60000	0	0	0	0	0	0	0	0	24000	30000	6000	0	60000
9	180000	0	0	0	0	0	0	0	0	0	72000	90000	18000	180000
10	450000	0	0	0	0	0	0	0	0	0	0	180000	225000	405000
11	370000	0	0	0	0	0	0	0	0	0	0	0	148000	148000
12	290000	0	0	0	0	0	0	0	0	0	0	0	0	0
Totals	1990000	0	0	0	0	0	40000	166000	255000	178000	127000	276000	391000	1433000

Note: A/R Carry-Over to next year would be $557,000.

INVENTORY COSTS:	One	Two	Three	Four	Five	Six	Seven	Eight	Nine	Ten	Eleven	Twelve	TOTALS
Supplier Products @ 50% COGS	0	0	0	0	50000	125000	75000	0	50000	125000	125000	125000	675000
Company Products @ 30% COGS	0	0	0	0	0	12000	30000	18000	24000	60000	36000	12000	192000
TOTAL COGS	0	0	0	0	50000	137000	105000	18000	74000	185000	161000	137000	867000

New Life Publications, Inc.
Marketing Expenses and Advertising Schedule - 1st Year of Operation

Month	One	Two	Three	Four	Five	Six	Seven	Eight	Nine	Ten	Eleven	Twelve	TOTALS
Marketing Exp's:													
Catalog Art/Printing	0	0	0	57200	0	0	0	57200	0	50700	0	0	165100
Cat Mail Labels	0	0	0	2875	0	0	0	2875	0	2875	0	0	8625
Cat Mail Prep	0	0	0	2500	0	0	0	2500	0	2500	0	0	7500
Cat Postage	0	0	0	20875	0	0	0	20875	0	20875	0	0	62625
Flyers Art/Printing	0	0	0	0	8000	0	0	16000	0	0	8000	0	32000
Flyers Mail Labels	0	0	0	0	1300	0	0	2600	0	0	1300	0	5200
Flyers Mail Prep	0	0	0	0	2000	0	0	4000	0	0	2000	0	8000
Flyers Postage	0	0	0	0	16700	0	0	33400	0	0	16700	0	66800
Ads in Publications	0	0	0	2500	0	2500	0	2500	0	2500	0	2500	12500
Inquiry Postage/Misc.	0	0	0	1440	1000	1000	1000	1000	1000	1250	1000	1000	9690
Total $	0	0	0	87390	29000	3500	1000	142950	1000	80700	29000	3500	378040
Advertising Schedule:													
Catalogs Mailed (Pcs)	0	0	0	125000	0	0	0	125000	0	125000	0	0	375000
Flyers Mailed (Pcs)	0	0	0	0	100000	0	0	200000	0	0	100000	0	400000
Catalogs for Inquiries	0	0	0	5000	0	0	0	5000	0	5000	0	0	15000
Ads in Publications	No	No	No	Yes	No	Yes	No	Yes	No	Yes	No	Yes	

Note: Press releases would be mailed to newspapers and magazines regarding the Company's published products.

New Life Publications, Inc.
Payroll - 1st Year of Operation

Month	One	Two	Three	Four	Five	Six	Seven	Eight	Nine	Ten	Eleven	Twelve	TOTALS
CEO/CFO	5000	5000	5000	5000	5000	5000	5000	5000	5000	5000	5000	5000	60000
Publishing Manager	1500	3000	3000	3000	3000	3000	3000	3000	3000	3000	3000	3000	34500
Accountant	1425	2850	2850	2850	2850	2850	2850	2850	2850	2850	2850	2850	32775
Ship/Rec Manager	0	0	2100	2100	2100	2100	2100	2100	2100	2100	2100	2100	21000
Admin Ass't	950	1900	1900	1900	1900	1900	1900	1900	1900	1900	1900	1900	21850
Sales/Order Entry	0	0	0	825	1650	1650	1650	1650	1650	1650	1650	1650	14025
Sales/Order Entry PT	0	0	0	0	0	825	825	825	825	825	825	825	5775
Accounting Clerk PT	0	0	0	0	0	850	850	850	850	850	850	850	5950
Shipper	0	0	0	800	1600	1600	1600	1600	1600	1600	1600	1600	13600
Shipper PT	0	0	0	0	0	800	800	800	800	800	800	800	5600
Sub Total	8875	12750	14850	16475	18100	20575	20575	20575	20575	20575	20575	20575	215075
Payroll Taxes	890	1275	1485	1650	1810	2060	2060	2060	2060	2060	2060	1060	20530
Hosp/Med/Life Ins.	425	650	800	950	1100	1100	1100	1100	1100	1100	1100	1100	11625
Total Payroll $	10190	14675	17135	19075	21010	23735	23735	23735	23735	23735	23735	23735	248230
Employees:													
Full-Time	4	4	5	7	7	7	7	7	7	7	7	7	
Part-Time	0	0	0	0	0	3	3	3	3	3	3	3	
Total	4	4	5	7	7	10	10	10	10	10	10	10	

Note: The Company may add 1 full-time order entry person and 1 full-time shipper by the 7th or 8th month if sales warrant.

New Life Publications, Inc.
Administrative Overhead - 1st Year of Operation

Month	One	Two	Three	Four	Five	Six	Seven	Eight	Nine	Ten	Eleven	Twelve	TOTALS
Rent	3500	3500	3500	3500	3500	3500	3500	3500	3500	3500	3500	3500	42000
Utilities	300	300	300	300	300	300	300	300	300	300	300	300	3600
Telephone	950	600	600	750	1200	1700	1700	1200	1400	2200	2200	2200	16700
Office Supplies	500	250	250	500	300	300	300	300	300	300	300	300	3900
Office Printing	400	200	200	500	200	200	200	300	300	300	300	300	3400
Office Postage	200	200	200	350	500	1000	900	900	900	1300	1300	1300	9050
Outside Services	1000	1000	1000	1000	1000	1000	1250	1250	1250	1250	1250	1250	13500
CEO Relocation Exp	10000	0	0	0	0	0	0	0	0	0	0	0	10000
Travel/Entertainment	500	500	500	500	500	750	750	750	750	750	750	750	7750
Business Insurance	2500	0	0	2000	0	0	0	0	0	0	0	0	4500
Legal Services	2500	200	200	200	200	200	200	200	200	200	200	200	4700
Mailing List Maint	0	0	0	500	500	500	500	500	500	500	500	500	4500
Employee Education	100	100	100	100	100	100	100	100	100	100	100	100	1200
Subs/Memberships	350	150	150	100	100	100	50	50	50	50	50	50	1250
Janitorial	300	600	600	600	600	600	600	600	600	600	600	600	6900
Equipment Maint	250	250	250	250	250	250	250	250	250	250	250	250	3000
Annual Acctg Audit	0	0	0	0	0	0	0	0	0	0	0	7500	7500
Miscellaneous	500	500	500	500	750	750	750	1000	1000	1000	1000	1000	9250
Total $	23850	8350	8350	11650	10000	11250	11350	11200	11400	12600	12600	20100	152700

New Product Development Expenses - 1st Year of Operation

	One	Two	Three	Four	Five	Six	Seven	Eight	Nine	Ten	Eleven	Twelve	TOTALS
NPD Exp $	0	0	6000	6000	6000	6000	6000	2000	2000	2000	2000	2000	40000

30

New Life Publications, Inc.
Proforma Cash Flow Statement - 2nd Year of Operation

Month	One	Two	Three	Four	Five	Six	Seven	Eight	Nine	Ten	Eleven	Twelve
Cash Bal Fwd	389780	120437	154607	202777	211447	265117	360537	406332	484877	582547	636092	710637
A/R's Collected	346000	282000	228000	267500	343500	306875	331250	395625	331875	335000	395625	331875
Investment/Loan	0	0	0	0	0	0	0	0	0	0	0	0
Cash Available	735780	402437	382607	470277	554947	571992	691787	801957	816752	917547	1031717	1042512
Less Operating Expenses:												
Payroll & Fringes	43155	43155	43155	43155	43155	43155	43155	43155	43155	43255	43155	43155
Admin Overhead	16641	16675	16675	16675	16675	16675	16675	16675	16675	16675	16675	26675
Marketing	81500	41000	5000	108500	45000	1000	112500	41000	5000	108500	45000	1000
Inventories	161000	137000	105000	80500	175000	140625	103125	206250	159375	103125	206250	159375
New Prod Dev	0	10000	10000	10000	10000	10000	10000	10000	10000	10000	10000	0
Equipment	20000	0	0	0	0	0	0	0	0	0	0	0
Profits Distribution	293047	0	0	0	0	0	0	0	0	0	0	0
Total Expenses	615343	247830	179830	258830	289830	211455	285455	317080	234205	281555	321080	230205
Cash Balance	120437	154607	202777	211447	265117	360537	406332	484877	582547	636092	710637	812307

Notes:

1. Operating expenses assume capitalization is an investment rather than a loan. If the $300,000 required is a loan, the interest would be paid monthly with a principal payment in the 12th month.
2. Cash balances do not reflect interest earnings.
3. The distribution of profits does not reflect possible bonus payments to officers, managers and key employees.

New Life Publications, Inc.
Sales, Accounts Receivable Collection Forecast and Inventory Costs - 2nd Year of Operation

Month	One	Two	Three	Four	Five	Six	Seven	Eight	Nine	Ten	Eleven	Twelve	TOTALS
SALES													
Catalog Sales @ $5	150000	125000	312500	187500	150000	375000	225000	150000	375000	225000	150000	375000	2800000
Ea. Average Return Product Flyer Sales @ $2.50 Ea. Avg. Return	100000	60000	62500	156250	93750	62500	156250	93750	62500	156250	93750	62500	1160000
TOTAL SALES	250000	185000	375000	343750	243750	437500	381250	243750	437500	381250	243750	437500	3960000

A/R's AS COLLECTED (40% in 30 Days; 50% in 60 Days and 10% in 90 Days)

Month	Sales	One	Two	Three	Four	Five	Six	Seven	Eight	Nine	Ten	Eleven	Twelve	TOTALS
10	45000	45000	0	0	0	0	0	0	0	0	0	0	0	45000
11	222000	185000	37000	0	0	0	0	0	0	0	0	0	0	222000
12	290000	116000	145000	29000	0	0	0	0	0	0	0	0	0	290000
1	250000	0	100000	125000	25000	0	0	0	0	0	0	0	0	250000
2	185000	0	0	74000	92500	18500	0	0	0	0	0	0	0	185000
3	375000	0	0	0	150000	187500	37500	0	0	0	0	0	0	375000
4	343750	0	0	0	0	137500	171875	34375	0	0	0	0	0	343750
5	243750	0	0	0	0	0	97500	121875	24375	0	0	0	0	243750
6	437500	0	0	0	0	0	0	175000	218750	43750	0	0	0	437500
7	381250	0	0	0	0	0	0	0	152500	190625	38125	0	0	381250
8	243750	0	0	0	0	0	0	0	0	97500	121875	24375	0	243750
9	437500	0	0	0	0	0	0	0	0	0	175000	218750	43750	437500
10	381250	0	0	0	0	0	0	0	0	0	0	152500	190625	343125
11	243750	0	0	0	0	0	0	0	0	0	0	0	97500	97500
12	437500	0	0	0	0	0	0	0	0	0	0	0	0	0
Totals		346000	282000	228000	267500	343500	306875	331250	395625	331875	335000	395625	331875	3895125

Note: A/R carry-over to next year would be $621,875.

INVENTORY COSTS:

	One	Two	Three	Four	Five	Six	Seven	Eight	Nine	Ten	Eleven	Twelve	TOTALS
Supplier Products @ 50% COGS	75000	62500	156250	93750	75000	187500	112500	75000	187500	112500	75000	187500	1400000
Company Products @ 30% COGS	30000	18000	18750	46875	28125	18750	46875	28125	18750	46875	28125	18750	348000
TOTAL COGS	105000	80500	175000	140625	103125	206250	159375	103125	206250	159375	103125	206250	1748000

Appendix A — The Private Placement Circular for New Life Publications, Inc. 49

New Life Publications, Inc.
Marketing Expenses and Advertising Schedule - 2nd Year of Operation

Month	One	Two	Three	Four	Five	Six	Seven	Eight	Nine	Ten	Eleven	Twelve	TOTALS
Marketing Exp's:													
Catalog Art/Printing	49920	0	0	75950	0	0	68200	0	0	75950	0	0	270020
Cat Mail Labels	2875	0	0	3450	0	0	3450	0	0	3450	0	0	13225
Cat Mail Prep	2500	0	0	3000	0	0	3000	0	0	3000	0	0	11500
Cat Postage	20875	0	0	25050	0	0	25050	0	0	25050	0	0	96025
Flyers Art/Printing	0	15000	0	0	15000	0	0	15000	0	0	15000	0	60000
Flyers Mail Labels	0	1625	0	0	1625	0	0	1625	0	0	1625	0	6500
Flyers Mail Prep	0	2500	0	0	2500	0	0	2500	0	0	2500	0	10000
Flyers Postage	0	20875	0	0	20875	0	0	20875	0	0	20875	0	83500
Ads in Publications	4000	0	4000	0	4000	0	11800	0	4000	0	4000	0	31800
Inquiry Postage/Misc.	1330	1000	1000	1050	1000	1000	1000	1000	1000	1050	1000	1000	12430
Total $	81500	41000	5000	108500	45000	1000	112500	41000	5000	108500	45000	1000	595000
Advertising Schedule:													
Catalogs Mailed (Pcs)	125000	0	0	150000	0	0	150000	0	0	150000	0	0	575000
Flyers Mailed (Pcs)	0	125000	0	0	125000	0	0	125000	0	0	125000	0	500000
Catalogs for Inquiries	3000	0	0	5000	0	0	5000	0	0	5000	0	0	18000
Ads in Publications	Yes	No	Yes	No	Yes	No	Yes	No	Yes	No	Yes	No	

Note: Press releases would be mailed to newspapers and magazines regarding the Company's published products.

New Life Publications, Inc.
Payroll - 2nd Year of Operation

Month	One	Two	Three	Four	Five	Six	Seven	Eight	Nine	Ten	Eleven	Twelve	TOTALS
CEO/CFO	6000	6000	6000	6000	6000	6000	6000	6000	6000	6000	6000	6000	72000
Publishing Manager	3300	3300	3300	3300	3300	3300	3300	3300	3300	3300	3300	3300	39600
Accountant	3300	3300	3300	3300	3300	3300	3300	3300	3300	3300	3300	3300	39600
Ship/Rec Manager	2500	2500	2500	2500	2500	2500	2500	2500	2500	2500	2500	2500	30000
Marketing Manager	2500	2500	2500	2500	2500	2500	2500	2500	2500	2500	2500	2500	30000
Purchasing Manager	2200	2200	2200	2200	2200	2200	2200	2200	2200	2200	2200	2200	26400
Personnel Admin Ass't	2000	2000	2000	2000	2000	2000	2000	2000	2000	2000	2000	2000	24000
Publishing Ass't	1750	1750	1750	1750	1750	1750	1750	1750	1750	1750	1750	1750	21000
Receptionist	1500	1500	1500	1500	1500	1500	1500	1500	1500	1500	1500	1500	18000
Sales/Order Entry	1850	1850	1850	1850	1850	1850	1850	1850	1850	1850	1850	1850	22200
Sales/Order Entry	1850	1850	1850	1850	1850	1850	1850	1850	1850	1850	1850	1850	22200
Sales/OE - PT	825	825	825	825	825	825	825	825	825	825	825	825	9900
Accounting Clerk	1900	1900	1900	1900	1900	1900	1900	1900	1900	1900	1900	1900	22800
Accounting Clerk - PT	800	800	800	800	800	800	800	800	800	800	800	800	9600
Lead Shipper	1800	1800	1800	1800	1800	1800	1800	1800	1800	1800	1800	1800	21600
Shipper	1600	1600	1600	1600	1600	1600	1600	1600	1600	1600	1600	1600	19200
Shipper - PT	800	800	800	800	800	800	800	800	800	800	800	800	9600
Shipper - PT	800	800	800	800	800	800	800	800	800	800	800	800	9600
Sub Total	37275	37275	37275	37275	37275	37275	37275	37275	37275	37275	37275	37275	447300
Payroll Taxes	3730	3730	3730	3730	3730	3730	3730	3730	3730	3730	3730	3730	44760
Hosp/Med/Life Ins.	2150	2150	2150	2150	2150	2150	2150	2150	2150	2150	2150	2150	25800
Total Payroll	43155	43155	43155	43155	43155	43155	43155	43155	43155	43155	43155	43155	517860
Employees:													
Full-Time	14	14	14	14	14	14	14	14	14	14	14	14	
Part-Time	4	4	4	4	4	4	4	4	4	4	4	4	
Total	18	18	18	18	18	18	18	18	18	18	18	18	

Note: The Company may add up to 6 full-time employees to the above schedule in the 2nd year if sales warrant.

New Life Publications, Inc.
Administrative Overhead - 2nd Year of Operation

Month	One	Two	Three	Four	Five	Six	Seven	Eight	Nine	Ten	Eleven	Twelve	TOTALS
Rent	3500	3500	3500	3500	3500	3500	3500	3500	3500	3500	3500	3500	42000
Utilities	350	350	350	350	350	350	350	350	350	350	350	350	4200
Telephone	2500	2500	2500	2500	2500	2500	2500	2500	2500	2500	2500	2500	30000
Office Supplies	700	700	700	700	700	700	700	700	700	700	700	700	8400
Office Printing	600	600	600	600	600	600	600	600	600	600	600	600	7200
Office Postage	2000	2000	2000	2000	2000	2000	2000	2000	2000	2000	2000	2000	24000
Outside Services	2000	2000	2000	2000	2000	2000	2000	2000	2000	2000	2000	2000	24000
CEO Relocation Exp	0	0	0	0	0	0	0	0	0	0	0	0	0
Travel/Entertainment	1250	1250	1250	1250	1250	1250	1250	1250	1250	1250	1250	1250	15000
Business Insurance	525	525	525	525	525	525	525	525	525	525	525	525	6300
Legal Services	400	400	400	400	400	400	400	400	400	400	400	400	4800
Mailing List Maint	500	500	500	500	500	500	500	500	500	500	500	500	6000
Employee Education	250	250	250	250	250	250	250	250	250	250	250	250	3000
Subs/Memberships	100	100	100	100	100	100	100	100	100	100	100	100	1200
Janitorial	750	750	750	750	750	750	750	750	750	750	750	750	9000
Equipment Maint	250	250	250	250	250	250	250	250	250	250	250	250	3000
Annual Acctg Audit	0	0	0	0	0	0	0	0	0	0	0	10000	10000
Miscellaneous	1000	1000	1000	1000	1000	1000	1000	1000	1000	1000	1000	1000	12000
Total $	16675	16675	16675	16675	16675	16675	16675	16675	16675	16675	16675	26675	210100

New Product Development Expenses - 2nd Year of Operation

	One	Two	Three	Four	Five	Six	Seven	Eight	Nine	Ten	Eleven	Twelve	TOTALS
NPD Exp $	0	10000	10000	10000	10000	10000	10000	10000	10000	10000	10000	0	100000

Appendix B

Prospectus For A Small Public Offering— Earth Stabilizers, Inc.

Highlights of the Prospectus Presented

1. The Company
2. Business of the Company
3. Management's Investment
4. Management's Background
5. Products, Services and Markets
6. Risk Factors
7. Underwriting Information
8. Audited Financial Statements

54 *Raising Capital: How To Write A Financing Proposal*

Prospectus

500,000 SHARES

EARTH STABILIZERS, INC.

Common Stock

THE SECURITIES OFFERED HEREBY ARE HIGHLY SPECULATIVE, INVOLVE A HIGH DEGREE OF RISK AND IMMEDIATE SUBSTANTIAL DILUTION. THEY SHOULD ONLY BE PURCHASED BY PERSONS WHO CAN AFFORD TO LOSE THEIR ENTIRE INVESTMENT.

Prior to this offering, there has been no public market for the Common Stock of the Company, and there can be no assurance that any such market will exist after this offering. The offering price of the Common Stock has been arbitrarily determined by negotiations between the Company and J. B. Owens & Co. (the "Underwriter") and does not bear any relationship to the Company's assets, book value, or other generally accepted criteria of value.

THE UNITED STATES SECURITIES AND EXCHANGE COMMISSION DOES NOT PASS UPON THE MERITS OF OR GIVE ITS APPROVAL TO ANY SECURITIES OFFERED OR THE TERMS OF THE OFFERING. NOR DOES IT PASS UPON THE ACCURACY OR COMPLETENESS OF ANY OFFERING CIRCULAR OR OTHER SELLING LITERATURE. THESE SECURITIES ARE OFFERED PURSUANT TO AN EXEMPTION FROM REGISTRATION WITH THE COMMISSION; HOWEVER, THE COMMISSION HAS NOT MADE AN INDEPENDENT DETERMINATION THAT THE SECURITIES OFFERED ARE EXEMPT FROM REGISTRATION.

	Price to Public	Underwriter's Commission (1)	Proceeds to the Company (2)
Per Share	$ 1.00	$ 0.10	$ 0.90
Total	$500,000	$50,000	$450,000

(see footnotes on next page)

The shares are being offered on a "Best Efforts" basis by the Underwriter subject to prior sale when, as, and if delivered to subscribers. The Company reserves the right to withdraw, cancel or modify this offering. The Underwriter and the Company reserve the right to reject at anytime, any order for the purchase of shares in whole or in part.

J. B. OWENS & COMPANY
100 VILLA AVENUE, MINNEAPOLIS, MINNESOTA 55401

The date of this Offering Circular is November 30, 199-

FOOTNOTES

(1) In addition, the Company has agreed to (i) issue to the Underwriter, for a nominal price, warrants to purchase 45,000 shares of the Company's Common Stock; (ii) pay to the Underwriter two and one half percent of the aggregate amount of the offering in non-accountable expenses; (iii) indemnify the Underwriter against certain liabilities; and (iv) grant to the Underwriter the right of first refusal for three years to represent the Company in connection with certain financings. See "Underwriting."

(2) Before deducting expenses payable by the Company related to the offering, including filing printing, legal, accounting and other miscellaneous fees and expenses estimated at $15,000 plus the non-accountable expense allowance to be received by the Underwriter.

The shares of Common Stock are offered subject to prior sale when, as and if delivered to and accepted by the Underwriter. It is expected that certificates for such shares will be ready for delivery in Minneapolis, Minnesota on or about December 30, 199-. The Underwriter reserves the right to withdraw, cancel or modify such offer and to reject orders in whole or in part.

NO PERSON HAS BEEN AUTHORIZED TO GIVE ANY INFORMATION OR TO MAKE ANY REPRESENTATION NOT CONTAINED IN THIS PROSPECTUS IN CONNECTION WITH THE OFFERING HEREIN, AND IF GIVEN OR MADE, SUCH INFORMATION OR REPRESENTATION MUST NOT BE RELIED UPON AS HAVING BEEN AUTHORIZED BY THE COMPANY OR THE UNDERWRITER. THIS PROSPECTUS DOES NOT CONSTITUTE AN OFFER OF ANY SECURITIES OTHER THAN THE SECURITIES TO WHICH IT RELATES OR AN OFFER TO ANY PERSON IN ANY JURISDICTION WHERE SUCH OFFER WOULD BE UNLAWFUL. THE DELIVERY OF THIS PROSPECTUS AT ANY TIME DOES NOT IMPLY THAT THE INFORMATION HEREIN IS CORRECT AS OF ANY TIME SUBSEQUENT TO ITS DATE.

UNTIL FEBRUARY 28, 199- (90 DAYS AFTER THE DATE OF THIS PROSPECTUS), ALL DEALERS EFFECTING TRANSACTIONS IN THE SECURITIES TO WHICH THIS PROSPECTUS RELATES, WHETHER OR NOT PARTICIPATING IN THIS DISTRIBUTION, MAY BE REQUIRED TO DELIVER A CURRENT PROSPECTUS. THIS IS IN ADDITION TO THE OBLIGATION OF DEALERS TO DELIVER A PROSPECTUS WHEN ACTING AS UNDERWRITERS AND WITH RESPECT TO THEIR UNSOLD ALLOTMENTS OR SUBSCRIPTIONS.

Summary of Prospectus

The following information is qualified in its entirety by the detailed information and financial statements appearing elsewhere in this Prospectus. Public investors should read the Prospectus in its entirety.

The Company

Earth Stabilizers, Inc. (the "Company"), will assemble certain high pressure pumping and earth probing equipment to be utilized in the application of a field tested and proven non-toxic and non-polluting sealant chemical manufactured by Preferred Chemical Corporation ("PCC").

Company trained personnel, operating this equipment, will provide contract services to rehabilitate and stabilize eroding and deteriorating properties exposed to continuous water infiltration and exfiltration. Prospective governmental, commercial and privately owned property sites requiring the Company's services include, but are not limited to, water reservoirs, dams, dikes, sea walls, canals, landscapes and building foundations throughout the United States and the world.

The Offering

Securities To Be Offered	500,000 shares of Common Stock - no par value (1)
Securities Outstanding	Before Offering: 750,000 shares After Offering: 1,250,000 shares
Approximate Net Proceeds	$422,500

(1) Does not reflect warrants to be issued to the Underwriter to purchase 45,000 shares; options issued to the founder, officers and directors to purchase 200,000 shares; and 300,000 shares reserved for issuance from time to time as options to purchase shares by certain key employees, officers and directors. See "Capitalization," "Underwriting," "Employee Stock Option Plan," and "Certain Recent Events."

Use of Proceeds

The proceeds of this offering will be used (1) to purchase component parts and assemble the Company's proprietary equipment (U. S. Patent Pending); (2) lease vehicles to trailer this equipment in the field; (3) to establish and train mobile service crews to provide contract services; and (4) for marketing, employee salaries and working capital purposes.

Certain Risk Factors

The Company does not have a operating history and the business is dependent upon key personnel. Additional financing may be required and the Company will be dependent upon its sealant supplier. For these and other reasons, an investment in the securities offered hereby involves a high degree of risk. See "Risk Factors."

The Offering

Type of Securities	Common Stock, No Par Value 5,000,000 Shares Authorized Upon Incorporation
Type of Offering	Regulation D, Rule 504
Shares Offered by the Company	500,000 (1)
Shares Outstanding Prior to Offering	750,000 (1)
Number of Shares to be Outstanding	1,250,000 (1)
Net Proceeds to the Company	$422,500
Use of Proceeds by the Company	To purchase parts and assemble equipment; train crews; lease trucks to transport equipment; marketing and for operating capital.

Shares and Percentages held by the Founder, Promoters, Directors and Officers:

	Shares	Percentages
Before Offering	750,000	100.0%
After Offering	750,000	60.0%

(1) Does not reflect stock options issued and to be issued, or warrants to be outstanding. See "Underwriting," "Certain Recent Events" and "Employee Stock Option Plan."

The Company

Earth Stabilizers, Inc. (the "Company), was incorporated in the State of Minnesota on September 1, 199- for the purpose of providing soil stabilization and rehabilitation services to governmental, commercial and private property owners in the United States and throughout the world.

These services, to be performed by Company trained personnel, will include the high pressure injection of non-toxic sealant chemicals that are activated by a controlled mix of water through a earth probe device. The utilization and application of these sealants — developed by the Preferred Chemical Corporation ("PCC") — will be used to saturate and fill voids and watercourses below ground caused by exposure to water infiltration and exfiltration. The procedure will reinforce structures retaining or restraining water movement, stabilize and seal eroding landscapes affected by heavy rainfalls and protect building foundation walls from water penetration, seepage and leaks. Such properties include, but are not limited to, water reservoirs, dams, dikes, sea walls, water channels, canals, landscapes and buildings with below ground foundations.

To facilitate the Company's ability to assure prompt and satisfactory completion of its contracting obligations, it plans to purchase the necessary components and assemble its own Mobile Equipment Units. These units will be completely self-contained systems, able to operate in remote areas when required. Each unit will include a high volume, heavy duty mixing pump, compressor, generator, water storage tanks, control panel, earth probes and other accessories which will be mounted in a small, towable utility trailer.

The Company will lease 4x4 pickup trucks to transport these units, spare parts and chemical storage containers to any work site accessible by road or trail. During the first year of operation, at least three (3) self-contained Mobile Equipment Units will be built at a cost of approximately $6,000 each. The three trucks required to tow the units will be leased at a annual cost of $4,200 each excluding licenses and insurance. See "Use of Proceeds."

Initially, the Company will establish three field crews to provide its services. The employees of these crews will be trained to operate and repair the equipment in the field. Each crew, consisting of one Crew Chief and One Field Assistant, will transport the equipment to the work site, establish a temporary base for operations in a local community and complete the contracted work. Additional field crews will be recruited and trained as the Company's business workload and revenues increase.

The Company intends to commence operations following the closing of the sale of the shares offered herein. A substantial investment of $100,000 will be made to promote and advertise the Company's capabilities. This marketing effort will include a vigorous sales effort to secure contract work through bids, direct invitation and negotiation.

The Company has $150,100 in current cash assets and has not engaged in operations since its incorporation. Selected key employees will be hired to staff the business as officers and managers who the Company believes have the necessary backgrounds, talents and expertise to conduct its business activities. See "Background of Management."

The Company believes the proceeds of this offering will satisfy its cash requirements for at least two years of operation. Its executive offices are located at 1002 Elm Street, Excelsior, Minnesota 55331 and its telephone number is (612) 424-0000.

Risk Factors

The shares offered hereby are highly speculative, involve a high degree of risk and should be purchased only by persons who can afford to lose their entire investment. Prospective investors should carefully consider the risks associated with this offering. Each offeree of the shares should, prior to purchase, carefully consider the following factors, as well as the other information contained in this Prospectus.

1. **Lack of Profitability**
   There can be no assurance that the Company will be able to commercially market its services or operate profitably.

2. **Absence of Operating History**
   The Company does not have a history of operating as a viable entity.

3. **Business is Dependent Upon Key Employees**
   The business of the Company is dependent upon the active participation of the Company's officers and managers. The loss of one or two of these individuals could adversely affect the conduct of the business.

4. **Additional Financing May Be Required**
   Although the Company believes that the funds raised in this offering will be sufficient for its growth needs over a two year period, the conduct of the Company's business may require the raising of additional funds.

5. **Non-Toxic Sealants**
   The Company will initially be dependent upon the Preferred Chemical Corporation for the chemical sealants used in conjunction with its soil stabilization equipment. Should this supplier cease to manufacture such sealants, there would be a period of downtime required to refurbish the Company's injection systems to accommodate other non-toxic, non-polluting chemicals on the market.

6. **Contractors Liability**
   Although the Company will maintain considerable insurance protection against liability claims, it will be required, on occasion, to post contractor performance bonds on certain projects. As a contracting Company, its exposure to lawsuits will be continually present.

7. **Warranty Obligation**
   The Company will not be in a position to guarantee that the sealants utilized will offer continuous protection against water infiltration and exfiltration. The policy of the Company will be to approach each job on its merits regarding any performance guarantee it may offer. In the case of sealing below ground walls of buildings or residential foundations, the Company intends to guarantee its workmanship for a period of five years against leaks which could occur. It will not guarantee possible leaks that could occur through the floors of a structure since high water tables could cause such leakage through no fault of the Company. The guarantee policy for building structures would be limited to the re-injection of sealants in the area where a leak has been verified and no other liability would be assumed.

8. **No Dividends**
   No dividends will be paid by the Company in the foreseeable future. Any future dividends will depend upon the earnings of the Company, its financial requirements and other factors. Investors who anticipate the need for immediate dividend income from their investment in the Company's Common Stock, should refrain from purchasing such shares. See "Description of Common Stock."

9. **Outstanding Warrants**
   The Company has granted warrants to purchase 45,000 shares of its Common Stock to the Underwriter for a nominal price. If these warrants are exercised, the percentage of Common Stock held by the public shareholders will decrease. See "Underwriting" and "Underwriter's Warrants."

10. **Competition**
    The Company will be in competition with several major drain tile installation companies and other companies offering a variety of chemical sealant services. See "Competition."

11. **Lack of Market Protection and Patent Applications**
    The basic business concept of soil stabilization or waterproofing through the use of injected chemical sealants is one which may be freely used by any firm. However, the Company has applied for patent protection on its unique sealant injection system which it believes is far superior to those currently used by other contracting firms.

12. **Control By Management**
    The 750,000 shares of the Company's Common Stock presently owned beneficially by the Company's founders will constitute in the aggregate 60% of the total shares to be outstanding upon the satisfactory completion of this offering, without giving effect to the possible exercise of warrants granted to the underwriter or stock options issued to the officers and directors. This percentage will allow the founder of the Company to control and exert significant influence over the business. In addition, and to the extent that 300,000 shares are available for issuance in the future to key employees, officers and directors — as options to purchase shares through the Employee Stock Option Plan, and should they be exercised, management will be able to increase its control and influence over the Company.

13. **Public Offering Price**
    The number of shares of Common Stock offered hereby and the public offering price were arbitrarily determined by negotiation between the Company and the Underwriter, and are not necessarily based on net worth or other generally accepted criteria of value.

14. **No Public Market**
    There is, at present, no market for shares of the Company's Common Stock. Although it is anticipated that the Underwriter and perhaps others may make a market in the shares of this stock, there can be no assurance that such a market will ever develop or that the shares offered hereby may be resold upon the completion of this offering. If such a market does develop, there can be no assurance that the shares purchased through this offering may be resold without incurring a loss thereon.

15. **Government Regulations**

    The sale and installation of certain chemical sealants to be used by the Company, in the performance of its contract work, are subject to federal, state and local environmental and safety codes which may vary significantly from community to community. While the Company has selected a high quality, non-toxic, non-polluting, inert chemical sealant product that complies with current underground 'use codes' of the federal, state and local governments nationwide, the possibility exists whereby new standards, laws and codes could be enacted that might affect the Company's business. See "Business of the Company."

Dilution

The Company has, as of November 30, 199-, 750,000 shares of its Common Stock outstanding with a net tangible book value (total assets less liabilities) of approximately $0.20 per share or $150,100.

Upon its incorporation on September 1, 199-, the Company issued 550,000 shares to the founder and president in exchange for $100,000 or approximately $.182 per share. On September 15, 199-, the Company sold an additional 200,000 shares to officers and directors for $50,000 or $0.25 per share. $100 was received from the Underwriter for warrants to purchase an additional 45,000 shares. See "Underwriter's Warrants." Cumulative voting is not allowed in the election of directors or officers and the holders of the above shares and warrants to purchase shares will be in a position to control the Company.

After the sale of the shares offered hereby, the public will own 500,000 shares or approximately 40% of the Company's outstanding Common Stock, for which they will have paid $1.00 per share or a total of $500,000. The Company, in this event, will have 1,250,000 shares outstanding with a net tangible book value after deducting discounts, commissions and other estimated expenses associated with this offering of $0.458 per share or a total of approximately $572,500.

The public shareholders will incur an immediate dilution or reduction in the present value of their investment of about $0.542 per share in the net tangible book value of the shares held by them, and present shareholders will benefit by an increase of about $.258 per share in the net tangible book value of the shares held by them.

Per Share Dilution

"Net Tangible Book Value" is the amount that results from subtracting the total liabilities and intangible assets of the Company from its total assets. "Dilution" is the difference between the public offering price and the net tangible book value of shares immediately after the public offering.

The following chart illustrates the percentage of equity in the Company purchased by the public investors and the percentage of total capital invested by them compared with the percentage of equity purchased by the founder, officers and directors, and the percentage of total capital invested by them — assuming that all shares offered are sold:

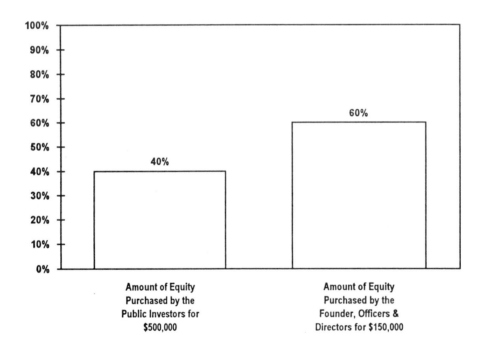

This chart does not give consideration to the warrants issued to the Underwriter to purchase 45,000 shares or the options to purchase 200,000 shares that have been issued to the directors and officers.

The following chart illustrates the public offering price paid by the public investors; net tangible book value before and after the sale of shares; the dilution for new investors and the gain realized by the present shareholders:

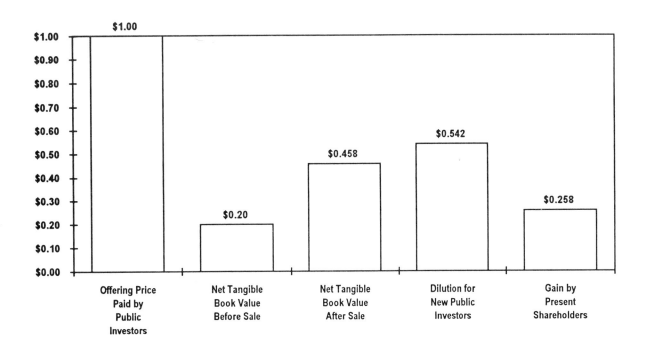

Use of Proceeds

The net proceeds to the Company, after deducting underwriting commissions and other expenses of this offering will be approximately $422,500 — assuming all of the 500,000 shares offered are sold. The following expenditures will be allocated and applied in the order of their priority:

To purchase various parts and components to assemble three (3) self-contained Mobile Equipment Units	$ 18,000
Spare Parts Inventory	8,500
To purchase initial chemical sealant inventories	15,000
To lease three (3) 4x4 pickup trucks to transport the Mobile Equipment Units — 3 Year Leasing Costs	37,000
Marketing and Advertising	120,000
Shop fixtures, tools, furniture and office equipment	26,500
Total	$ 225,000

The balance of the proceeds and other cash assets of the Company totaling $346,700 will be utilized for general corporate purposes, including the payment of employee salaries and for working capital. The Company will further seek to establish credit lines with banks and other institutions to insure that sufficient working capital is available. The Company, however, does not have any present intention to borrow funds except as may be necessary to develop the business. Accordingly, and because presently unforeseen circumstances may cause some variation in the allocation of the proceeds of this offering, the Company reserves the right to make such variations as the situation may warrant.

To the extent that the foregoing proceeds and other cash assets of the Company are not immediately used, they will be invested in money market accounts, government and other highly rated securities.

Business of the Company

General

The Company will be engaged in contracting soil stabilization and rehabilitation services to government agencies, commercial and private property and building owners. Marketing will first focus on developing project contracts in the United States, however, expansion to the international community is planned once the Company has earned a solid reputation for its work in the domestic market, and has accumulated the necessary capital to establish field crews and their equipment in other areas of the world.

The Company intends to assemble its own self-contained Mobile Equipment Units and will continually improve this equipment and its injecting systems as new technologies become available.

The Company may 'joint venture' certain contracting assignments with other reputable domestic and international contracting companies on projects requiring their assistance, expertise and services. Such joint ventures, if any, will be entered into if it is beneficial and in the best interests of both parties or a requirement of a municipality, the federal government or a general contractor.

To enhance the Company's services, it plans to engage the full-time services of a qualified geological engineer to provide government, commercial and residential property owners with a professional evaluation and feasibility report for sites being considered for sealant injection and rehabilitation.

Services

During the first year of operation, the Company will recruit, train and equip at least three field crews. These 'home based' crews will transport their equipment and supplies to the work site; establish a temporary base near the area where the work is to be performed; and will stay on location until the job is completed.

Management believes that a single crew, using the Company's equipment, can complete a minimum of 2,500 lineal feet of underground or barrier injection sealing per month at a contracted fee of $20 per foot. This rate is somewhat lower than prevailing rates for cement grouting and certain drain tile applications.

Although the Company may establish permanent regional service crews in the future — as the volume of work increases — management does not believe such centers would be cost effective at this time. By operating with home based field crews and assigning them to the various job sites, the Company's field operating expenses will be easier to estimate and control.

The Company may also consider establishing selected subcontractors to service certain geographical areas through a licensing agreement, but has not and does not plan to enter into these possible agreements in the near future.

Potential Markets

There are many areas in the United States and around the world where the Company's services are needed because of severe water problems. The actual geographical locations for the marketing effort have not been finalized, but the following regions in the domestic market are currently being studied: (1) Mid-Atlantic (Virginia, North and South Carolina); (2) Florida; (3) The Southeast (Alabama, Mississippi and Tennessee); (4) Midwest (Iowa, Minnesota, Illinois, Indiana and Ohio); (5) The Northeast (New England States and Upstate New York); (6) South Central (Southeast Texas and Louisiana); and (7) West (Arizona, California, Oregon and Washington).

Possible international locations include: (1) Canada; (2) Northern Europe; (3) Far East (Japan); and (4) North Atlantic (England, Ireland and Scotland).

The state-of-the-art in soil stabilization, rehabilitation and erosion control is not new although there has been a lack of reliable systems, technical expertise and non-toxic, environmentally acceptable products to surmount the problems of water damage. The Company believes that by using its high pressure Mobile Sealing System, it will have the capability to 'get to the problem' underground. By offering a reputable chemical sealant product and the technical expertise needed to analyze and correct a damaged property or provide a barrier to check further damage, management believes the Company can make a significant contribution to the industry and its clients.

Equipment and Products

To provide prompt and reliable services, the Company will manufacturer its own proprietary equipment.

The Mobile Sealing System

The Mobile Sealing System ("MSS") incorporates several prefabricated components including a high volume, heavy duty mixing pump, compressor, generator, water storage tanks, electronic control panel, earth probes, high pressure hoses and other accessories. The system is assembled and mounted in a small utility type trailer that can be easily towed by a pickup truck. The combination of the MSS and a truck is called the Mobile Equipment Unit. The Company has build one MSS which has been successfully field tested and has applied for patent protection for the system and the unique Earth Probe Device it has invented and developed. The single MSS owned by the Company will be used for training purposes.

To activate the MSS, water, under high pressure, is first pumped through a hose to the earth probe causing it to penetrate the earth utilizing the principle of water powered jet action. When the probe reaches the depth level required, the operator injects, through a series of procedures, a combination of water and a non-toxic sealant chemical. As the earth probe is slowly withdrawn from the ground, the chemical, activated by water, is pumped under pressure into the earth until the exiting probe nears the surface and the procedure is terminated. The probe is then repositioned for the next insertion.

After about 10 to 15 minutes, the activated sealant expands and forms a tight, open-cell type of gasket which fills all underground voids and previous water-courses. In addition, and because the chemical is pumped under pressure with water, the soil below ground is sealed tightly, thus blocking all avenues for water to flow into the immediate area. By injecting the chemical at closely spaced intervals, a barrier is formed underground that will check future water infiltration and stop the erosion of soil through water exfiltration. The Mobile Sealing System, mounted in a utility trailer, cost approximately $6,000 to build.

Chemical Sealants

The Company will use Preferred Chemical Corporation's non-toxic sealant chemicals in conjunction with its Mobile Sealing System. This product line is currently available direct from PCC who manufacturers the sealants primarily for underground pipeline repair companies. The Company has secured a national distributorship agreement with PCC to market the sealants throughout the world, and as a result, will be able to realize substantial savings on its own inventory costs — in addition to serving as PCC's sole international distributor.

The Company has chosen PCC's products because they are considered safe, tough, durable, will not crumble, shrivel, crack or wash away, and they are resistant to common soil acids and to extremes in soil temperature. PCC's sealants have proven reliable for over ten (10) years in the field and have been accepted and approved in the United States for use in soil stabilization projects and to repair leaks in underground wastewater and freshwater pipelines. If for some reason, the Company was unable to obtain these sealant products in the future, it would be necessary to refurbish its equipment to accommodate other products available in the marketplace.

Pickup Trucks

The Company will lease 4x4 3/4 ton pickup trucks to transport the crew, chemical supplies, spare parts and the Mobile Sealing Systems. They will be equipped with lockable bed toppers, standard accessories and air conditioning. The Company will seek competitive bids for its truck requirements. The per unit lease cost is expected to be about $350/month or $4,200 per year. At least three trucks will be leased immediately at a estimated cost of $12,600 per year or $37,800 over a three year period.

Marketing

The Company will promote its services to local, state and federal agencies, commercial and private property owners, and actively solicit contract work by direct invitation, negotiation and specific project bids. In connection with its 'joint venture' plans, the Company will seek other reputable contracting companies who are working on projects where the Company's services are needed and where joint participation is deemed beneficial and in the interests of both parties.

A substantial investment will be made in regional and national trade publication advertising, direct mail and personal contact with potential clients. The Company intends to employ experienced sales representatives to call on prospects rather than utilize independent or manufacturers' representatives to promote and sell its services.

The goal of the Company is to build a international reputation as a skilled and reliable soil stabilization and rehabilitation contractor.

Pending Contract

While the Company has not entered into any contracts for its services or engaged in any operations since its incorporation except to build one Mobile Sealing System, it has been offered a contract by the State of North Carolina to repair a six mile sea wall using its MSS and PCC chemical sealants. This pending contract, should it be accepted, is valued at over $600,000.

Competition

The Company's major competitors are drain tile installation contracting companies located throughout the world and many of them have enjoyed consistent growth and a good reputation for their work.

A limited number of firms operate as 'waterproofing' contractors who utilize cement type grouts which are currently unacceptable for restoring potable water storage facilities and above or below ground water pipelines. Although the use of these grouts will seal voids underground, they will not bind the soil to prevent new watercourses from developing.

The urgent need is for reliable systems designed to inject environmentally safe sealing products that will provide lasting results. The Company's Mobile Sealing System is a state-of-the-art technology, designed to meet today's environmental concerns and provide a new level of expertise in controlling underground water problems. By offering the technical support of a qualified geological engineer, the Company will operate in areas where its competition has little expertise or the ability to execute the work.

In regard to those firms which install drain tile, the Company believes its methods will produce superior results, are cost competitive and offer the important advantage of not destroying the surface of a property to remedy the water problem. While drain tile will direct water flow away from a affected area, it will not stabilize underground sites that have suffered from erosion, nor can drain tile reinforce barriers or structures such as sea walls, dikes and dams designed to restrict or confine water movement.

An unconventional method of 'waterproofing' has surfaced in recent years whereby the installer digs a trench around a home or building and pours chemicals into it. When mixed with water, it is suppose to percolate down into the earth and seal the foundation from further water penetration and leaks. The Company does not support this technique and is highly skeptical regarding the results of such an application.

Employees

After the sale of shares offered herein, the Company will employ: (1) President/CEO to supervise all business operations; (1) Chief Financial Officer to manage the accounting department and office administration; (1) National Sales Manager; (1) Geologist for engineering and sales support; (3) Crew Chiefs; (3) Crew Assistants; (1) Mechanic; and (1) Administrative Assistant. A total of 12 full-time employees. Additional personnel will be recruited as the needs of the business develop and its financial condition warrants. See "Background of Management."

The Company is not a party to any union or collective bargaining agreement affecting its employees and believes its relationship with them will be satisfactory.

Property

The Company's executive offices, shop and warehouse are presently located at 1002 Elm Street, Excelsior, Minnesota 55331 and occupy a total of 1,500 square feet. This space has been provided free-of-charge by David O. Williamson, President of the Company until this public offering has been successfully completed. After the closing of the offering, the business will lease approximately 3,000 square feet of office, shop and warehouse space in a western suburb of Minneapolis at an estimated cost of $1,500 per month plus utilities. This new location is expected to be adequate for the needs of the business for at least two years.

Intangible Assets

The Company has applications pending at the U. S. Patent Office on its Mobile Sealing System and unique Earth Probe Device and will continue to file patent applications for any product or improvements it develops in the future. The Company believes that patent protection, while important, is not the deciding factor in determining whether or not it will develop a new product or service technique.

Management and Controlling Shareholders

The names and resident addresses of the founder, directors, officers, promoters and shareholders holding Common Stock in the Company as of the date of this Prospectus are as follows:

Name, Address and Office	Shares owned of record and beneficially	% of Shares owned prior to Offering	% of Shares owned after Offering	% of time devoted to Company
David O. Williamson (1) 23 Oak Street Edina, MN 55345 Founder, Chairman, President/CEO & Promoter	550,000 Shares	73.333%	44.000%	100%
John P. Budd 421 Cedar Hopkins, MN 55334 Director, CFO & Promoter	100,000 Shares	13.333%	8.000%	100%
James A. Richardson 63391 Bradley Tonka Bay, MN 55331 Director & Secretary	50,000 Shares	6.666%	4.000%	1%
Philip N. Kreuger 7550 1st Ave., Edina, MN 55345 Director	50,000 Shares	6.666%	4.000%	1%

(1) David O. Williamson is the founder of the Company within the meaning of the Securities Act of 1933 and may be deemed a controlling entity and founding shareholder.

Remuneration of Officer and Directors

As Chief Executive Officer of the Company, David O. Williamson will receive a salary of $39,000 plus Company paid medical and life insurance benefits as remuneration during the first year of operation. John P. Budd, Chief Financial Officer, will receive a salary of $36,000 plus Company paid medical and life insurance benefits. Annual bonuses may be paid to the officers and key employees based on the profits of the Company, however, no bonus plan has been approved by the Board of Directors. The Directors will receive no fees for attending meetings of the Board of Directors and when performing their duties in behalf of the Company as its representatives.

Background of Management

David O. Williamson, age 44, is the founder, chairman of the board, president, chief executive officer and promoter of the Company. Prior to founding Earth Stabilizers, Inc., he was the former general manager of Arco Pipeline Corporation in Golden Valley, Minnesota and developed that company's underground pipeline repair systems. From 1968 to 1975, he was a consulting engineer for the Rand Pipeline Development Company in Dallas, Texas and participated in the design of undersea pipelines for off shore drilling operations. Mr. Williamson is a 1968 graduate engineer from the University of Michigan and has published several papers on pipeline construction in professional industry journals.

John P. Budd, age 39, is a director, chief financial officer and promoter of the Company. Prior to joining the Company, he was employed as the controller for the Kalstead Corporation in Minneapolis, Minnesota for the past 17 years. He is a 1973 graduate from the University of Minnesota and holds a BS degree in Accounting. Mr. Budd is a member of the National Association of Accountants and the Institute of Management Accounting.

James A. Richardson, age 52, is a director and serves as the corporate secretary for the Company. He is an attorney at law and has been in private practice since 1963. received his Juris Doctorate from Hamline University School of Law in 1963 (cum laude) and his BA degree in Psychology from the University of Minnesota in 1959.

Philip N. Kreuger, age 49, is a director of the Company. Mr. Kreuger has been a free-lance water management consultant for the past 28 years and is a 1963 engineering graduate from the University of Southern California. He has written numerous papers and articles published in several international trade journals and publications, and is the author of two books on fresh water management.

Additional candidates for the Company's Board of Directors will be sought to provide counsel and the appropriate expertise for continued development and growth. Management will, from time to time, seek to utilize the securities of the Company as incentives for its directors, officers and key employees through its Employee Stock Option Plan.

Capitalization

The capitalization of the Company on September 1, 199-, and as adjusted to reflect the sale of subsequent shares and the sale of shares offered hereby, is set forth in the following table:

Title and Class	Amount Authorized	Amount Outstanding Before Offering	Amount to be Outstanding After Offering
Stockholders' Equity, Common Stock, No Par Value (1)	5,000,000	750,000	1,250,000
Underwriter's Stock Purchase Warrants (2)	45,000	0	45,000
Incentive Stock Options to Directors & Officers (3)	200,000	0	200,000
Employee Stock Options for Key Employees, Officers & Directors (3)	300,000	0	300,000

(1) Does not include 45,000 shares for issuance upon exercise of the Underwriter's stock purchase warrants or the incentive stock options on 200,000 shares to be issued to the Directors and Officers or the options to purchase up to 300,000 shares to be issued under the Employee Stock Option Plan.

(2) See "Underwriting."

(3) See "Certain Recent Events and Transactions" and "Employee Stock Option Plan."

Certain Recent Events and Transactions

As the founder and promoter of the Company, David O. Williamson received 550,000 shares of its Common Stock for which he paid $100,000 in cash on September 1, 199-. John P. Budd received 100,000 shares for which he paid $25,000 on September 15, 199-, and on September 15, 199-, James A. Richardson and Philip N. Kreuger each received 50,000 shares for which they both paid $12,500 in cash. On September 25, 199-, the Underwriter paid a $100 fee for Warrants To Purchase up to 45,000 shares of the Company's Common Stock. See "Underwriter's Warrants."

On September 15, 199-, the Board of Directors elected to provide Incentive Options to the Directors and Officers of the Company to purchase up to 200,000 shares of its Common Stock at $1.00 per share. Such options must be exercised within a two year period beginning March 1, 199-. Any portion of the Incentive Options that are not exercised by March 1, 199-, will be automatically revoked. Mr. Williamson, Mr. Budd, Mr. Richardson and Mr. Kreuger each received options to purchase up to 50,000 shares under this plan. The options are not assignable and may only be exercised by the directors who received them.

Employee Stock Option Plan

An Employee Stock Option Plan was adopted by the Board of Directors on September 15, 199-. Under the plan, options to purchase shares of the Company's Common Stock may be granted from time to time to directors, officers and key employees up to a maximum aggregate total of 300,000 shares subject to adjustment in case of stock splits and stock dividends. For details about this plan, please see "Description of Common Stock."

Description of Common Stock

General

The Company's authorized capital stock consists of 5,000,000 shares of its no par value Common Stock. Warrants to purchase up to 45,000 such shares, a Incentive Stock Option Plan to purchase up to 200,000 shares and a Employee Stock Option Plan to purchase up to 300,000 shares are included. See "Underwriting," "Certain Recent Events and Transactions," and "Employee Stock Option Plan."

Dividends

Holders of the Company's Common Stock are entitled to receive dividends when and as declared by the Company's Board of Directors out of funds legally available therefor. Any such dividends may be paid in cash, property or shares of the Company's Common Stock. The Company presently anticipates that all earnings, if any, will be retained for development of the Company's business and that no dividends on its Common Stock will be declared in the foreseeable future. Any future dividends will be subject to the discretion of the Company's Board of Directors, and would depend upon, among other things, future earnings, the operating and financial condition of the Company, its capital requirements, and its general business condition. Therefore, there can be no assurance that any dividends on the Company's Common Stock will be paid in the future.

Voting Rights

All shares of the Company's Common Stock have equal voting rights, and, when validly issued and outstanding, have one vote per share on all matters to be voted upon by the stockholders. Cumulative voting in the election of Directors is not allowed.

Miscellaneous Rights and Provisions

Shares of the Company's Common Stock have no preemptive or conversion rights, no redemption or sinking fund provisions, and are not liable to future call or assessment. The outstanding shares of the Common Stock are, and any shares sold pursuant to this offering will be, fully paid and non-assessable. Each share of the Company's Common Stock is entitled to share ratably in any assets available for distribution to holders of its equity securities upon liquidation of the Company.

Incentive Stock Option Plan Terms

An Incentive Stock Option Plan was adopted by the Board of Directors. Under the plan, four directors received options to purchase up to 50,000 shares each at $1.00 per share within a period of two years commencing March 1, 199-. These options are not assignable and may only be exercised by the four directors who received the "Options to Purchase." Any portion of the options issued and not exercised within a two year period will be automatically revoked by the Company and will not be reinstated. The Incentive Stock Option Plan was approved because the Company does not intend to pay its directors fees for attending board meetings and because the Company places a high value on the services that have been and will be provided by its directors in the future.

Employee Stock Option Plan Terms

An Employee Stock Option Plan was adopted by the Board of Directors. Under the plan, options may be granted to key employees, officers and directors up to a maximum aggregate of 300,000 shares of the Company's Common Stock subject to adjustments in case of stock splits and stock dividends. Options may be granted for terms up to six years and the option price must not be less than the fair market value of the stock at the time the option is granted. Additionally, the plan requires that the aggregate fair market value of eligible stock, determined at the time of grant of the option, may not exceed $100,000 per calendar year, and the total amount of options granted to any employee, officer or director for all years cannot exceed $500,000.

Underwriter's Warrants

In connection with this offering, the Company has agreed to sell to the Underwriter — for a fee of $100 — Warrants to Purchase up to 45,000 shares of its Common Stock at exercise prices formally agreed upon. See "Underwriting."

Escrow of Shares

All of the Common Shares of the Company issued and outstanding prior to the offering made hereby will be held in escrow by the Cummings National Bank of Minneapolis, Minnesota for 13 months from the date of this Prospectus and will be released to the owners of those shares upon written advice by the Company after that time. The Company and the shareholders represent that none of the interests of the shares have been transferred, assigned or otherwise disposed of.

Report to Shareholders

The Company intends to furnish annual reports to its stockholders containing financial statements reported upon by independent certified public accountants, and may also issue unaudited quarterly or other interim reports to its stockholders as it deems appropriate.

Transfer Agent

The Company has retained Jackson Stock Transfer Company, Minneapolis, Minnesota as its transfer agent and registrar of its Common Stock.

Limitations of Officers' and Directors' Liability

As permitted by governing provisions of Minnesota Law, the Company's Articles of Incorporation provide that no director of the Company shall be personally liable to the Company or its shareholders for monetary damages for any breach of fiduciary duty by such a person in his or her capacity as a director. The Company's Articles of Incorporation and Bylaws also provide for indemnification of the Company's officers, directors, employees and agents to the fullest extent permitted by law. Such limitations of liability will not affect the availability of equitable remedies such as injunctive relief or rescission. Insofar as indemnification for liabilities arising under the Securities Act of 1933 may be permitted to officers and directors, the Company has been informed that in the opinion of the Securities and Exchange Commission, such indemnification is against public policy as expressed in the Act and is therefore unenforceable.

Underwriting

Subject to the terms and conditions of the Underwriting Agreement between J. B. Owens and Company (the "Underwriter") and the Company, the Underwriter has agreed to purchase from the Company the 500,000 shares of the Company's Common Stock offered hereby. The following is a summary of the principal terms of the Underwriting Agreement and the Underwriter's Warrants, and does not purport to be complete. Reference is made to a copy of the Underwriting Agreement and to the form of Warrant which has been filed as exhibits to the Registration Statement of which this Prospectus is a part. See "Additional Information."

The Underwriter is obligated to purchase all of the shares offered hereby, if any are purchased, subject to the terms and conditions set forth in the Underwriting Agreement, at the public offering price set forth on the Cover Page of this Prospectus less the 10 percent ($0.10) per share underwriting discount. The Underwriter proposes to reoffer part of the shares directly to the public at the public offering price set forth on the Cover Page of this Prospectus and the balance thereof to selected dealers who are members of the National Association of Securities Dealers, Inc. at the public offering price, less a negotiated concession per share, from which concession an amount to be negotiated may be allowed by such dealers to certain other brokers and dealers.

The Underwriting Agreement provides that for a period of three years from the closing of this offering the Underwriter will have the right of first refusal with respect to any public offering or private placement by the Company or any of its affiliates, excluding bank or institutional debt financing, in excess of $300,000.

The Underwriting Agreement provides for reciprocal covenants of indemnification against certain liabilities, including civil liabilities under the Securities Act of 1933, as amended. In addition, the Underwriting Agreement provides that the Company will pay to the Underwriter, for its out-of-pocket expenses (including attorneys' fees), a non-accountable expense allowance of two and one half percent of the aggregate amount of the offering. The Underwriter is to bear the expenses, including attorneys' fees and disbursements incurred in connection with the qualification of the shares offered hereby with the regulatory agency of the State of Minnesota.

The offering of the shares covered by this Prospectus is made by the Underwriter subject to prior sale, the approval of certain legal matters by counsel, withdrawal, cancellation, modification or termination of this offering without notice and the right to reject subscriptions in whole or in part.

Underwriter's Warrants

The Company has agreed, upon consummation of the offering of the shares, to sell to the Underwriter, for a fee of $100, warrants to purchase 45,000 shares of its Common Stock ("Warrants"), exercisable in whole or in part, at any time during a period of four years beginning the first anniversary date of issuance thereof at an exercise price of $1.07 during the first 12 month period; $1.14 during the second 12 month period; $1.21 during the third 12 month period and $1.28 during the fourth 12 month period during which such warrants are exercisable.

The exercise price and the number of shares of Common Stock which may be purchased upon the exercise of the Warrants are subject to adjustment upon the occurrence of certain events, including stock dividends, stock splits, stock reclassification, and any combination of the Common Stock or the merger, consolidation or disposition of substantially all the assets of the Company.

No adjustment of the exercise price of the Warrants will be made in connection with the exercise of the issuance of shares of Common Stock upon the exercise of stock options heretofore outstanding or granted pursuant to the Company's Incentive Stock Option Plan and the Employee Stock Option Plan. The Warrants are not transferable except to individuals who are both stockholders and officers of the Underwriter or who are employees of the Underwriter. The Warrants and the shares issuable upon the exercise thereof have been included in the Registration Statement of which this Prospectus is a part.

Determination of Public Offering Price

The initial offering price of the shares offered hereby has been established by negotiations between the Company and the Underwriter. The primary factors involved in establishing the offering price were the amount of funds necessary for the Company to undertake the activities referred to herein and the percentage of the total equity of the Company that management believes should be publicly offered pursuant to this offering. The value that the public offering price purports to place on the Company's securities may bear no relationship to the assets or other criteria of value applicable to the Company. See "Dilution."

Legal Matters

The validity of issuance of the Common Stock offered hereby will be passed upon for the Company by Moffitt, Blaine and McNoll, Professional Association, 75531 Parkway Avenue, Minneapolis, Minnesota 55401. Certain legal matters will be passed upon for the Underwriter by Tyson, Smith and Waters, PA, 122 Brand Building, Minneapolis, Minnesota 55402.

Registration Statement

The Company has filed with the Securities and Exchange Commission, Chicago, Illinois 66610, a Registration Statement under the Securities Act of 1933, as amended, with respect to the securities offered hereby. This Prospectus omits certain information contained in said Registration Statement, of which this Prospectus is a part, and the exhibits hereto, and reference is hereby made to such Registration Statement and exhibits. The Registration Statement may be examined without charge by anyone at the offices of the Chicago Regional Office of the Commission, Room 1204, Everett McKinley Dirksen Bldg., 220 South Dearborn Street, Chicago, Illinois 60604, and copies of all or any part of such Registration Statement may be obtained from the Securities and Exchange Commission, 500 N. Capitol Street, Washington, DC 20549 upon payment of the appropriate fees.

Litigation

No legal proceedings to which the Company is a party or which any of its property is the subject are pending or known to be contemplated, and the Company knows of no legal proceedings pending or threatened, or judgements entered against any director or officer is his capacity as such.

Experts

The financial statements of the Company and the financial information appearing under the caption "Selected Financial Information" included in this Prospectus have been examined by Canter, Scott and Company, independent certified public accountants, to the extent set forth in their report which appears herein. These financial statements have been included in the Prospectus and in the Registration Statement, of which this Prospectus is a part, in reliance upon the report and upon the authority of such firm as experts in auditing and accounting.

***

Independent Auditor's Report

To the Board of Directors
Earth Stabilizers, Inc.
Excelsior, Minnesota 55331

October 27, 199-

Gentlemen:

We have audited the accompanying balance sheet of Earth Stabilizers, Inc. (a development stage, non-operating company) as of October 1, 199-, and related statements of operations for the period from September 1, 199- (date of incorporation) through October 1, 199-. These financial statements are the responsibility of the Company's management. Our responsibility is to express an opinion on these financial statements based on our audit.

We conducted our audit in accordance with generally accepted auditing standards. Those standards require that we plan and perform the audit to obtain reasonable assurance about whether the financial statements are free of material misstatement. An audit includes examining, on a test basis, evidence supporting the amounts and disclosures in the financial statements. An audit also includes assessing the accounting principles used and estimates made by management, as well as evaluating the overall financial statement presentation. We believe that our audit provides a reasonable basis for our opinion.

In our opinion, the financial statements referred to above present fairly, in all material respects, the financial position of Earth Stabilizers, Inc. as of October 1, 199-, in conformity with generally accepted accounting principles.

The Company is in the development stage and has not engaged in business as of October 1, 199-. Therefore it does not have any revenues or expenses, other than those expenses incurred as prepaid expenses in preparation for its public offering of Common Stock shares; to develop one prototype Mobile Sealing System, and its Startup Organizational Expenses. The balance sheet reflects the Company's financial condition accurately as of October 1, 199-.

CANTER, SCOTT AND COMPANY
Certified Public Accountants
620 Federal Arts Building
Minneapolis, Minnesota 55401

Earth Stabilizers, Inc.
(a development stage company)

BALANCE SHEET
as of
October 1, 199-

ASSETS

CURRENT ASSETS	
Cash	$ 122,000
Prepaid Public Offering Expenses	20,000
TOTAL CURRENT ASSETS	$ 142,000
OTHER ASSETS	
One (1) Mobile Sealing System (at cost)	6,000
Organizational Costs	2,000
TOTAL OTHER ASSETS	$ 8,000
TOTAL ASSETS	**$ 150,000**

LIABILITIES AND SHAREHOLDERS' EQUITY

CURRENT LIABILITIES	
Trade Accounts	$ 0
Notes Payable	0
TOTAL LIABILITIES	$ 0
SHAREHOLDERS' EQUITY	
Common Stock, No Par Value: 5,000,000 shares authorized, 750,000 shares issued and outstanding.	150,000
TOTAL SHAREHOLDERS' EQUITY	$ 150,000
TOTAL LIABILITIES & SHAREHOLDERS' EQUITY	**$ 150,000**

Earth Stabilizers, Inc.
(a development stage company)

STATEMENT OF SHAREHOLDERS' EQUITY
For the Period of September 1, 199-
(Date of Incorporation)
to
October 1, 199-

	Common Stock Number of Shares	Amount	Total
Initial issuance of common stock on September 1, 199- for $0.182 per share	550,000	$100,000	$100,000
Issuance of common stock on September 15, 199- for $0.25 per share	200,000	$ 50,000	$ 50,000
Balance, October 1, 199-	750,000	$150,000	$150,000

Earth Stabilizers, Inc.
(a development stage company)

STATEMENT OF CASH FLOW

For the Period from September 1, 199-
(Date of Incorporation)
to
October 1, 199-

CASH FLOW FROM FINANCING ACTIVITIES	
Sale of Common Stock	$ 150,000
NET CASH PROVIDED BY FINANCING ACTIVITIES	$ 150,000
CASH FLOW FROM INVESTING ACTIVITIES	
Prepaid Public Offering Expenses	20,000
Purchase of Components to Build Mobile Sealing System	6,000
Organizational Costs	2,000
NET CASH USED BY INVESTING ACTIVITIES	$ 28,000
CASH, BEGINNING OF PERIOD	$ 150,000
CASH, END OF PERIOD	$ 122,000

Notice to Reader

Other Statements

If a Company has an operating history, other statements would include a Statement of Operations for at least three previous fiscal years (all must be audited) and would show for each of those years: Sales, Cost of Sales, Gross Profit, Operating Expenses (selling, general operating, administrative and interest payments), Profit or (Loss) from the Operation, Other Income, Profit or (Loss) Before Income Taxes, Provision for Income Tax Payments, Net Profit or (Loss) After Tax Payment, Profit or (Loss) Per Share (for each year presented) based on the weighted average number of shares outstanding during the respective periods, and the Average Number of Shares Outstanding for each year.

Another statement that can be included is the Statement of Changes in Financial Position which provides detailed information regarding a Company's Sources of Working Capital, Applications of Working Capital, Increase or Decrease in Working Capital and Changes in Components of Working Capital.

Notes to Financial Statements

The auditor will include notes to the financial statements which would include the activities of the Company; the basis of their presentation; inventory information; methods of depreciating office and other equipment and organizational costs; related party transactions; commitments of the Company; Shareholders' Type of Equity; Type of Public Offering; Income Tax Status; Outstanding Loans and Notes Payable and any other event that may affect the financial condition of the Company.

Table of Contents

In most prospectuses, the table of contents appears on one half of the back page. The other half is used to announce the offering and includes the number of shares offered, the name of the Company, type of stock, the words "Offering Circular," the name of the Underwriter and the date of the offering.

Use of Photographs

Photographs and drawings may be included in a prospectus if they relate directly to the Company's products or services.

Appendix C
A Limited Partnership Circular —
VBF American Ginseng Crop 1991

Highlights of the Circular Presented

1. Business of the Partnership

2. General Partner's Investment

3. Products and Markets

4. Risk Factors

5. Subscription Information

6. Proforma Financial Projections

Limited Partnership Circular

VBF AMERICAN GINSENG CROP 1991

A Minnesota Limited Partnership

The date of this Circular is March 1, 1991

Offeree Name:
Date:

Vermilion Botanical Farms, Inc., The General Partner
5300 Melody Hills Drive, Shorewood, Minnesota 55331
Telephone: (612) 935-0000

THE UNITS OFFERED HEREBY HAVE NOT BEEN REGISTERED UNDER THE SECURITIES ACT OF 1933, AS AMENDED (the "ACT"), OR THE SECURITIES LAWS OF CERTAIN STATES, AND ARE BEING OFFERED AND SOLD IN RELIANCE ON EXEMPTIONS FROM THE REGISTRATION REQUIREMENTS OF THE ACT AND SUCH LAWS. THE UNITS HAVE NOT BEEN APPROVED OR DISAPPROVED BY THE SECURITIES AND EXCHANGE COMMISSION, ANY STATE SECURITIES COMMISSION OR OTHER REGULATORY AUTHORITY, NOR HAVE ANY OF THE FOREGOING AUTHORITIES PASSED UPON OR ENDORSED THE MERITS OF THIS OFFERING OR THE ACCURACY OR ADEQUACY OF THIS CIRCULAR. ANY REPRESENTATION TO THE CONTRARY IS UNLAWFUL.

THIS CIRCULAR DOES NOT CONSTITUTE AN OFFER OF UNITS TO YOU UNLESS YOUR NAME AND AN IDENTIFICATION NUMBER APPEAR ON THE FRONT COVER. THIS OFFERING IS MADE SUBJECT TO WITHDRAWAL, CANCELLATION OR MODIFICATION BY THE GENERAL PARTNER WITHOUT NOTICE. THE GENERAL PARTNER RESERVES THE RIGHT TO REJECT ANY SUBSCRIPTION IN WHOLE OR IN PART OR TO ALLOT TO ANY PROSPECTIVE INVESTOR LESS THAN THE NUMBER OF UNITS APPLIED FOR BY SUCH INVESTOR.

THE UNITS ARE BEING OFFERED THROUGH THIS CIRCULAR TO A LIMITED NUMBER OF INVESTORS MEETING CERTAIN SUITABILITY STANDARDS. NO ONE SHOULD INVEST IN THE UNITS WHO IS NOT PREPARED TO LOSE HIS OR HER ENTIRE INVESTMENT.

PROSPECTIVE INVESTORS ARE NOT TO CONSTRUE THE CONTENTS OF THIS CIRCULAR OR ANY PRIOR OR SUBSEQUENT COMMUNICATIONS FROM THE PARTNERSHIP, THE GENERAL PARTNER, OR ANY OF ITS RESPECTIVE OFFICERS, EMPLOYEES OR REPRESENTATIVES AS LEGAL OR TAX ADVICE OR AS INFORMATION NECESSARILY APPLICABLE TO EACH PROSPECTIVE INVESTOR'S INDIVIDUAL FINANCIAL SITUATION. EACH INVESTOR SHOULD CONSULT WITH HIS OR HER OWN FINANCIAL ADVISOR, COUNSEL AND ACCOUNTANT AS TO THE TAX IMPLICATIONS AND RELATED MATTERS CONCERNING INVESTMENT IN THIS LIMITED PARTNERSHIP.

NO DEALER, SALESPERSON OR REPRESENTATIVE IS AUTHORIZED TO GIVE ANY INFORMATION OR MAKE ANY REPRESENTATION IN CONNECTION WITH IS OFFERING OTHER THAN AS AUTHORIZED IN THIS CIRCULAR OR IN THE EXHIBITS HERETO. THIS CIRCULAR DOES NOT CONSTITUTE AN OFFER OR SOLICITATION IN ANY JURISDICTION IN WHICH SUCH AN OFFER OR SOLICITATION IS NOT AUTHORIZED.

THE PURCHASE OF THESE SECURITIES WILL ENTAIL A HIGH DEGREE OF RISK. SEE "RISK FACTORS."

THE INFORMATION CONTAINED IN THIS CIRCULAR HAS BEEN FURNISHED BY VERMILION BOTANICAL FARMS, INC., A MINNESOTA CORPORATION ("VBF," the "COMPANY" and the "GENERAL PARTNER"), AND IS INCLUDED HEREIN IN RELIANCE UPON THEIR ADVICE AND EXPERTISE.

Limited Partnership Circular

$234,000

VBF AMERICAN GINSENG CROP 1991

$39,000 Per Unit — Minimum Investment

Vermilion Botanical Farms, Inc. ("VBF," the "Company" and the "General Partner"), is a Minnesota Corporation which has organized for the purpose of producing American Ginseng and other botanical cash crops in a forest environment. See "The General Partner."

The Limited Partnership as referred to herein is offered with the investment objective of realizing income from the production of American Ginseng (*Panax Quinquefolium L. — Araliaceae*) and is limited to one crop to be planted in September/October 1991 and harvested and sold during the fall of 1996. Therefore, and upon distribution of the proceeds received from the crop sale, VBF American Ginseng Crop 1991, this Limited Partnership, will automatically expire.

Limited Partnership interests are being offered to qualified investors in Units of $39,000 — which is the minimum investment per investor, payable entirely in cash at the closing. The General Partner reserves the right, in its sole discretion, to accept or reject each subscription.

	Unit Price to Investors (1)	Placement Fees (2)	Proceeds to the Partnership (3)
Minimum Investment	$ 39,000	$ 5,850	$ 33,150
Total	$234,000	$35,100	$198,900

(1) The Minimum Investment is One Unit.
(2) Placement Fees are payable by the Partnership to Representatives authorized to represent this offering.
(3) Proceeds are shown after deducting expenses for the Placement Fees but before other expenses related to this offering and payable by the Partnership.

Investment Suitability

Investment in the Units is suitable for persons of adequate financial means who have no need for liquidity with respect to this investment. Units offered hereby will be sold only to an investor who: (a) represents that he or she is acquiring a Unit or Units for his or her own account, for investment only and now with a view toward the resale or distribution thereof; (b) represents that he or she is aware that his or her transfer rights are restricted by the Act and applicable state securities laws, the Partnership Agreement/Certificate of Limited Partnership and the absence of a market for the Units; (c) has such knowledge and experience in business and financial matters that, together with his or her advisors, he or she is capable of evaluating the merits and risks of this investment; and (d) the Partnership believes that the investor is able to bear the economic risk of complete loss of his or her investment because of crop failure.

The suitability standards referred to above represent the minimum suitability requirements for prospective investors and the satisfaction of such standards by a prospective investor does not necessarily mean that the Unit(s) are a suitable investment for such investor.

Subscription Procedures

In order to subscribe for Unit(s), please contact the General Partner or the authorized representative for the necessary legal documents. Each prospective investor will be required to complete, execute and deliver the following documents to the General Partner:

1. Two (2) signed copies of the Partnership Agreement/Certificate of Limited Partnership.

2. Two (2) signed and notarized copies of the Subscription Agreement Signature Page, which incorporates a power of attorney and makes certain representations concerning such investor's subscription.

3. One (1) signed copy of the Investor Letter.

4. A check payable to "VBF American Ginseng Crop 1991; A Limited Partnership" — in the amount of $39,000 for each Unit subscribed for. (The minimum investment is $39,000 for One Unit).

Table of Contents

Limited Partnership Circular Announcement	1
Investment Suitability	4
Subscription Procedures	4
Ginseng Plant Drawing	6
Glossary	7
Summary of the Partnership and the Offering	8
Risk Factors	11
Fiduciary Responsibility of the General Partner	14
No Further Contributions	14
Accounting	15
Table I — Summary of Estimated Cash Proceeds	16
Table II — Potential Return on Investment	17
The Partnership	18
The General Partner/Vermilion Botanical Farms, Inc./The Company	18
Business of the Partnership — General Background	20
Stratified Seed	22
Marketing	23
Competition	23
Directors, Officers and Shareholders' of Vermilion Botanical Farms, Inc.	24
Shareholders' of Vermilion Botanical Farms, Inc. — Ownership	25
Balance Sheet of Vermilion Botanical Farms, Inc.	26
Auditor's Opinion Letter	27
Exhibit A — Partnership Agreement/Certificate of Limited Partnership	28
Schedule A To Partnership Agreement	32
Exhibit B — Subscription Agreement	33
Exhibit C — Investment Letter	35
Exhibit D — Estimated Expenses of the General Partner	36

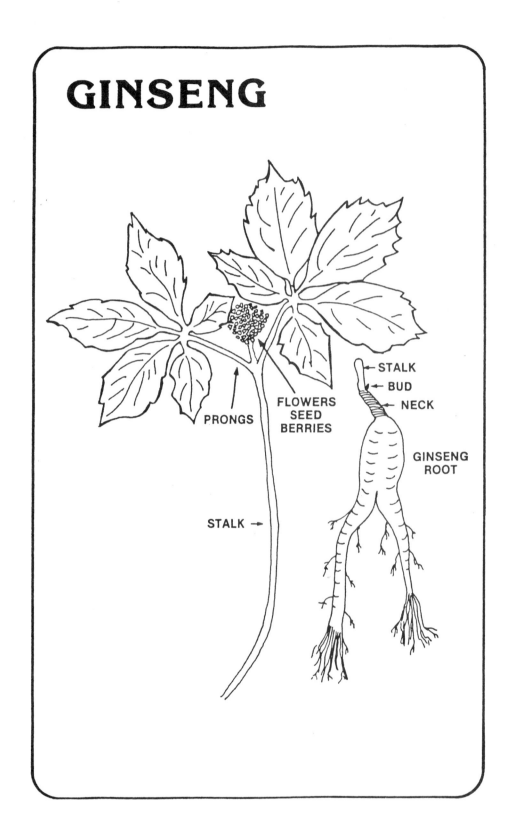

Glossary

Stratified Seed: American Ginseng seed collected from the berries; placed in a fine-grade sand box, covered and allowed to remain dormant for one year prior to planting.

pH: Used to indicate the degree of acidity or alkalinity on a scale where the values range from 0 to 14 with 7 representing neutrality. Numbers less than 7 indicate decreasing acidity, and numbers greater than 7 indicate increasing acidity.

Virgin Forest: Forested land which has never been cultivated to produce agricultural crops.

Perennial: A plant which continues to live from year to year. The surface plant may die annually, but the root continues to live (although sometimes dormant) and develops a new surface plant the following year.

Optimum Maturity: The most advantageous time to harvest American Ginseng roots as a cash crop.

Crop Beds: Specially designed sections of land prepared to receive a specific number of plants and that provide easy access for crop maintenance and inspection.

Proper Environment: In reference to the context used herein, a proper environment includes an area forested by Birch, Maple or Aspen trees; a near neutral soil pH; rich humus deposits; sand base for drainage; adequate rainfall and approximately 60% sunlight penetration through the tree canopy for the necessary crop bed shading.

Summary of the Partnership and the Offering

The Partnership

The Partnership is offered by Vermilion Botanical Farms, Inc., a Minnesota Corporation. Their executive offices are located at 5300 Melody Hills Drive, Shorewood, MN 55331 and their farm is located in St. Louis County, Cook, Minnesota.

The Partnership's Business

The business of the Partnership is to prepare, plant and maintain one American Ginseng Crop to be planted in the fall of 1991 and harvested and sold during the fall of 1996.

The Partnership Offering

Six (6) Investment Units are being offered at $39,000 per Unit with a maximum purchase of One Unit per investor. Once the crop is harvested, sold and the proceeds of the sale are distributed to the partners, this Limited Partnership will automatically expire.

Contributions of the General Partner

The General Partner will contribute a lease for land upon which the 1991 crop will be planted and grown, certain equipment, labor to maintain the crop and management of the Limited Partnership.

Use of Proceeds

The net proceeds of the Partnership Offering, after payment of the placement fees, but before other offering expenses, will be approximately $198,900 which will be used to compensate the General Partner for installation of the crop, use of equipment, purchase of supplies, operating and administrative expenses and to establish a reserve maintenance fund to provide crop maintenance services over a five (5) year period.

Compensation of the General Partner

The General Partner shall be compensated for the initial crop site preparation, seed, planting, mulching, general administrative and operational expenses, equipment use, maintenance and other crop related expenses of the Limited Partnership including legal and offering expenses as incurred to organize this Limited Partnership.

Reserve Maintenance Fund

The General Partner will maintain a reserve maintenance fund of at least 15% of the net proceeds of this offering for crop security, maintenance, labor and disease control which will be utilized over the growing cycle of the crop prior to its harvest, sale and distribution of the sale proceeds in 1996. The Limited Partners will not be entitled to any monetary distribution until the crop is harvested, sold and the profits, if any, are distributed.

Allocation of Proceeds

Upon the sale of the crop, projected to take place during the fall of 1996, the net profit or loss, after the harvesting expenses of the Partnership have been deducted, shall be divided between the Limited Partners and the General Partner as follows:

1. The General Partner shall receive, as a management and sales commission fee, 25% of the net sale proceeds realized from the sale of the crop.

2. The Limited Partners shall divide and receive the remaining 75% of the net proceeds upon the sale of the crop according to their equity ownership of Units in the Limited Partnership.

No Offer of Ownership in Vermilion Botanical Farms, Inc.

No offer of ownership, equity or partial equity in Vermilion Botanical Farms, Inc., its equipment, supplies, land, buildings or other assets is intended in this offering. Land use as furnished and supplied by the General Partner is limited to the sole production of one (1) American Ginseng Crop as described herein which is to be managed by the General Partner. The land cannot be used for any other purpose by the Limited Partners and no share or equity is offered or intended in any other botanical crops that are owned or may be owned in the future by Vermilion Botanical Farms, Inc. or in any other limited partnership agreements that may be organized to produce other crops in the future.

Commissions

Placement fees of 15% or $5,850 per Unit sold will be paid to the Representative(s) authorized by the General Partner to secure private investment subscriptions. Such fees will be paid only if all Units offered are purchased as a direct result of the representatives' efforts.

Expiration of the Limited Partnership

The Partnership will automatically expire after the crop planted in 1991 and harvested in 1996 or thereafter has received the sale proceeds, if any, from same and the profits or losses have been distributed to the General Partner and the Limited Partners. Such distribution will constitute fulfillment and the expiration of the Partnership Agreement as described herein.

Offering Closing Date

The closing date for this offering is June 30, 1991 unless extended by the General Partner to a date not later than August 1, 1991. On or before the closing date, and if all of the Units have been subscribed to, the investor(s) will become Limited Partners under the Limited Partnership Agreement. If all of the Units are not sold, the proceeds actually received will be refunded in full to the Limited Partners who did subscribe and the offer will be withdrawn.

Risk Factors

The purchase of the Units offered hereby involve a number of risks, which include, but are not limited to, the risks summarized as follows:

1. **Crop Failure.** American Ginseng crops have been known to fail for a variety of reasons and although the General Partner will utilize its best efforts to produce the crop, it cannot guarantee success to the Limited Partners.

2. **Fire.** Many forest fires sweep through the woods and in this event, the roots of the American Ginseng plants could escape damage because they are below the surface of the ground. The top plants would be destroyed, but the roots would likely send up new plants the following Spring. A more conventional method of shading the plant beds would become necessary if the trees (used for shading), were destroyed by fire. A deep burning peat fire would destroy the roots and a crop under cultivation would end in failure. Fire is a serious threat because the General Partner will produce the crop in a forest setting. by brushing-out the Ginseng beds and service paths, some protection can be realized against a "sweeping" type of forest fire.

3. **Disease.** There are some diseases that can attack American Ginseng, however, most can be controlled with a variety of chemical spray formulas which are commercially available. By placing the crop in separate beds, the chance of a large loss due to disease is greatly reduced but not eliminated. Most diseases of Ginseng plants are caused by the use of animal waste fertilizers. the General Partner will not use any fertilizers (animal or chemical) to produce the crop, but will rely instead upon the natural, rich forest floor and leaf-mulch for the proper pH and plant mulch.

4. **Rodents.** Field mice and moles may cause minor damage to Ginseng plants and roots but can be controlled in several ways if necessary.

5. **Drought.** Northern Minnesota's annual rainfall is adequate for American Ginseng to thrive; however, in case of a severe drought in any given year, the General Partner has access to two, year-around flowing creeks, a large three acre beaver pond and a deep water well located near the crop site. The well is equipped with a jet pump and the site has a irrigation system in place should it be needed.

6. **Delayed Harvest.** If the General Partner believes that a substantially increased return could be realized by leaving the crop in the ground for another year, it would notify the Limited Partners and not harvest the crop until the following year.

7. **Vandalism, Theft and Acts of God.** The crop will be located in a remote area of northern Minnesota — 20 miles from the town of Cook, Minnesota. Certain security precautions will be taken to provide an efficient security system that will ensure crop protection from vandalism and theft. These security measures will not be disclosed in this Circular, but will be discussed with those actually purchasing Units of ownership in the crop. The General Partner has had other American Ginseng crops under cultivation on the Company's farm and has not experienced any problems with vandals or theft.

High winds, heavy rains, hail and tornadoes could cause damage to the surface plants, but as with the fire threat, the roots would send up new plants either in mid-Summer or the following Spring. The crop beds are heavily mulched in the fall months to protect the roots from the winter snow. To kill this plant species, the root must be destroyed.

8. **Business of the Partnership is Dependent Upon Key Employees.** The Partnership will be dependent upon the active participation of Vermilion Botanical Farms, Inc., its officers and employees. Loss of two or more of these individuals could adversely affect the Limited Partnership.

9. **Competition.** The General Partner believes there is little competition in regard to producing American Ginseng in an actual forest environment in the United States and the method it intends to use in its production. There are several "commercial growers" in the country who produce Ginseng crops in a three year period using various chemicals and animal waste to cause rapid root development. Conversely, the General Partner plants its crops in the habitat where American Ginseng is still found growing wild and it produces crops without the aid of chemicals or other fertilizers so that the "wild tasting character" of the herb will not be changed.

The General Partner believes that in following this "mother nature" approach of production, albeit a continuous maintenance program that requires a five year growing cycle to obtain salable roots, it will produce Ginseng roots equal to those still found growing wild in a few American forests. Such roots are in great demand and currently command prices of $160 to $170 per pound as of this Offering. Roots produced by the "commercial growers" sell for $50 to $60 per pound depending upon the demand at harvest time.

10. Internal Revenue Service Tax Treatment. As of this offering, the Internal Revenue Service will permit the Limited Partners to deduct the expenses of planting the crop and to maintain it as the funds are expended over a five year growing period. Proceeds received after the sale of the crop are currently treated as ordinary income. The General Partner recommends that all Limited Partners consult with their own tax attorney or accountant for tax advice concerning this Offering. Please see "Table II — Potential Return Per Unit" which provides an estimate of potential return on investment and when the investment in each Unit may be deducted as a crop expense.

11. Audit of the Limited Partnership's Tax Returns. There is a possibility that the tax returns of the Partnership may be examined by the IRS. Such an examination could result in adjustments to the tax consequences initially reported by the Partnership and could also result in audits of the Limited Partners personal income tax returns. Any such audits could involve items not related to the investment in the Partnership as well as Partnership items. The cost of any individual audit would be borne solely by the Limited Partners involved.

12. Restrictions on Transferability — No Market for the Units. The sale of the Units is not registered under the Securities Act of 1933, as amended, and the Units may not be resold unless such sale is subsequently registered thereunder or an exemption from registration is made available. The Limited Partners have no right to require such registration. Moreover, there is no existing public or other market for the Units and it is not anticipated that any such market will develop in the future. The transferability of the Units is subject to certain restrictions, including the consent of the General Partner, which may be withheld in its absolute discretion. Consequently, investors may not be able to liquidate their Units in the event of a personal financial emergency or for any other reason.

13. Lack of Management Control by Investors. The investors will become Limited Partners in the Partnership and be subject to the restrictions of the Partnership Agreement. They will have no right or power to take part in the management or control of the business of the Partnership. The business of the Partnership will be managed solely by the General Partner.

14. Conflicts of Interest. The Partnership may be subject to certain conflicts of interest arising out of its relationship with the General Partner. In view of these potential conflicts, certain provisions of the Partnership Agreement are designed to protect the interests of the Limited Partners. All agreements and arrangements between the affiliates are not, and will not be, the result of arms-length negotiations.

Shareholders of the General Partner own 100% of its capital stock. Situations may arise under the Partnership Agreement in which the General Partner would be making a determination on a issue where the interests of the General Partner and those of the Limited Partners may be in conflict. Therefore, all determinations with respect to the expenditure of funds and crop management will be made by the General Partner.

Fiduciary Responsibility of the General Partner

The General Partner is accountable to the Partnership as fiduciary and consequently must exercise good faith judgement and integrity in managing the Partnership's affairs. The definition of a general partner's responsibilities is a changing area of law, and investors who have questions concerning the duties of the General Partner should consult with their counsel. If the General Partner fails to perform its obligations as fiduciary, there can be no assurance that adequate remedies will be available to the Limited Partners.

The General Partner may not be liable to the Partnership or Limited Partners for errors in judgement or other acts or omissions not amounting to negligence or willful misconduct, because provision has been made in the Partnership Agreement for exculpation of the General Partner in such circumstances. Therefore, Limited Partners may have a more limited right of action than would have existed in the absence of the limitation set forth in the Partnership Agreement.

Furthermore, under the terms of the Partnership Agreement, the General Partner will be indemnified by the Partnership for certain liabilities it may incur in dealing with third parties on behalf of the Partnership.

No Further Contributions

No further contributions shall be required of the Limited Partners except for the initial purchase price of the Units in the Partnership. Vermilion Botanical Farms, Inc. may offer investment opportunities in future crop plantings as the General Partner under other Limited Partnership Agreements. In this event, Limited Partner participants in VBF American Ginseng Crop 1991 will be afforded first option to participate in such Partnership Agreements as investors.

Accounting

The General Partner shall keep full and correct books of accounting at the principal office of the Partnership, and these books shall record all financial transactions relating to the Partnership. All Limited Partners shall have access to such books during normal business hours. The General Partner shall also prepare, or have prepared, any financial and operating statements and such other statements as it or the Limited Partners shall deem desirable. Copies of all such statements shall be supplied by the General Partner to the Limited Partners at least annually during the term of the Partnership Agreement, and the General Partner will file the appropriate "information tax returns" concerning the Partnership with the Internal Revenue Service and the State of Minnesota in a timely manner.

***

TABLE I

SUMMARY OF ESTIMATED CASH PROCEEDS FROM THE SALE OF VBF AMERICAN GINSENG CROP 1991

Crop Sale Price	$ 1,236,900 (A)
Less: Estimated Harvest Expenses	25,000
Net Sale Proceeds for Distribution	$ 1,211,900
Limited Partners Share @ 75%	$ 900,925
Distribution Per Unit to Limited Partners	$ 151,488
General Partner's Share @ 25%	$ 302,975

(A) Crop Sale Proceeds Are Based On The Following:

1. That 300,000 American Ginseng seeds are planted in 1991 and that 95% survive to maturity and harvest in the fall of 1996.

2. That 50 Ginseng dried roots will equal one pound and the total crop's dried weight will be approximately 5,700 pounds.

3. Historically, the wholesale price of "woods grown" American Ginseng has kept pace with world inflation trends. As of this Offering, the current price paid is $160 to $170 per pound. If inflation should continue, even at an annual rate of 5%, a crop started in 1991 would have a selling price of $217 or more per pound when harvested and sold in 1996. (i.e., $217/lb. x 5,700/lbs. = $1,236,900).

The above estimated crop yield and selling price reflects a return of 288% on an original investment of $39,000 per Unit. This return cannot be guaranteed by the General Partner. Certain risk factors are involved in the production of American Ginseng crops. See "Risk Factors."

TABLE II

POTENTIAL RETURN PER UNIT
AND TAX DEDUCTIONS

Year	Date of Investment	Amount	Potential Tax Deduction	Potential Cash Distribution
1991	Mar/Aug	$39,000	$29,000	$ 0
1992	-	-	2,000	0
1993	-	-	2,000	0
1994	-	-	2,000	0
1995	-	-	2,000	0
1996	-	-	2,000	$151,488

The Partnership

Introduction

The Partnership will be formed as a Limited Partnership under Minnesota Law if subscriptions are accepted for the six (6) Units offered hereby. The terms of the Partnership are outlined in detail in the Partnership Agreement/Certificate of Limited Partnership attached hereto as Exhibit A.

The Partnership is being formed to prepare, plant, maintain, harvest and sell one (1) American Ginseng Crop which will be planted in the Fall of 1991 and tentatively harvested and sold in the Fall of 1996.

The General Partner of the Partnership is Vermilion Botanical Farms, Inc. See "The General Partner/Vermilion Botanical Farms, Inc./The Company" below and "Business of the Partnership."

The General Partner — Vermilion Botanical Farms, Inc. — The Company

Vermilion Botanical Farms, Inc. (the "Company," "General Partner" and "VBF"), was incorporated in the State of Minnesota on November 17, 1985 for the purpose of producing salable American Ginseng cash crops (*Panax Quinquefolium L. — Araliaceae*) in a compatible forest environment. The Company owns 600 acres of virgin forest land located near Cook, Minnesota in St. Louis County and currently has under cultivation, a five year old American Ginseng crop of 600,000 plants located on a six acre parcel of the farm. The Company also has a crop drying and equipment storage building, a house and garage on the property together with its farming equipment. The farm is accessible only by a 1/4 mile private road which the Company also owns. This road is secured by a large iron gate and joins a secondary State forest road owned and maintained by the Minnesota Department of Natural Resources.

Upon sale of the Units offered herein, VBF will lease three acres of land to the Limited Partnership to plant its crop and will provide: use of the Company's equipment, irrigation system, deep water well, the seed and labor necessary to plant the crop and will provide the maintenance services required until the crop is ready to harvest in 1996 for a single prepayment of $198,900 — assuming all six (6) Units are purchased. Any additional proceeds realized from this offering that are not paid out in the form of commissions to those representing the sale of the Units, or used to pay the expenses associated with this offering, will be placed in a "crop maintenance fund" to be used at the discretion of the General Partner for added crop maintenance and operating expenses of the Partnership and/or to pay a portion of the anticipated harvesting costs in 1996.

Once the three (3) acre crop site and the planting beds are prepared, the General Partner will plant 300,000 stratified American Ginseng seeds in them. This crop will be designated as "VBF AMERICAN GINSENG CROP 1991" and appropriately mapped and marked.

After a sixty (60) month development period or growing cycle, which is necessary for ginseng roots to reach maturity, the harvested dry weight of the roots is expected to be about 5,700 pounds. The current price offered for "woods grown" American Ginseng ranges between $160 and $170 per pound. Historically, prices have risen with world inflation and because it will require at least five years to produce a salable crop of roots, and should inflation continue, even at a rate of 5% per year, a crop started in 1991 could have a value of $217 per pound or more when harvested and sold in 1996.

The Company intends to be simultaneously engaged in the experimental production of other botanical cash crops which may prove beneficial to the Company's business development while it is also servicing the Partnership as the General Partner. Such operations will be kept separate from the Partnership and will not, under any circumstances, be considered a part of the Partnership as described herein.

Vermilion Botanical Farms, Inc. has $508,500 in assets and at this time has four directors who act in behalf of the business. Two of these directors serve the Company on a full-time basis as working officers and managers. Additional employees are hired for seasonal Summer and Fall employment.

The General Partner plans to commence operations of **VBF American Ginseng Crop 1991** following the closing of the sale of all Units offered hereby. A substantial expense will be made in the preparation of the forested land for the crop's installation. This includes, but is not limited to, the brushing-out of the acreage, tree root removal, roto-tilling and bed construction for planting. The irrigation system will be installed for emergency watering purposes and drain tile laid where necessary to protect the beds. The planting of seed will begin during the month of September, 1991 utilizing hand operated planting equipment. Annual maintenance of the crop will include plant inspection, weeding, water (if required), mulching and disease control. Hand-harvesting of this crop is necessary to prevent damage to the roots and will be undertaken starting in September, 1996 (if the crop is approved for harvesting by the General Partner). The Company will pay for the harvesting expenses estimated to be about $25,000. These advanced monies will be reimbursed to the Company by the Partnership from the sale proceeds of the crop before they are to be distributed to the Limited Partners and the General Partner.

Upon harvesting, the ginseng roots are carefully washed, dried and bulk packed for shipment in barrels. If at harvest time, the market price is considered to be fair by the General Partner, the crop will be harvested and sold to the highest domestic or international bidder. Conversely, if the market is not considered to be at peak price, the General Partner will so advise the Limited Partners that the crop will not be harvested and the Partnership will wait at least one year for improved market conditions. If for some reason the crop is harvested but not sold immediately, the roots can be safely stored indefinitely to await better market conditions and prices. In the event the crop is not harvested in 1996 as planned, the Company will continue to provide crop maintenance services at no further charge to the Partnership and until such time as the crop can be harvested and sold.

The General Partner believes that the proceeds of this Offering will satisfy the cash requirements of the Partnership to produce and maintain the crop described herein.

Business of the Partnership

General Background

American Ginseng (*Panax Quinquefolium L. Araliaceae*), is a smooth textured, light colored, root herb. From seed germination, it produces a surface plant about 12 to 18 inches tall over a period of approximately 60 months. Because it is a perennial, the top or surface plant dies each Fall and the root enters a dormant stage during the winter months. In the Spring, a new plant is produced by the root and the cycle is repeated from year to year. Leaves on the mature Ginseng plant usually consist of five ovate leaflets — sometimes called the "Hand" — and it blooms yellow/green flowers in midsummer. Seed borne by the mature plant forms in a cluster of berries on the seed stem or stalk. They turn a bright red in August or September and each berry produces two seeds about the size of a pea.

American Ginseng still grows wild in a few of America's northern forests. It is dependent upon the forest floor for its nutrition and requires considerable tree shade to thrive. Unfortunately, this natural forest plant has become very rare because during the past 200 years, thousands of "foragers" and "wild-crafters" have harvested its valuable roots to sell. Millions of the plants were removed out-of-season, and as a consequence, were unable to reseed themselves. Millions more were harvested before their roots reached maturity even though the prices paid for them were extremely low. According to the U. S. Department of Agriculture, trade in Ginseng roots actually exceeded America's international commerce in furs during the 18th century.

Farming Ginseng crops started in the United States in the early 1800s, although it has been a respected profession in the orient since history was first recorded. Korea produces the most prized roots in the world, but America ranks a solid second because of our rare woods grown species. Farming this unique herb has been a lost art, especially in this country, because most would-be farmers prefer to turn their money over as fast as possible in agricultural enterprises today. To produce a successful Ginseng crop requires considerable capital, the proper environment, suitable soil composition, a thorough knowledge about the species and a minimum of 60 months to raise a crop. There are some shortcuts that one can take in the production of Ginseng, but the resulting crop value is greatly reduced in the marketplace. More about this method of production will follow shortly.

Ginseng is prized by the Chinese and many other oriental and European cultures who use the dried roots to make numerous blends of tea, medicines and to chew much the say way we enjoy chewing gum. In America, it is used in tea production, some eye medications and it is sold as a vitamin supplement in capsule or tablet form by most drug and health food stores nationwide. According to the U. S. Department of Agriculture, at least $60 million dollars of domestically produced Ginseng was exported in 1988, and America still imports over $15 million dollars of Korean produced roots each year.

American Ginseng is a labor intensive crop requiring many man hours in its cultivation. It must be planted, maintained and harvested by hand. Once harvested, the roots are washed carefully to prevent damage to the roots, kiln dried thoroughly, bulk packed in waterproof barrels or cartons and sold to international or domestic buyers (or brokers) who represent clients around the world.

Ginseng is an attractive cash crop because the prices paid for it have consistently increased with world inflation trends. Historically, the prices paid for "woods grown" roots have continued to increase, partly because of this consistent demand and inflation. For example: In 1977, the average price paid on the wholesale level was $115/lb. Today, the average is $160 to 170/lb. although some buyers are willing to pay as high as $260/lb. for top quality roots. Prices are usually set annually in the oriental markets but can rise during any given year when the supply is short. Even in 1933 during the depths of the Great Depression, American Ginseng roots were selling for an unbelievable price of $3.62/lb.

As previously discussed in this Prospectus, there are several "commercial" Ginseng growers in the United States who produce a plant in only three years time. These particular plants are developed by using chemical and animal waste fertilizers to obtain rapid root growth. Artificial lathe structures are constructed over the plant beds to simulate a forest shaded environment. Roots grown by this method have a value of $50 or slightly more per pound, depending upon current demand.

Ginseng produced in a natural woods habitat, without the aid of chemicals or other fertilizers, does require more time to reach maturity, but the demand for it has always been excellent. Any expert Ginseng buyer can tell the difference immediately between the two methods of production by examining the root color, texture, taste and root weight. They prefer the "woods grown roots" and are willing to pay up to five times more to obtain them.

In regard to the physical enhancement claims made for Ginseng and the products it is used in, the General Partner does not support them. The Chinese have said for centuries that it relieves or cures a multitude of ailments, however, the American Medical Association has not concurred with or supported these claims. Recently, the Russian government conducted a research project using a Ginseng extract to control the heart palpitation problems of a large test group of patients, and claimed the program was extremely successful in their medical journals. Whether or not the medical community in the United States will attempt to duplicate this research is unknown, but similar projects are being conducted in Denmark, Sweden and England.

As with any agricultural enterprise, the General Partner cannot guarantee crop success, yields or final root weights after drying. Some of the factors that govern Ginseng survival and good root development are: Site Selection; Forest Floor pH Composition; Bed Drainage; Types of Tree Cover; Shading; Disease Control and Botanical Knowledge.

Stratified Seed

The General Partner has ample supplies of stratified seed on hand to produce the crop described herein. Additional supplies can be purchased from seed suppliers for $120 per pound. The yield is approximately 7,500 seeds per pound.

To promote improved root development, the General Partner purposely pinches off the flower/berry pods on the stalks of each plant in mid-summer. This procedure allows the root to spend its energies developing itself rather than sending up the nutrients required to produce seed on the surface plants. The end result is a larger, heavier root with greater value at harvest time.

Marketing

The General Partner will market the crop directly to companies purchasing American Ginseng to manufacture their respective products. Several United States buyers of Ginseng roots do exist, but are considered to be commissioned brokers who represent clients around the world. To avoid paying these additional "middlemen" commissions, the General Partner will sell the crop to its contacts in Hong Kong, Taiwan, Singapore, Tokyo, Paris and London. By selling the crop direct, the Partnership's net proceeds will be much greater.

When such a crop is ready for sale, the procedure is to invite representatives of several international firms to inspect it *before harvesting*. At that time, bids are presented and the highest bid is accepted. Before harvesting, the sale proceeds are deposited in a U. S. bank. The crop is then harvested, washed, dried and packed for shipping. The company purchasing the crop then takes charge of the shipment and the sale proceeds are immediately released to the General Partner.

Competition

The General Partner has very little competition in regard to producing American Ginseng crops in an actual forest environment. The General Partner further believes that its method of production will develop salable roots equal to those still found growing wild in a few north American forests, and has been advised by several prospective international companies that they are willing to pay top prices for them. Some of these firms include the Tai Kwong Company, Hong Kong; Chow Lia Company, London and the Dalaisee Tea Company in Paris. Copies of their letters are on file at the General Partner's executive offices and will be made available to prospective investors upon request.

Commercial growers of Ginseng are scattered throughout the United States, however, Wisconsins' Marathon County produces most of the commercially grown Ginseng in the nation. The growers produce and sell their crops in three year cycles as previously mentioned. Their crop selling prices range up to $60 per pound depending upon the current demand. It is estimated that there are between 250 and 300 Ginseng growers in Marathon County alone. All are small growers, yet they produce as much as 650,000 pounds of dried roots per year according to the U. S. Department of Agriculture.

Directors, Officers and Shareholders' of Vermilion Botanical Farms, Inc.

Michael A. Bennett is Chairman, Director and Chief Executive Officer of the Company. Mr. Bennett began preparations for planting the Company's first American Ginseng crop in 1984 and planted it in 1985. He has since managed its development on a part-time basis but intends to devote his full-time services to the business of VBF after the successful completion of this Offering. Mr. Bennett is a botanist and has conducted extensive research on the production of American Ginseng in a forest setting for seven years. He has been a botanist for the Randal Research Institute, St. Paul, Minnesota since 1965 and holds a Ph.D. in Botany from the University of Minnesota which he earned in 1964.

Joseph A. Andrews is a Director and the Chief Financial Officer for the Company. He is presently employed by the Borst Manufacturing Company in Minneapolis as their controller and has been in their employ since 1975. He is a 1969 graduate of the University of Colorado at Denver and holds a BS Degree in Accounting. Mr. Andrews has been a director and shareholder of VBF since its incorporation and has acquired the essential knowledge required for the production of American Ginseng. He will also provide his full-time services to the Company upon the successful completion of this Offering.

Craig D. Logan is a Director and Secretary for the Company. Mr. Logan has been self-employed as a business consultant in the Minneapolis area since 1970. He will continue to serve the Company as a director and will assist management from time to time as required. Mr. Logan is a 1971 graduate of Harvard and holds an MBA in Marketing.

Mark S. Stevens is a Director for the Company. Mr. Stevens is a Attorney-At-Law and has been in private practice in Rochester, Minnesota since 1971. He received his Juris Doctorate Degree from the University of Southern California at Los Angeles in 1971 and his BA Degree in Journalism from the University of Arizona in 1967.

Shareholders' of Vermilion Botanical Farms, Inc.

The following shareholders' of Vermilion Botanical Farms, Inc. are listed as follows:

Shareholder & Residence	Shares Held	Percent of Ownership
Michael A. Bennett 7251 Wildhurst Road Edina, MN 55343	1,108,896	60%
Joseph C. Andrews 207 Smithtown Way Bloomington, MN 55441	554,448	30%
Craig D. Logan 87910 Georgia Street St. Louis Park, MN 55337	92,408	5%
Mark S. Stevens 1002 Mallard Road Rochester, MN 55701	92,408	5%
Totals	1,848,160 /Shares Outstanding	100%

Vermilion Botanical Farms, Inc.
Audited Balance Sheet
As Of January 31, 1991

ASSETS
Current Assets:
  Cash on Hand/Savings Accounts $ 285,000
  Seed Supplies (Current Market Value)   25,000

Total Current Assets $ 310,000

Other Assets:
  Land — 600 Acres (No Mortgage)   90,000
  Buildings (No Mortgage)   61,850
  Farm Equipment (Purchased 1-1-91)   40,900
  Office Furniture & Equipment (Purchased 1-1-91)   5,750

Total Other Assets $ 198,500

TOTAL ALL ASSETS   **$ 508,500**

LIABILITIES & STOCKHOLDERS' EQUITY:
Current Liabilities:
  Total Current Liabilities $ 0

Stockholders' Equity:
  Common Stock, No Par Value, 5,000,000 Shares
  Authorized: 1,848,160 Shares Issued & Outstanding $ 508,500

TOTAL LIABILITIES & STOCKHOLDERS' EQUITY   **$ 508,500**

Note: The Company has a five year old American Ginseng crop under cultivation that will be harvested and sold in the Fall of 1991. This crop is valued at $1,938,000 but has not been included as an asset of the Company.

  Upon incorporation in 1985, the Company was formed as a Sub Chapter "S" Corporation. Management has changed this status to a "C" Corporation to be effective in tax year 1991. This change will not affect the Limited Partnership offered herein.

Opinion of Independent Certified Public Accountants

Board of Directors
Vermilion Botanical Farms, Inc.

We have examined the balance sheet of Vermilion Botanical Farms, Inc. and related financial statements. Our examinations were made in accordance with generally accepted auditing standards and, accordingly, included such tests of the accounting records and such other auditing procedures as we considered necessary under the circumstances.

In our opinion, the above mentioned financial statements present fairly the financial position of the company as of January 31, 1991 and conform with generally accepted accounting principles applied on a consistent basis.

SPARKS, WELLS AND ANDERSON
Certified Public Accountants
February 19, 1991

Reader Notice:

Additional financial statements can be included in a Limited Partnership Offering Circular and may be required by the securities laws of your state if full disclosure of the General Partner's financial condition is required. Consultation with your legal counsel is strongly recommended.

EXHIBIT A
PARTNERSHIP AGREEMENT
CERTIFICATE OF LIMITED PARTNERSHIP
VBF AMERICAN GINSENG CROP 1991

The undersigned, being desirous of forming a limited partnership under the provisions of Chapter 322A of the Minnesota Statutes, does hereby make and sign the following Certificate of Limited Partnership Agreement for that purpose:

1. The name of the partnership shall be VBF AMERICAN GINSENG CROP 1991: A Limited Partnership.

2. The character of the business to be transacted by the Partnership shall be the preparation, planting, maintenance, production, harvest and distribution of American Ginseng and the conducting of all related and necessary business to the planting, growing, harvesting and distribution of the crop produced by the Partnership, and the entering into of any and all contracts related to such business.

3. The location of the principal place of business of the Partnership shall be in the City of Shorewood, Minnesota at 5300 Melody Hills Drive, Hennepin County, Minnesota 55331. For purposes of service under Minnesota Statutes Section 322A.04, the agent designated shall be the General Partner and the address shall be that address as designated in Schedule A of said General Partner.

4. The name, address and capital contribution of the General Partner and the name, address and capital contribution of the Limited Partners are as set forth on Schedule A attached hereto and incorporated herein by reference.

5. The term of the Partnership shall be from the date hereof to January 1, 1997, unless sooner terminated as herein provided, or as provided in Chapter 322A of the Minnesota Statutes, or amendments thereto or as may be extended by the General Partner. The General Partner is hereby authorized to raise capital for the Partnership by offering and selling interest in the Partnership and by admitting the purchaser(s) of said interest as a Limited Partner for proper Partnership purposes, including registration, legal and accounting expenses.

6. The Limited Partner shall contribute the minimum sum of $39,000 per Unit purchased to the Partnership which contribution shall consist solely of cash. Such contribution shall be made at the time the Limited Partnership herein is formed. The maximum number of Units to be offered for investment in this Partnership to Limited Partners is six (6).

7. No further contribution shall be required of the Limited Partners, except as set forth in the paragraph above, but additional contributions may be made from time to time by the Limited Partners for future American Ginseng crops that may be planted with the consent and under such conditions as may be agreed upon by the General Partner.

8. The contribution of the Limited Partner is to be returned to him or her upon the dissolution or termination of the Partnership, but only after all liabilities of the Partnership, except liabilities to the General Partner on account of his contribution, have been paid.

9. The General Partner shall contribute to the Partnership a lease of land upon which the crop will be grown, certain expertise and equipment, and management of the business of the Limited Partnership, and the control and management of the Partnerships affairs. (Lease set forth on Schedule A hereto).

10. The General Partner shall be compensated for the initial crop preparation, seed, planting, mulching, general administrative, equipment lease, maintenance and other crop related expenses from the capital contribution of the Limited Partners, and legal and offering expenses, including placement fees (if any) shall therefrom be deducted also. The General Partner shall maintain an initial minimum fund of 15% of the net proceeds of this offering for crop security, maintenance, labor and disease control to be expended over the growing cycle of the crop and prior to harvest, sale and distribution of the crop proceeds, profits or losses. The Limited Partners shall not be entitled to any distribution until the crop is sold and profits or losses are taken.

11. The balance of the net profits or losses of the Partnership remaining after the payments mentioned above shall be divided as follows between the Limited Partners and General Partner:

   a. The General Partner shall receive as a management and sales commission fee 25% of the net sale proceeds after harvesting expenses and upon sale of the crop; and

   b. The Limited Partners shall divide and receive the remaining 75% of the net proceeds of the net profits or losses after harvesting expenses and upon sale of the crop, according to their equity ownership of Units in the Limited Partnership.

12. The General Partner shall plant a minimum crop of 300,000 American Ginseng stratified seeds which will comprise VBF AMERICAN GINSENG CROP 1991: A Limited Partnership, during the Fall of 1991.

13. The General Partner shall keep full and correct books of account at the principal office of the Partnership, which books shall record all financial transactions relating to the Partnership. A Limited Partner shall have access to such books at all times during normal business hours. The General Partner shall also prepare, or have prepared, any financial and operating statements and such other statements as it or the Limited Partners shall deem necessary. Copies of all such statements shall be supplied to all partners in the Limited Partnership.

14. The Limited Partners shall not participate in the management or control of the Partnership's business, nor shall they transact any business for the Partnership, nor shall they have the power to act for or by the Partnership, said powers being vested solely and exclusively in the General Partner. Limited Partners shall have no interest in the stock or assets of the Corporate General Partner, or in any proceeds of any sale thereof by virtue of acquiring or owning interest in the Partnership.

15. It is acknowledged that the transfer ability of the interests herein are restricted, and it is not anticipated that there will be a public market for these interests and that it may not be possible to sell or dispose of the Partnership interests being acquired herein.

16. The occurrence of any one of the following events shall work an immediate dissolution of the Partnership:

   a. Bankruptcy, dissolution or withdrawal of the last remaining General Partner; or

   b. The termination of the Partnership pursuant to any applicable statutory provisions in the Minnesota Statutes.

17. The Limited Partners shall look solely to the assets of the Partnership for all distributions with respect to the Partnership and their capital contribution thereto and share of the profits or losses thereof and shall have no recourse therefore against the General Partner or any other Limited Partner that the General Partner may enter into agreement with in the future.

18. The Limited Partner, by execution hereof, jointly and severally hereby irrevocably constitutes and appoints the Corporate General Partner, with full power of substitution, their true and lawful attorney-in-fact, in their name, place and stead to make, execute, sign, acknowledge, record and file, on behalf of them and on behalf of the Partnership, the following:

a. The Partnership/Certificate of Limited Partnership, a Certificate of Doing Business Under An Assumed Name, and any other certificates or instruments which may be required to be filed by the Partnership or the Partners under the laws of the State of Minnesota and any other jurisdiction who's laws may be applicable.

b. A Certificate of Cancellation of the Partnership and such other instruments or documents as may be deemed necessary or desirable by the Corporate General Partner upon the termination of the Partnership's business.

c. Any and all amendments required by law to be filed, or are consistent with this Agreement (including, without limitation, any amendments admitting or substituting assignees of interests as a Limited Partner or admitting or substituting an additional or successor General Partner), or have been authorized by this particular Limited Partner or Partners.

d. Any and all such other instruments as may be deemed necessary or desirable by the Corporate General Partner to carry out fully the provisions of this Agreement in accordance with its terms.

Agreement made this _____ day of _____ , 1991.

General Partner:

_____

Vermilion Botanical Farms, Inc.
By: Michael A. Bennett
Its: Chairman and Chief Executive Officer

Notary Witness: Limited Partner:

_____   _____

_____   _____

_____   _____

(Notary Signature, Seal and   (Signature and Address of Current Residence
Commission Expiration   and Social Security Number)
Date)

Schedule A
To
Partnership Agreement
Certificate of Limited Partnership
VBF American Ginseng Crop 1991

Name and address of the Corporate General Partner:

Vermilion Botanical Farms, Inc.
5300 Melody Hills Drive,
Shorewood, Minnesota 55331
Telephone: (612) 935-0000

Capital Contribution of the General Partner:

> Lease of three (3) acres of forested land located within the Southerly 600 feet of the Northerly 800 feet of the NW 1/4 of the NE 1/4 Section 10, Township 61, Range 14 lying West of the Fourth Meridian and according to the United States Government Survey thereof, use of certain farm/garden equipment, water well and certain crop irrigation equipment for the production of the crop.

Name, address and capital contribution of the Limited Partner(s):

_____
_____
_____
_____
_____
_____

EXHIBIT B
SUBSCRIPTION AGREEMENT
VBF AMERICAN GINSENG CROP 1991:
A LIMITED PARTNERSHIP

LIMITED PARTNER SIGNATURE PAGE
AND
POWER OF ATTORNEY

The undersigned, desiring to become a Limited Partner of VBF AMERICAN GINSENG CROP 1991: A Limited Partnership, pursuant to its Partnership Agreement/Certificate of Limited Partnership dated _____, 1991, of VBF American Ginseng Crop 1991, hereby agrees to all of the terms of said Agreement and Certificate and agrees to all of the terms and provisions thereof. The undersigned further, by executing this Signature Page and Power of Attorney, hereby executes, adopts and agrees to all terms, conditions and representations of the Subscription Agreement/Offering of the Partnership. The Undersigned further constitutes and appoints the Corporate General Partner of VBF American Ginseng Crop 1991, with full power of substitution, his true and lawful attorney for him or her in his/her name, place and stead to make, execute, sign, acknowledge, swear to, deliver, record and file any documents or instruments which may be considered necessary or desirable by the Corporate General Partner to carry out in full the provisions of such Agreement, including, without limitation, an amendment or amendments to such Agreement and the Certificate of Limited Partnership of VBF American Ginseng Crop 1991, for the purpose of adding the undersigned and others as Limited Partners to the Partnership as contemplated in said Agreement (which amendment(s) the undersigned hereby joins in and executes, hereby authorizing this Signature Page to be attached to any such amendment), and of otherwise amending said Agreement and Certificate, from time to time, or canceling the same. The power of attorney hereby granted shall be deemed to be coupled with an interest and shall be irrevocable and survive the death, incapacity, insolvency, dissolution or termination of the undersigned or any delivery by the undersigned of an assignment of the whole or any portion of his or her interest. The place of residence of the undersigned is as shown on the Subscription Agreement. (Check must be made payable to: "VBF American Ginseng Crop 1991: A Limited Partnership").

_____   _____   _____
Signature of Limited Partner   No. of Units   Dollar Amount Paid

_____   _____
Signature of Joint Partner   Residence
If Joint Partner, check one:
__ Joint Tenants with Right of Survivorship   _____
__ Tenants in Common   City, State and Zip Code
__ Community Property   _____
                                 Social Security or Taxpayer ID Number

If Fiduciary or Corporation, check one:
__ Trust   __ Power of Attorney
__ Estate   __ Corporation

— Continued on next page —

If signing as a trustee, indicate the state whose law governs the trust instrument:
_____
_____

===

ACKNOWLEDGMENT

This document must be acknowledged before a Notary Public.

    State of:)SS.
    County of:)

On this _____ day of _____ in the year 1991, before me, the undersigned, a Notary Public of said State, duly commissioned and sworn personally appeared: _____ and _____ known to me to be the person (or persons) whose name acknowledged under oath before me that he (or she or they) executed the same as his (or her or their) free and voluntary act in the capacities therein expressed and pursuant to proper authority.

In WITNESS WHEREOF, I have hereunto set my hand and affixed my official seal the day and year on this certificate of acknowledgment, first above written.

My Commission Expires: _____

_____
Notary Public in and for said State.

           — SEAL —

EXHIBIT C
INVESTMENT LETTER

Date: _____

To: VBF American Ginseng Crop 1991: A Limited Partnership

Gentlemen:

By executing the Subscription Agreement Signature Page and Power of Attorney attached, I hereby subscribe for _____ Limited Partnership Unit(s) of VBF American Ginseng Crop 1991 at a purchase price of $39,000 per Investment Unit as set forth in the Offering.

I further:

(a) acknowledge receipt of the Offering Circular of the Partnership and understand that the Unit(s) being acquired will be governed by the terms of the Partnership Agreement/Certificate of Limited Partnership thereof by which I agree to be bound in all respects;

(b) represent and acknowledge that (i) I have received the Offering; (ii) I understand that the transferability of the Unit(s) of Investment is restricted; that it is not anticipated that there will be any public market for the Interest being acquired; (iii) I understand that the management and control of the Partnership is vested in the management of the Partnership's Corporate General Partner and, (iv) I have reviewed and understand the Federal income tax aspects of investment in the Partnership and such advice from qualified sources such as an attorney, accountant or tax advisor as I deem necessary;

(c) if executing the Investment Letter in a representative or fiduciary capacity, I represent and warrant individually that I have full power and authority to execute and deliver this Investment Letter on behalf of the subscribing individual, ward, partnership, trust, estate, corporation or other entity and have full right and power to execute, deliver and perform pursuant to such Investment Letter and become a limited partner in the Partnership pursuant to the Partnership Agreement/Certificate of Limited Partnership; and

(d) acknowledge that this purchase and subscription for Unit(s) in VBF American Ginseng Crop 1991 is made as an investment.

It is understood that the Partnership shall have the right to accept or reject this subscription in whole or in part. As used above, the singular includes the plural in all respects if Interests are being acquired by more than one person. This Agreement and all rights hereunder shall be governed by, and interpreted in accordance with the laws of the State of Minnesota.

_____
Signature of Limited Partner

_____
Signature of Joint Partner if Joint Ownership

EXHIBIT D
ESTIMATED EXPENSES OF THE GENERAL PARTNER
FOR
VBF AMERICAN GINSENG CROP 1991:
A LIMITED PARTNERSHIP

Investment of the Limited Partners	**$ 234,000**

Less Operating Expenses:

*Placement fees	$ 35,100
Offering and Legal	3,600
Land Lease (Contribution from Corporate General Partner)	0
Initial Crop Site Preparation, Planting, Mulching — General Labor, includes Payroll Taxes	59,165
Stratified Seed (300,000)	3,720
Crop Related Expenses (Drain Tile, Fuel, Fencing, Irrigation System Installation, Equipment Insurance, Supplies, Contract Labor & Misc)	16,580
Equipment Maintenance/Replacement	3,500
Crop Management Fees & Accounting	35,000
Estimated 1991 Expenses	**$156,665**

Expenses 1992 — 1996:

A 15% Reserve Crop Maintenance Fund to be expended by the General Partner for crop security, maintenance labor, disease control, supplies and related expenses	29,835
Crop Management Fees & Accounting	47,500
TOTAL	**$ 234,000**

* Any placement fees that the Partnership is not obligated to pay as the result of this Offering will become part of the Reserve Crop Maintenance Fund. If any funds are remaining when the crop is to be harvested, they will be applied to the harvesting expenses. Any funds not immediately used will be invested in a short-term money market account and the interest earnings will be added to the Maintenance Fund.

Appendix D
A Private Placement Circular — Shorewood Press, Inc.

Highlights of the Circular Presented

1. The Company

2. Production Costs

3. Risk Factors

4. Dilution

5. Use of Proceeds

6. Financial Statements

		6216	10 1/8	−1/4
1.30	17	490	58 1/2	−3/8
.50	11	1640	73 7/8	+1/2
3.25		569	67 1/2	+1/2
1.94	14	672	36	−3/8
		166	15 3/4	+1/8
	25	954	19 5/8	+1/8
.60	7	905	27 1/8	+1/8
1.32	18	1440	47 7/8	−1/4
.22	19	479	25 7/8	−1/4
.68	24	647	33 3/4	+1/8
		3048	11 3/8	
.40	19	429	17 7/8	−1/2
		1314	17 1/4	+1/4
	19	1117	36	+1/8
.20	12	449	80 7/8	−1/4
3.50		534	56 3/8	−1/8
		2866	14	−3/8
.80a	7	873	24 1/4	+1/4
D				
1.60	13	379	36 1/8	
1.60	35	544	57 1/2	−5/8
		440	9 7/8	+1/8
1.60	14	941	68 5/8	−1 3/8
.10e	15	1618	43 1/4	−3/8
2.06	52	1429	72 5/8	−1/4
.20		1100	52 1/4	+1/8
1.44	18	576	35 3/8	−5/8
2.06	10	556	34 1/8	
1.94		385	26	
.88	25	367	22 3/4	−1/4
	131	3248	15 3/4	+1/4
12	43	972	38 1/2	−1 5/8
		352	12 3/8	+1/8
		344	18 5/8	−1/8
		1217	36 5/8	−3/8
.08	17	777	36 3/8	−1/8
		1722	7 5/8	−1/8
.25	21	3829	37 3/4	−1/4
2.46	16	357	48 3/8	−1/8
.56	26	1442	29 5/8	−1/4
2.60	38	1503	58 1/8	+3/8
.80	27	257	33	+1/4
.60	39	3729	21 1/2	+1/8
.76	17	451	43 1/2	+1/4
1.76	19	4516	46 7/8	−1/4
.78e		372	10 7/8	−1/8
1.88	17	393	43 3/8	−1/8
		1374	24 1/2	−1/4
2.44	20	350	62 3/4	+1/4
.64	33	1391	36 3/8	+3/8
E				
.52	10	999	16 1/8	
	56	1384	35 3/4	−3/8
1.10	12	363	43 5/8	−3/8
2.00	19	1952	59 3/8	+1/2
1.20	20	385	50	
.70	19	x952	30 5/8	+3/8
.60	11	382	29 5/8	−3/8
	12	539	8 5/8	+1/8
70e	10	2305	37 1/4	+1/4
1.44	19	780	58 3/4	−1/2
	23	853	34 5/8	−1/4
.20	38	938	20 7/8	−1/8
1.60	15	761	38 7/8	
.56	22	434	24 7/8	−1/8
.20		358	30 1/4	−1/8
1.08	18	162	40 7/8	+1/2
		375	31 1/8	−3/8
.60	7	503	17 3/4	+1/4
2.88	17	4491	66 1/4	−3/8
F				

Herculs	2.24	21	961	90 1/4	+1/2
HewlPk	1.00	18	3194	68 3/8	+1/2
Hexcel			1511	6	+3/8
Hibern	.03e		1287	8 3/8	−1/8
Hilton	1.20	23	658	48 3/4	−5/8
HmeDp s	.12	41	6768	38 7/8	
HomeSh	.21t		2385	11 1/8	
Hmstke	.10		3807	16 5/8	+1/2
Honywl s	.89	15	1856	35 7/8	+5/8
HK Tel	1.68e	24	861	49 5/8	+1/4
Horsh	.05e	27	2603	11 1/4	
HospFS n		41	851	46 1/2	−1 1/8
Houlnd	3.00	16	481	46 3/4	+1/8
Humana		18	1310	13	+1/8
HypT97 n	.70		521	8 7/8	
HypT99	.72		614	7 5/8	−1/8
HypT02 n	.80		776	8 3/8	−1/8
I					
IMC Frt	.27j	18	1538	33 3/4	+1/8
IdahoP	1.86	17	788	32 7/8	
IlliCtr	.68	18	436	32 3/8	−1/8
IllPowr	.80	16	464	24 5/8	
Imcera	.44		848	32 5/8	−1/8
ICI n	.77i		668	43 5/8	−1/8
INCO	.40		646	17 5/8	
IncOp2	.70		256	9 1/2	
IngerRd	.70	32	742	37 1/2	
InldStl			577	27 3/4	
InstSy		13	1215	8 5/8	−1/8
Intelcal			546	12 5/8	+3/8
IBM	1.00		6137	42	+3/8
IntFlav	3.00	21	372	101 7/8	+7/8
IGame s	.06i	46	3246	40 1/8	−3/4
IntPap	1.68	23	1307	60 1/8	+1/4
IT Crp			380	4 3/8	+1/8
IntpbGp	.50	19	441	30 5/8	+1/8
J					
JWP			738	1 1/4	+1/8
JNuveen	.56	20	502	35 3/4	−7/8
JohnJn	1.04	15	3925	39 7/8	+3/8
JonesAp		16	403	28	−3/4
K					
K mart	.96	14	5985	24 3/8	+1/4
Kellogg	1.36	18	955	50 1/4	+3/8
Kennemt	1.16	20	400	37 1/4	+1/8
Keycp	1.24	11	894	38	+1/8
KimbClk	1.72	24	1078	49 1/4	+1/2
Kohls		36	492	47 5/8	−1/8
L					
LAC g	.06		1347	8	+1/8
LSI Lg			1744	16 3/4	−1/4
LTV n			2547	10 7/8	+7/8
LaidlwB	.16	11	579	5 3/4	
LakehdP	2.36	14	408	32 1/2	+5/8
vjLesFay			896	3 1/2	+1/8
LfePart n	.05		385	23	+1 1/8
Lilly	2.42	19	1532	50 1/8	+3/8
Limitd	.36	18	6711	22 1/2	+3/8
Litton		13	722	59 3/8	−5/8
LizClab	.45	9	1151	19 3/4	+1/4
LomasFn		11	2451	8 5/8	−1 3/4
LILCo	1.78	13	824	27 1/4	−1/8
LongvF	.40a	20	75	16 7/8	+1/8
Loral	1.12	13	410	62 1/2	+1 1/2
LaLand	1.00	45	1368	44 1/2	+1 1/2
LaPac	.44	15	978	33 1/4	+1/2
Lowes	.32	32	893	45 5/8	−3/8
M					
MCR	.88		349	10	
MGF	.58		1326	7 1/4	
MIN	.62		993	7 5/8	

Norwst s	.66	14	937	27 1/4	+1/4
Nucor s	.16	47	916	52 3/4	
Nutmeg		22	669	14 7/8	−1/8
NvIMO	.96a		443	15 3/4	+1/8
NuvMu	.68		440	11 5/8	
Nynex s	2.36	14	1351	46 1/8	+1/8
O					
OakInd s		19	961	18 1/4	+1 1/4
OcciPet	1.00		3692	20 5/8	−1/4
Ogden	1.25	17	446	25 1/8	+1/8
OhioEd	1.50	14	244	25 1/8	
OklaGE	2.66	14	124	38	
Omncre	.16	18	598	24	−1/8
OpnhCa	1.85a	16	51	29 3/4	−1/8
OrbEng			403	12 5/8	+1 7/8
OreStl	.56	31	213	22 5/8	+3/8
Oryx	.40	110	3565	24 1/4	+1/8
OwensIll		11	1381	9 7/8	
P					
PNC s	1.14	12	1075	30 3/4	+1/4
PPG	2.16	20	571	65 3/8	−1/4
PSI	1.12	15	475	25 7/8	
PacEnt	.30e	16	406	27 1/8	+1/8
PacGE	1.88	15	945	35 1/2	−1/4
PacTel	2.18	25	2189	53 7/8	−1/4
PacifCp	1.08	19	1463	19 5/8	+1/8
PanBev n			422	28 5/8	−1/8
ParagT n		11	366	23 5/8	+1/2
ParCom	.80	38	2559	79 1/8	−1/4
ParkPar	.10e	23	482	34 1/2	+3/4
ParkDrl		102	360	7 1/8	
PatPtr			451	2 7/8	+3/4
PatPrll	.90a		418	12 7/8	
Patten	.13t	18	852	4	+1/4
PayCsh n			582	11 5/8	
PencpF n	.03e		872	20 3/4	
Penney s	1.44	14	1528	46 3/4	−5/8
Pennzol	3.00	34	2631	63 3/4	+1/4
PepBoy	.15	24	850	23	−3/8
PepsiC	.64	23	3739	39 1/2	−1/4
PerkEl	.68	58	742	31 3/8	−1/8
Pet	.28	16	487	16 7/8	+1/8
Pfizer	1.68	17	4317	59 7/8	+1/4
PhelpD	1.65	13	1966	39 5/8	−1/2
PhilaEl	1.40	14	709	32 5/8	−1/8
PhilMr	2.60	9	5940	46 1/8	+1/4
PhilNV			1371	20 3/8	+1/8
PhilPet	1.12	20	5915	33 7/8	
Pier 1	.10	19	743	10	+1/8
PinWst		12	588	24 1/4	
PionFS			383	10 7/8	+1/4
PitnyBw	.90	18	887	38 1/4	+1/8
PlacerD	.26	43	5122	19 3/8	+3/8
PlumCr	4.00	11	64	64	−3/8
PogoPd		19	731	18 7/8	+3/8
Polaroid	.60	26	376	33 3/4	−1/4
Polygr	.37e	20	359	34 3/8	−1/8
PopeTal	.76	14	221	21 3/8	−1/4
Potash g	.72		838	18 1/2	+1/8
Potltch	1.56	23	38	42 1/4	+3/8
PotmEl	1.64	15	492	28 3/4	
Praxair	.25	15	577	15 3/8	+1/8
PrecCst	.12	170	40	25 1/2	+1/8
PrmHsp			2817	4 3/4	+1/4
Primca s		15	2177	48 3/4	−3/8
ProctGm	1.24	148	1508	47 1/2	+3/8
Promus s		80	1151	77 3/8	+3/8
PSEG	2.16	15	563	35	
PugetP	1.84	12	414	26 1/8	+1/8
PMIIT	.72		369	8 3/8	+1/8
PPrIT	.75		440	8 3/8	+1/8
Q					

Sunstrnd	1.20	13	1517	38 3/8	−1/4
SunMn			2051	2 1/4	
SunTrst	1.12	13	515	44 1/4	+1/8
Supval	.88	13	951	32 5/8	−1/8
SurgAf	.16	22	1871	19 1/4	+1/2
SyblTc			364	13 1/2	−1/4
Syntex	1.04	13	2275	17 3/8	−1/8
Sysco	.28	25	496	27 1/4	
T					
TIS	.20		407	2 1/8	+1/8
TJX	.50	20	981	30 1/4	+1/8
TRW	1.88	21	586	67 1/8	+3/8
Tambd	1.68	18	754	42 1/4	
Tandem		18	2884	12 1/4	−1/8
Tandy	.60	55	389	36 1/4	+1/8
Taubmn n	.88		1227	13 7/8	−1/8
Tektrnx	.60		41	24	
Telef	1.40e		565	35 3/4	
TelMex	.96e	12	6937	50 7/8	−1/4
Templl	1.00	20	805	40 5/8	+1/8
TmpCh n			348	15 3/8	−1/8
TEMIF n			468	15	
TmpGlb	.60		704	8 1/8	
Tepco	2.20	13	18	27 5/8	
Terdyn		41	755	28 3/8	+3/4
Terra		8	177	4 5/8	−1/4
Texaco	3.20	15	2770	67 5/8	+1/8
TexInst	.72	22	3210	76 3/8	−1/4
TexUtil	3.08	14	1835	46	−1/4
Textron	1.24	15	898	58 1/4	+1/4
Tidwtr	.40	37	582	22 3/4	+1 1/4
TimeWa	.32		2305	41	−5/8
TmMir	1.08	73	1213	28 1/2	−1/8
TollBro		20	3789	14	+3/8
Total	.97e	10	593	27 1/4	−1/4
ToyRU		24	2018	36 1/2	
Transm	2.00	14	781	59 5/8	−1/8
Travler	1.60		2000	38 3/8	−3/8
Tremnt			10	7 5/8	+1/8
Tribune	.96	24	602	53 3/4	+3/4
TritEng			1268	32 1/8	+3/4
TucsEP			653	3 5/8	
U					
UAL Cp			811	139 3/8	−1 5/8
UGI	1.34	23	107	24 3/4	−1/8
UNUM	.80	14	531	54 5/8	+1/4
USWst	2.14	19	4675	49 1/4	+1/4
USFG	.20	54	8998	14 5/8	−1 5/8
UST	.96	17	1060	27 5/8	+1/4
USXMar	.68		2428	19 3/4	+1/8
USXUSS	1.00		635	31 3/4	
Unifi s	.56	12	1448	22 1/2	+1/4
UnCmp	1.56	60	428	42 3/8	+1/8
UCarb	.75	15	1685	19 3/8	
UnElec	2.32	14	618	44 1/8	−1/8
UnPac	1.60	17	1608	62 3/4	−3/4
UnfedF s			387	1 3/4	
Unisys		10	403	11 3/4	
Unit		35	812	4 1/4	+1/4
UHltCr	.03	35	2133	69	+7/8
UsairG			2732	12 1/2	−1/8
US Bknt		16	558	7 1/8	−1/8
US Surg	.30	14	1325	20 3/4	−1/8
UnTech	1.80		1053	55 1/2	−1/2
UWR	.92	19	84	15 1/4	
Unocal	.80	25	7692	28 3/8	−3/8
Upjohn	1.48	9	1112	28 3/4	+1/8
V					
VF Co	1.20	10	388	44 1/4	+1/4

Wa
roun

The Wall Str

Prudenti
unit agreed
charges of i
ited partne
to pay pena
$345 millio
the case sa

Disney a
than 350 m
dia's pay-T
term relati
Showtime,
uation said.

United A
union abr
labor-conc
cluded a pl
low-fare ai
the giant c

Stock mu
record $12.
24 percent
almost half
funds that i

The Pritzl
get back int
with a $15C
control of A

Private Placement Circular
The date of this offering is September 24, 199-

Shorewood Press, Inc.
Publisher of:
The National Sales Journal
5000 Wedgewood Drive,
Victoria, Minnesota 55339
Tel: (612) 479-1000

===

Purchase Price:	$7,500 Per Unit of 5,000 Shares Each
Common Stock:	$.01 Par Value Per Share
Units Offered:	30 Units Maximum
	15 Units Minimum

===

The securities offered hereby are highly speculative, involve a high degree of risk and immediate dilution, and should be purchased only by persons who can afford to lose their entire investment. See "Dilution" and "Risk Factors."

Prior to this private offering, there has been no market for the Common Stock Shares of the Company. The offering price of the Units offered hereby was arbitrarily determined by the Company and there can be no assurance that the shares can be resold at the offering price or that a trading market will develop. This Private Placement Offering is made on a "best efforts" basis and there can be no assurance that all of the units of shares offered will be sold. This offering involves substantial dilution in that the book value of the shares after the offering will be less than the offering price.

	Private Offering Price	Proceeds to the Company
Per Unit of 5,000 Shares	$ 7,500	$ 7,500
30 Units Maximum	$ 225,000	$ 225,000
15 Units Minimum	$ 112,500	$ 112,500

These securities have not been approved or disapproved by the Securities and Exchange Commission nor the securities division of any state, nor has the commission of any state passed upon the accuracy or adequacy of this Offering Circular. Any representation to the contrary is a criminal offense. This Private Placement Offering is made in accordance with the Minnesota Securities Act as a transactional exemption found in Minnesota Statutes 80A.15, subd.2(h) for private placements by the issuer with limited distribution within the State of Minnesota.

Offeree: _____ Number: _____

Table of Contents

Private Placement Circular Announcement	1
Summary of Private Placement Offering	3
The Company	6
Risk Factors	10
Business of the Company	11
Marketing	12
NSJ Production Costs	13
Costs of Booklet Publishing	13
Competition	14
Employees	15
Property	15
Intangible Assets	15
Other Tangible Assets	16
Dilution	16
Use of Proceeds	18
Background of Management and Employees	19
Company Management and Controlling Shareholders	20
Capitalization	21
Remuneration of Officers and Directors	21
Description of Common Stock	22
General	22
Dividends	22
Voting Rights	22
Report to Shareholders	22
Legal	23
Financial Reports and Experts	23
Private Offering Plan	23
Procedures for Subscribers	24
Subscription Agreement	24
Report of Independent Certified Public Accountants	25
Current Balance Sheet	26
Current Income Statement	27
Current Stockholders' Equity	28
Balance Sheet for Period December 17, 199- to December 31, 199-	29
Income Statement — December 17, 199- to December 31, 199-	30
Proforma Profit and Loss Statement	32

Summary of the Private Placement Offering

The information set forth below is intended to supply, in summary form, certain information and highlights from material contained in this Private Placement Circular and should be read in conjunction with, and is qualified in its entirety by the detailed information appearing elsewhere in this circular and the financial statements attached hereto.

The Company

Shorewood Press, Inc. (the "Company"), and formerly called General Admissions, Inc., was incorporated as a Subchapter "C" Corporation in the State of Minnesota on December 17, 199-. The Company has 5,000,000 shares of Common Stock authorized, par value $.01/share, with 100,000 shares currently issued and outstanding.

After completing 18 months of development, the Company has commenced publishing a bimonthly, copyrighted, tabloid newspaper entitled *The National Sales Journal* (the "NSJ" or the "Journal"). The Journal's audience includes sales, marketing, advertising, finance and business executives nationwide. The Company plans a circulation of 100,000 copies per issue and is estimating a national readership of 300,000. The September/October 199- issue (the first edition), is attached to this circular as Exhibit A.

The Company sells display and classified advertising space in the Journal; sells single and multiple subscriptions to the NSJ; sells subscriptions to other well known publications through co-op advertising in the NSJ; represents other book publishers, audio production companies and a mailing list compiler as a national distributor, and, plans to publish a series of professionally authored business booklets for the retail and wholesale markets.

The Offering

Securities Offered	30 Units of 5,000 shares per Unit for a total of 150,000 shares at a offering price of $7,500 per Unit. See "Description of Common Stock" and the "Private Offering Plan."
Private Placement	This is a Private Placement Offering and the Units of shares are being sold by the Company on a "best efforts" basis with 15 Units as a Minimum and 30 Units as a Maximum. See "Private Offering Plan."

Approximate Net Proceeds	$225,000 providing all 30 Units are purchased; $112,500 if the Minimum of 15 Units are sold. See "Use of Proceeds."
Use of Proceeds	To be added to the general operating funds of the Company (i) for publication expansion; (ii) for marketing and promotion; (iii) for publishing a series of professional publications; (iv) for working capital; and (v) for general and administrative expenses including salaries. See "Use of Proceeds" and "Business of the Company."
Number of Shares Outstanding	Assuming 30 Units or 150,000 shares are sold: Before Offering: 100,000 Shares After Offering: 250,000 Shares See "Dilution."
Risk Factors	The Company is dependent upon key personnel; absence of operating history; additional financing may be required. For these and other reasons, investment in the securities offered involve a high degree of risk. See "Risk Factors."

"Before" and "After" shares and percentages held by the founder, directors and officers assuming 30 Units totaling 150,000 shares are sold:

	Outstanding Shares	Percentages
Before Private Offering	100,000	100.0%
After Private Offering	100,000	40.0%

"Before" and "After" shares and percentages held by the founder, directors and officers assuming 15 Units totaling 75,000 shares are sold:

	Outstanding Shares	Percentages
Before Private Offering	100,000	100.0%
After Private Offering	100,000	57.1%

Financials

The Company's revenues, development and operating expenses, profits and losses are reported and projected briefly as follows:

	*199- Actuals	199- Projected	199- Projected	199- Projected
Revenues	$ 84	25,066	966,175	2,534,625
Less Expenses	16,603	65,083	889,315	1,834,505
Profit or (Loss) Before Taxes	$ (16,519)	(40,017)	76,860	700,120
Profit Percent	-	-	7.96%	27.62%

* 12 and 1/2 months of operation.
Please see the attached current balance sheets and audited income statements for 199- and 199-, and the proforma profit or loss statements projected for 199-, 199- and 199-.

How to Subscribe for Units of Shares

Please see "Procedures for Subscribers" for detailed information regarding the procedure for purchasing the Units of Shares as described in this Circular.

The shares of Common Stock are offered by the Company subject to prior sale, when, as and if delivered to and accepted by the subscribers, acceptance of the subscriptions by the Company, and approval of certain legal matters by counsel to the Company.

This Circular has been prepared by the Company and all of the information contained herein, including the financial information, is provided by the Company and its auditors.

Subscribers are urged to read this Circular carefully, and may obtain additional details about the Company upon request. Investing subscribers will be asked to acknowledge in the Subscription Agreement that they were given the opportunity to obtain additional information and that they did so to their satisfaction.

***

The Company

On December 17, 199-, William C. Foster founded and incorporated General Admissions, Inc. as a Subchapter "C" Corporation in the State of Minnesota. On January 3, 199-, the Company's name was changed to Shorewood Press, Inc. to better reflect its publishing business.

Upon incorporation, the Company was authorized 5,000,000 shares of Common Stock, par value $.01/per share and issued 100,000 shares to its directors. Mr. Foster currently holds 98,000 shares as the founder, chairman and chief executive officer and Jack W. Olson holds 2,000 shares as corporate secretary and legal counsel to the Company.

After incorporation, Mr. Foster planned to complete the preliminary work necessary to publish a tabloid newspaper to be called *The National Sales Journal* (the "NSJ" or the "Journal"). Due to unexpected limitations on his time during 199-, he was unable to devote his attention to the publishing effort until the spring of 199-.

Since then, he has made a considerable investment, both in time and capital, to develop the publication. This work included:

1. Researching several markets to determine the potential opportunities of readership, distribution and advertising space sales.

2. Recruiting a qualified executive editor.

3. Securing a printing supplier that could provide all of the services required to lay out, typeset, print, label and mail the publication in a timely manner.

4. Establishing a reliable relationship with publishers of other magazines, journals and newspapers in order to secure permissions to reprint articles and feature stories previously published in their publications.

5. Locating professional writers in the fields of sales, marketing, advertising and finance to produce the columns for the NSJ on a regular basis.

6. Building a listing of prospective advertisers and advertising agencies representing prospective clients.

7. Establishing distributorship agreements with selected publishers of books, educational audio program producers and with a compiler of mailing lists which the Company could represent as a seller of those products to its readers through the NSJ.

8. Locating a suitable mailing list of prospective subscribers.

The foregoing and many other details had to be completed prior to actually publishing the first edition.

The first issue of the Journal (September/October 199-), was published and distributed to 13,300 prospective subscribers nationwide during the 2nd week of August, 199-. This twelve page edition included eight business articles reprinted with the permission of other publishers, one feature article on a manufacturing business and introduced a new column concerning business travel called *Travel Beat*, written by Joe Lenning, a owner and vice president of a successful Minneapolis travel agency. His travel column will become a regular feature in the NSJ. The reprint articles used in this particular issue originally appeared in *The Wall Street Journal, Industry Week* and *The Minnesota Business Journal*.

New columns concerning marketing, sales, advertising, finance and business management will begin to appear in subsequent issues. *Focus on Marketing*, for example, will be written by Philip Canter, vice president of marketing for Taylor Manufacturing Corporation in Detroit. Other writers, who are professionals in their respective fields, are actively being recruited by the Company at this time.

While the first issue of the Journal did include some advertising, it was designed primarily as a prototype edition since many prospective advertisers wanted to see what the publication looked like before making a advertising decision. As a result, many advertisers and agencies representing a number of clients have expressed interest in the Journal and are reserving space for future editions.

Normally, and when the proper mix of advertising is achieved, the Journal will range in size from 24 to 48 pages. Approximately 25% to 30% of each issue will be devoted to columns, articles and feature stories of interest to its readers, and 70% to 75% will be devoted to advertising.

The Company has secured a national distributorship with a computerized mailing list compiler enabling it to purchase their lists for resale at a discount of 54%. As a result, management believes the Company can build a client following for these mailing lists. Please refer to the ad appearing in the Journal that the Company is currently using to promote these low-cost lists.

The Company has established distributorships with several publishers to promote and sell their books and audio educational tapes to the Journal's readers. See the back page of the September/October issue — "From the Publisher's Library." After shipping expenses, the Company will earn a gross profit margin on these products ranging from 40% to 65%.

The Company has also established a co-op advertising relationship with Dow Jones & Company, Inc., publishers of *The Wall Street Journal* — to run selected advertisements in the NSJ for their publication called *The National Business Employment Weekly*. The Company receives $13 for each 8 week subscription received, and plans to develop similar co-op advertising programs with the publishers of other journals, magazines and newspapers that its readers may wish to subscribe to.

The Journal will become a subscription oriented publication, however, during the first full year of building its circulation, several thousand copies will be mailed free-of-charge to prospective subscribers. The Company believes that the subscription rate of $6.50/per year and $11.70 for two years is a very attractive offer for this caliber of bimonthly publication. Due to increasing postal rates, the subscription price will be raised by March, 199-. At that time, the Company will begin publishing the Journal on a monthly basis and the tentative subscription rates will be $12 per year and $20 for two years. Discounts off the subscription rates are offered to companies ordering multiple issues for their employees.

Management believes that although the Journal's rates are somewhat below other such publications, a more reasonable price plus multiple subscription discounts will enable the Company to reach its goal of 100,000 subscribers more quickly.

Ideally, the Company would prefer to have 100% of the Journal's circulation sold on a subscription basis, however, and as previously mentioned, management also views this publication as a marketing vehicle for the Company's product line. Therefore, the Company will promote subscriptions aggressively, but has forecast a relatively low revenue estimate for subscription sales and will continue to do so until the Journal becomes more established.

The Company plans to begin publishing a series of professional booklets ranging in size from 25 to 75 pages that focus on the vocations of sales, marketing, advertising, finance and business management. These booklets will be written by individuals who are presently executives in these respective fields, and who, through their expertise and experience, can offer solid how-to information and advice to others wishing to learn, improve or expand their career skills.

The Company will market these booklets through the Journal and by direct mail catalog to prospective buyers and the wholesale book market. The average retail selling prices for these publications will range from $4.95 to $9.95 each; however, actual prices will depend upon the publishing and marketing costs. After royalties, production and marketing expenses, these booklets are expected to show a gross profit margin of 65% to 75%. The Company has started advertising for manuscripts in the Journal and will utilize other sources to locate its authors.

Now that the Company has commenced publishing the Journal, and upon the successful completion of this offering to private investors, management believes there is every opportunity for the business to become a viable entity within a relatively short period of time.

To accomplish its goals, the Company, through this Private Placement Offering, is selling up to 30 Units of 5,000 Common Stock shares each at a price of $7,500 per Unit. Each Unit represents 2% of the shares to be outstanding after the offering is closed provided all 30 Units are sold. Should a maximum number of Units be purchased by investors, the Company's total proceeds will be $225,000. Since it is selling these Units direct to investors, it will not incur expenses for underwriting or be required to pay commissions on the sales. To comply with Minnesota Law, the Company intends to maintain under 35 private investors as shareholders and should all of the Units be sold, the Company will have 32 investing participants or less should some investors purchase two or more Units each.

Should the minimum of 15 Units be purchased, the total proceeds to the Company will be $112,500. Management believes this is the minimum capital needed to conduct the Company's business and still achieve its goals albeit at a reduced rate of growth.

The proceeds of this offering will be used to: (1) improve the circulation of the Journal; (2) change the publishing frequency from bimonthly to monthly; (3) expand the marketing and promotion program; (4) begin publishing a series of new booklets and other publications; and (5) pay personnel salaries and improve the general working capital funds of the business.

Management believes that this additional capital will satisfy the Company's growth needs for the next three years, but the Company may, at some later date, seek to raise additional funds for possible acquisitions or to expand the business of the Company. In this event, management would consider commercial loans, further private equity investment or a public offering of the Company's Common Stock.

The Company currently has $19,166 in assets. Mr. Foster's cash and tangible asset investment through July 31, 199- has been $44,660 during the Company's development stage. Key employees are presently working in a non-paid, volunteer capacity for the Company and will join the business on a full-time and part-time basis as its growth needs warrant. See "Background of Management and Employees."

The Company's temporary executive offices are located at 5000 Wedgewood Drive, Victoria, Minnesota 55339 and its telephone number is (612) 479-1000.

***

Risk Factors

The shares of Common Stock offered herein as Units for private investment are speculative, involve a high degree of risk and should be purchased only by persons who can afford to lose their entire investment. The following risk factors should be considered carefully as well as the other information contained in this Offering Circular.

1. **Lack of Profitability.** There can be no assurance that the Company will be able to commercially market The National Sales Journal, its other products or operate profitably in the future.

2. **Absence of Operating History.** The Company does not have a history of operating as a viable entity other than in its current development stage.

3. **Business Dependent Upon Key Employees.** The business of the Company is dependent upon the participation of its chief executive officer and supporting personnel. Loss of one or two of these individuals could adversely affect the conduct of the Company's business.

4. **Additional Financing May Be Required.** Although the Company believes that the funds raised in this offering will be sufficient for its early growth needs, the conduct of the Company's business may require the raising of additional capital in the future.

5. **Competition.** The Company will be in competition with several other publishing companies. See "Competition."

6. **Private Offering Price.** The Unit price of the Common Stock shares offered hereby was arbitrarily determined by the Company and is not necessarily based on net worth or other generally accepted criteria of value.

7. **Control By Management.** The 100,000 shares of the Company's Common Stock presently owned beneficially by the founder, officers and directors will constitute in the aggregate 40% of the shares to be outstanding upon the satisfactory completion of this private offering. This percentage will allow management to exert significant influence over the activities of the Company and its business.

8. **No Public Market.** There is at present no market for shares of the Company's Common Stock and, there can be no assurance that such a market will ever develop or that the shares offered hereby can be resold. If such a market does develop, there can be no assurance that the shares purchased by the investors can be resold without incurring a loss thereon.

9. **Dividends.** Any future dividends paid by the Company will depend upon its earnings, its financial requirements and other factors. Investors who anticipate the need for immediate dividend income from their investment in the Company's Common Stock should refrain from purchasing the shares offered hereby. See "Description of Common Stock."

Business of the Company

The Company's principal publication, *The National Sales Journal*, is a copyrighted, bimonthly, 6 column wide, tabloid newspaper, printed on 32 inch newsprint stock. Display advertising space is sold in full page units (10 3/8" x 15" deep) to one column inch (1 9/16" x 1" deep). The Journal's advertising rates vary depending upon the number of ad insertions purchased by a advertiser, but typically, a full page ad sells for $1,413.13 after discounts and agency commissions, and a one column inch ad sells for $28.26 after discounts and commissions are paid.

Classified advertisements are accepted and the rate is $1.25 per word ($1.05 per word for three or more consecutive insertions). The Journal offers a variety of classified ad headings from which to choose. For more detailed information, please refer to the center page spread in the September/October 199- issue which also includes the Journal's mechanical, production and deadline requirements.

Advertising for each issue of the Journal is secured by soliciting advertising agencies who purchase space on behalf of their clients, and the Company also promotes the publications directly to prospective advertisers who sell products or services the Company believes would appeal to the Journal's readers.

Editorial content is written by several professionals in the form of columns which address a variety of subjects that will interest NSJ's readership. Features and articles that have appeared in other publications will be selected for reprint in the Journal when the stories are of special interest. The NSJ obtains permission rights to reprint these articles from such periodicals as *The Wall Street Journal, Barron's, Forbes, Fortune, Venture, Industry Week, Business Week, Sales and Marketing Management, Selling Direct, The New York Times, The Washingtonian, Agency Sales Magazine*, and many others.

NSJ's circulation will continue to be composed of subscribers and a rotating list of prospective subscribers who will infrequently receive issues of the Journal free-of-charge. The Company estimates that there are in excess of 10,000,000 individuals in the United States who are potential subscribers and buyers for the products and services of the Journal's advertisers and the products sold by the Company.

Management believes that the Company can achieve 100,000 plus subscriptions within three years, but is projecting only 24,000 subscribers beginning in 199-. Should the Journal's subscription sales develop more quickly, the Company will then expand the circulation accordingly. For example, if 50,000 subscriptions are sold, the Company may elect to expand the actual circulation to 200,000 plus per issue. This expansion in issues distributed would enable the Company to charge more for display and classified advertising space, and ultimately, an increased subscription rate could be asked without damaging the publication's circulation goals.

As an authorized representative to secure subscriptions for other publications, management is negotiating the exchange of ads with several publications to promote the Journal to their readers.

By acting as a national distributor for other book publishers, audio training tape producers and mailing list houses, management believes these sales will significantly boost the revenue base of the Company. See "Competition."

The Company is presently advertising in the Journal for manuscripts it can publish in booklet form — from 25 to 75 pages in length. These booklets will focus on specific career skills, insights, how-to's and experiences in the fields of marketing, sales, advertising, finance and business management. The marketing of these booklets will be conducted through the Company's ads in the Journal's "From the Publisher's Library" and by catalog or flier mailings to prospective buyers. The Company plans to enter the wholesale book markets with its booklets in mid 199-.

Marketing

The lists of prospective subscribers are purchased from National Business Lists, Inc. under a Master Mailer contract agreement. Management has also compiled a list of approximately 6,500 advertisers and advertising agencies that the Company will utilize continuously to promote its advertising space in the NSJ.

By March, 199-, the Journal will be published and distributed monthly to at least 100,000 recipients. Media kits will be developed and furnished to selected advertising agencies to assist in building the Journal's advertising base.

At this time, management is negotiating with two subscription service companies to promote the Journal in their mass marketing programs.

The Company has established a merchant agreement with Visa and MasterCard through the National Bank of Victoria, Victoria, Minnesota. Credit card purchases for books, audio cassettes and subscriptions will be accepted. The servicing fee ranges from 2.2% to 3.5% depending upon the monthly sales volume.

The Company has a policy of offering credit terms only to accounts that furnish at least three trade references and a bank reference. The Company's credit terms to "open account customers" is Net 30 Days.

The goal of the Company is to build the image of *The National Sales Journal* as a informative, useful and reliable publication. As a publishing business, the Company intends to demonstrate that it is able to provide its customers with a wide variety of professional, up-to-date publications and other products that will directly aid in upgrading their career skills and general knowledge.

NSJ Production Costs

The direct costs of publishing the Journal with a circulation of 100,000 copies, including reprint and author fees, art work, typesetting, stripping, printing, mail lists, mail preparation and bulk rate postage are as follows:

	Total Direct Costs
24 page Unit with 17 potential revenue pages	$23,500/per 100M
28 page Unit with 20 potential revenue pages	$25,500/per 100M
32 page Unit with 23 potential revenue pages	$29,200/per 100M
40 page Unit with 28 potential revenue pages	$32,000/per 100M

All typesetting, art work, printing and mailing services are presently contracted with the Maxwell Printing Company, Victoria, Minnesota.

Costs of Booklet Publishing

An example of costs to publish a 52 page, softcover booklet, purchased in quantities of 3,000 copies per printing — in comparison to selling prices — is illustrated as follows:

	Retail	Wholesale
Estimated Selling Price Per Booklet	$4.95	$2.52
Less:		
Typesetting, Printing and Binding	.74	.74
Author's Royalty (15% of Net Sale)	.74	.38
* Gross Profit	$3.47	$1.40
Percent Gross Profit	70.1%	55.6%

* Before editing, selling and administrative expenses.

The Company would like to publish up to 35 booklets in 199- and 25 more in 199-. No assurances can be given that this goal will be achieved; however, since the Company began advertising for manuscripts, it has received 119 to date and at least 22 of them are considered to be good publishing candidates.

Competition

The Company's competitors include many well known publishers of bimonthly, monthly and weekly publications and several publishers of books. And, while many have considerable assets to their credit, management believes that the Company can compete effectively with them.

The NSJ, for example, offers advertising rates that the Company's competitors cannot afford to provide because of their high, fixed overhead expenses. The NSJ can offer a national circulation comparable to many other publications, and many of them only serve a small portion of NSJ's intended market. One national magazine currently serves about 50% of the NSJ's planned audience and their advertising rates are approximately three (3) times higher than those charged by the Company. The Journal is also able to offer its advertisers more space to present their products and services (because it is a tabloid publication) for fewer advertising dollars. For example, the NSJ now offers 90 column inches of space when an advertiser wants a full page for an ad while most magazines are limited to the equivalent of 70 column inches or less.

The Company has established relationships with several of its competitors to reprint selected articles and feature stories and is negotiating with others to exchange subscription advertising as previously mentioned. The Company has secured distributorships with such competitors as Barnsworth Publishing Company, Quality Books, Trainer Books, BranDenBerg Publishing Company, Phillips-Hall Publishing Corp., Science Press, Inc., Grand Almanac Publications, William Nash Publishers, Inc., and the World Educational Institute to name only a few. As a distributor for these and other publishers and producers, the Company will be in a position to offer their products at the same retail prices they list and still earn a satisfactory profit.

As a publisher of professional business booklets, the Company will focus on specific topics that will aid individuals in building their career skills. Although the Company may, in the future, consider publishing full length books, management believes that a strong market currently exists for short and informative works that address the needs of the Journal's readers.

Employees

The business is managed by its chief executive officer and vice president of production on a part-time (non-paid) basis. Upon the satisfactory completion of this offering, the Company will employ a staff of full-time and part-time employees to conduct its operations. Should all 30 Units of the Company's Common Stock be sold, it will employ 3 full-time employees (CEO, CFO and Vice President of Production) and one part-time secretary during the balance of 199-. In 199-, the Company expects to employ up to 6 full-time and 3 part-time employees, and in 199-, up to 12 full-time and 4 part-time staffers. These employment estimates do not include the Company's Executive Editor and Art Director who work for the business as independent free-lancers on a work-for-hire basis and not as employees.

The Company is not a party to any union or collective bargaining agreement affecting its employees and believes that its relationship with them will be satisfactory.

Property

The Company's executive offices, presently located in Victoria, Minnesota occupy a total of 750 square feet. This space has been provided free-of-charge by Mr. Foster until the business has located a suitable office facility in the western suburbs of Minneapolis. After the successful completion of this offering, the Company will lease office space of about 1,500 square feet at a estimated cost of $1,250 per month.

This new location is expected to adequately serve the Company's growth needs for at least two years. In 199-, management believes the business will need an additional 1,200 square feet of office and warehouse space for a combined monthly lease expense of $2,250 plus utilities.

Intangible Assets

The Company holds a copyright for *The National Sales Journal* and will follow a policy of filing copyright applications for any new publications it creates and/or publishes.

Other Tangible Assets

The Company has compiled a computerized mailing list of 6,500 advertisers and advertising agencies which it uses to promote the NSJ.

Dilution

As of September 24, 199-, the date of this offering, the Company has 100,000 shares of its Common Stock outstanding with a current net tangible book value (total assets less liabilities and intangible assets) of $19,166 or $.192 per share.

Upon incorporation, the Company was authorized 5,000,000 shares and issued 100,000. 98,000 shares were issued to William C. Foster, founder, promoter, chairman and chief executive officer for cash and other tangible assets. 2,000 shares were issued to Jack W. Olson, secretary and director for the corporation in exchange for legal services rendered. Up to September 24, 199-, Mr. Foster has contributed a total of $44,660 in cash and other tangible assets as his investment in the Company without issuing additional shares of its Common Stock. Therefore, the cash value of his and Mr. Olson's investment to date is $.4466 per share, however for purposes of computing the current book value, $.192 reflects the book value as of September 24, 199- and after the Company's development expenses have been deducted. Cumulative voting is not allowed in the election of directors and officers and the holders of the above shares are in a position to influence control of the Company.

In the event 30 Units totaling 150,000 shares are purchased by private investors, the purchasers will own 60% of the Company's outstanding shares for which they will have paid $1.50 per share. The Company, in this event, will have 250,000 shares issued and outstanding with a net tangible book value (current book value plus the investment) of $.977 per share. The private investors will incur an immediate dilution of approximately $.523 per share in the net tangible book value of the shares held by them, and the present shareholders will benefit by an increase of approximately $.785 per share in the net tangible book value of the shares held by them.

In the event only 15 Units totaling 75,000 shares are purchased by private investors, the purchasers will own 42.85% of the Company's outstanding shares for which they will have paid $1.50 per share. The Company, in this instance, will have 175,000 shares issued and outstanding with a net tangible book value of $.752 per share. The private shareholders will then incur an immediate dilution or reduction in the present value of their investment of approximately $.748 per share in the net tangible book value of the shares held by them, and the present shareholders will benefit by an increase of approximately $.56 per share in the net tangible book value of the shares they hold.

"Net Tangible Book Value" is the amount that results from subtracting the total liabilities and intangible assets of a Company from its total current assets. "Dilution" is the difference between the private offering price and the net tangible book value of shares immediately after the private investment is made and the offering expenses have been deducted.

***

Use of Proceeds

In the event all 30 Units totaling 150,000 shares of the Company's Common Stock are sold, the proceeds will be $225,000 (Maximum). Should only 15 Units be sold totaling 75,000 shares, the proceeds will be $112,500 (Minimum). Both the Maximum and Minimum distribution of these funds and how they will be applied is described as follows:

	Maximum	Minimum
For general development of *The National Sales Journal* and to change its publication from bimonthly to monthly ...	$ 85,000	$ 40,000
To develop a series of new booklet publications for the retail and wholesale markets ...	20,000	12,500
For promoting *The National Sales Journal* to prospective advertisers and agencies and to develop its subscription base ...	40,000	20,000
For personnel salaries and working capital ...	80,000	40,000
Total	$ 225,000	$ 112,500

Any unused balance of the proceeds and other cash assets of the Company will be utilized for general corporate purposes. The Company will further seek to establish credit lines with banks, other lending institutions and its suppliers to insure that sufficient working capital is available. The Company does not have any present intention to borrow funds except as may be necessary for its business development. Accordingly, and because presently unforeseen circumstances could cause some variation in the allocation of the proceeds indicated above, the Company reserves the right to make such variations as the circumstances warrant.

To the extent that the foregoing proceeds are not immediately used, they will be invested in a short term money market account or government securities to produce additional revenues for the Company.

Background of Management and Employees

William C. Foster, age 46, is the founder, chairman of the board, publisher and chief executive officer of the Company. Mr. Foster is currently employed by the Merrill Institute in Minneapolis as its director of administration. The Institute is recognized worldwide for its educational training, publishing, film production and consulting services in the field of continuing education programs for sales, marketing and advertising professionals. From 198- to 199-, he served as a consultant to the Wild Wood Corporation to assist with preparing a public offering of their common stock shares. From 197-to 198-, he was the president of Research Marketing, Inc., in Minneapolis and from 197- to 197-, he was the director of marketing for the Kohl Manufacturing Company in Racine, Wisconsin. Mr. Foster is a 196- graduate of the University of Minnesota and holds a BA degree in Accounting. He is a published author and has written several articles on business management. Upon receipt of the proceeds of this offering, Mr. Foster will direct his full-time efforts to the Company.

Moreen C. Foss, age 42, is a director and the vice president of advertising for the Company. Since 197-, she has been employed as the advertising manager for the Minneapolis Herald. Mrs. Foss is a 197- graduate of the University of Minnesota and holds a BA degree in Journalism. She will join the Company on a full-time basis upon the successful completion of the offering.

Thomas T. Sommers, age 32, will be the production manager for the Company on a consultant basis. He is currently employed as the production manager for Forest Management Magazine in St. Paul, Minnesota. Mr. Sommers is a graduate of the University of Wisconsin and holds a BS degree in Journalism.

Jack W. Olson, age 51, is a director and secretary for the Company. He is an attorney-at-law and is a partner of the firm Olson, Jarvis and Brenner, PA in Minneapolis. He received his Juris Doctorate from the University of Minnesota in 196- and holds a BA degree in Accounting. Mr. Olson devotes about 1% of his time to the Company and serves as its legal counsel.

Theodore T. Wright, age 39, is the executive editor for the Company. Mr. Wright has been a free-lance editor of scholarly works and publications for the past 15 years and has proven to be an asset in the creation and publication of *The National Sales Journal*. He will continue to work for the Company as a consultant and executive editor on a work-for-hire basis.

Julia A. Elliot, age 43, is the accountant for the Company and will be appointed as its chief financial officer on a full-time basis after the offering has been successfully completed. Mrs. Elliot has considerable experience in business, accounting, inventory control, forecasting and cash management and recently directed the reorganization of the Robertson Crane Corporation in St. Paul. She is a graduate of the University of North Dakota and holds a BS degree in Accounting. Mrs. Elliot is presently studying for the Minnesota CPA examination to be given in the spring of 199-.

Additional candidates for the Company's Board of Directors will be sought to provide counsel and the appropriate expertise for its continued development and growth. Management will, from time to time, seek to utilize the securities of the Company as incentives or bonuses for its executives and key employees, however, no Employee Stock Option Plan has been adopted by the Board of Directors prior to this offering.

Company Management and Controlling Shareholders

The names and resident addresses of the founder, directors and officers holding Common Stock shares of the Company as of September 24, 199- are as follows:

William C. Foster 6800 Teal Place Victoria, MN 55339	Founder, Chairman, Publisher, CEO/CFO	98,000 Shares 98% of Equity
Jack W. Olson 15300 Bell Heights Road Mound, MN 55333	Director, Secretary, Legal Counsel	2,000 Shares 2% of Equity

William C. Foster is the founder of the Company within the meaning of the Securities Act of 1933, as amended, and may be deemed a controlling entity and founding shareholder.

The Directors of the Company receive no fees for attending meetings, but are reimbursed for expenses incurred to attend such meetings and for their out-of-pocket expenses when performing their duties in behalf of the Company. Mr. Olson will receive a retainer of $200 per month for his services as legal counsel after the offering is successfully completed.

Capitalization

The capitalization of the Company is presented as follows to reflect the sale of the shares offered hereby:

	Shares Outstanding Before Offering	Shares Outstanding With 30 Units Sold	Shares Outstanding With 15 Units Sold
Stockholders' Equity Common Stock, $.01/Par Value Authorized: 5,000,000 Shares			
Current Shareholders'	100,000	100,000	100,000
Private Investors	-	150,000	75,000
Shares Outstanding	100,000	250,000	175,000

Remuneration of Officers and Directors
First Year After Offering

Name	Position	Salary	Benefits
William C. Foster	Chairman, CEO and Publisher	$3,250/Mo.	$200/Mo.
Moreen C. Foss	Director and VP of Advertising	$2,250/Mo.	$175/Mo.
Julia A. Elliot	CFO	$2,250/Mo.	$175/Mo.
Jack W. Olson	Director, Secretary, and Legal Counsel	$ 200/Mo.	$ 0/Mo.

Description of Common Stock

General

The Company's authorized capital stock consists of 5,000,000 shares, par value $.01/per share, Common Stock.

Dividends

Holders of the Company's Common Stock are entitled to receive dividends when and as declared by the Company's Board of Directors out of the funds legally available therefor. Any such dividends may be paid in cash, property or shares of the Company's Common Stock. Any future dividends will be subject to the discretion of the Company's Board of Directors and would depend upon, among other things, future earnings, the operating and financial condition of the Company, its capital requirements and general business conditions. The Company therefore, can give no assurance that any dividends on its outstanding shares of Common Stock will be paid.

Voting Rights

All shares of the Company's Common Stock have equal voting rights, and, when validly issued and outstanding, have one vote per share on all matters to be voted upon by the stockholders. Cumulative voting in the election of Directors and Officers is not allowed.

Miscellaneous Rights and Provisions

Shares of the Company's Common Stock have no preemptive or conversion rights, no redemption or sinking fund provisions, and are not liable to further call or assessment. The outstanding shares of the Company's Common Stock are, and any shares sold pursuant to this Private Offering of Investment will be fully paid and non-assessable. Each share of the Common Stock is entitled to share ratably in any assets available for distribution to holders of its equity securities upon liquidation of the Company.

Report to the Shareholders

The Company will furnish annual reports to its shareholders containing financial statements and may in the future issue quarterly or other interim reports to them as it deems appropriate.

Legal

Legal matters in connection with the Company's securities will be passed upon for the Company by Olson, Jarvis and Brenner, PA, 740 Keller Building, Minneapolis, MN 55301.

Litigation

The Company knows of no legal proceedings pending or threatened, or judgements entered against it, or any director or officer.

Financial Reports and Experts

The audited balance sheets and income statements provided herewith have been completed using acceptable accounting practices and are submitted by the accounting firm of Lincoln, Dell and Ryder, CPAs. The proforma statements of profit or loss are provided by the Company for the benefit of the investors to better understand the goals of the business. They are forecasts and as such, may not develop as planned or projected.

Private Offering Plan

The Company is hereby offering 30 Units of its Common Stock Shares, Par Value $.01/per share. Each Unit consists of 5,000 shares and are offered at $7,500 per Unit or the equivalent of $1.50 per share. No partial purchases of these Units may be made.

The Units will be offered and sold pursuant to a continuing offer over a period of 90 days after the date of this Private Placement Circular by authorized officers of the Company without special compensation. Should all 30 Units be sold prior to the end of the 90 day sale period, this offering will automatically be considered completed and fulfilled.

There is no maximum to the number of Units an investor may purchase; however, no more than 30 Units are available for purchase through this private offering.

In the event the Company does not sell at least 15 Units (Minimum) as offered herein, those proceeds received from investors for 14 Units or less will be refunded in full to those investors concerned at the end of the 90 day period.

Procedures for Subscribers

Investors should fill out the following Subscription Agreement and return it with a check for the amount of Units purchased — payable to "Shorewood Press, Inc.":

===

Subscription Agreement

Date: _____

From: _____
        _____
        _____
        _____
        Telephone: _____

To: The Board of Directors of Shorewood Press, Inc.,
      5000 Wedgewood Drive, Victoria, MN 55339

I/We hereby make application to purchase _____ Unit(s) totaling _____ Shares of Shorewood Press, Inc. Common Stock Shares and have enclosed a check in the amount of $_____ as payment in full for the Unit(s) purchased.

I/We have carefully read the Private Placement Circular provided by the Company and acknowledge the risk factors associated with the business and have been afforded the opportunity to inspect the Company's records further to My/Our satisfaction, and further understand that I/We may have the opportunity to do so at any time in the future during normal business hours by appointment.

It is further understood that in the event fourteen (14) or less Units of the Common Stock Shares are sold by the Company as a result of this Private Placement Offering, that My/Our full investment stated above will be refunded within 90 days or shortly thereafter from the date of the Private Placement Circular.

_____

Notary Public Signature, Date & Seal

                                        _____

                                        Purchaser(s) Signature(s)

Appendix D — A Private Placement Circular — Shorewood Press, Inc.

Report of Independent Certified Public Accountants

Board of Directors
Shorewood Press, Inc.
Victoria, MN 55339

We have examined the balance sheet of Shorewood Press, Inc. as of September 1, 199- and related statements of operations, stockholders' equity, and changes in financial position to the period ending September 1, 199-. Our examinations were made in accordance with generally accepted auditing standards and accordingly, include such test of the accounting records and such other auditing procedures as we consider necessary in the circumstances.

The Company has incurred losses from inception due to development costs which have resulted in a deficit in Stockholders' Equity as of September 1, 199-. Realization of the Company's assets, principally accounts receivable, is dependent upon successful future operations.

In our opinion, subject to the realization of the Company's assets as described in the preceding paragraph, the financial statements referred to above present fairly the financial position of Shorewood Press, Inc. on September 1, 199- and the results of its operations and changes in its financial position for the period ending September 1, 199- and fiscal year periods from December 17, 199- through December 31, 199- are in conformity with generally accepted accounting principles applied on a consistent basis.

LINCOLN, DELL AND RYDER
Certified Public Accountants

St. Paul, Minnesota
September 10, 199-

Balance Sheet
Shorewood Press, Inc.
(Audited)
as of
September 1, 199-

ASSETS:

Cash	$ 3,385.44	
Office Supplies	100.00	
Taxes Receivable	15,557.00	
Furniture & Equipment	1,530.00	
Less: F & E Deprec.	(791.00)	
Mail List	3,000.00	
Less: Deprec.	(377.00)	
Organizational Fees	85.00	
TOTAL ASSETS		**$ 22,489.44**

LIABILITIES AND STOCKHOLDERS' EQUITY:

LIABILITIES:

Accounts Payable   3,323.00

STOCKHOLDERS' EQUITY:

Common Stock, Par Value $.01/Share; 5,000,000 Shares Authorized; 100,000 Shares Outstanding	1,000.00	
Capital In Excess of Par Paid In	43,660.36	
Retained Earnings	(25,493.92)	
TOTAL STOCKHOLDERS' EQUITY		19,166.44
TOTAL LIABILITIES AND STOCKHOLDERS' EQUITY		**$ 22,489.44**

Current Book Value Per Share = $.192

Income Statement
Shorewood Press, Inc.
(Audited)
For Period of January 1, 199- to September 1, 199-

Revenues	$ .00
Expenses:	
Cost of Goods Published	$ 3,583.00
Selling	3,061.09
Administrative	14,674.17
Interest	536.81
Income Taxes	(12,880.00)
Total Expenses	$ 8,975.07
Net Loss for Period	$ (8,975.07)
Net Loss Per Share	$ (.09)

Notes:

Tax on Income:
The tax effect of items in the Statement of Income (Loss), are recognized in the current period. The tax loss in 199- is expected to be carried forward to 199- and is therefore reported as Taxes Receivable.

Property:
The Mail List was transferred by William C. Foster to the Company after incorporation in January, 199- in exchange for stock equity. Depreciation and amortization are computed on a straight line basis as follows:

> Furniture & Equipment — 3 years
> Mail List — 3 years
> Organizational Fees — 5 years

Net Income (Loss) Per Share:
Net Income (Loss) Per Share is computed by dividing the net income (loss) by the number of common stock shares outstanding and was rounded off.

Note Payable and Interest Payable:
In July, 199-, Mr. Foster elected to forgive the note payable and interest payable in exchange for stock equity. Interest was charged at an annual rate of 12%.

Stockholders' Equity
(Audited)

Capital contributions are as follows:

199-	William C. Foster	- Furniture & Equipment	$	1,530
		Salaries		9,970
		Rent		3,125
	Jack W. Olson	- Services		400
			$	15,025
199-	William C. Foster	- Mail List	$	3,000
		Rent		1,750
		Note Payable/ Cash Contribution		13,513
		Interest Forgiven		872
			$	29,635
	Total Capital Contributions Through 9-1-9-		$	**44,660**

Balance Sheet
Shorewood Press, Inc.
formerly
General Admissions, Inc.
(Audited)
For Period of December 17, 199- to December 31, 199-

ASSETS:

Cash	$ 98.20	
Office Supplies	70.00	
Furniture & Equipment	1,530.00	
Less: F & E Deprec.	(500.00)	
Organization Fees	85.00	
Less: Amortization	(17.00)	
Taxes Receivable — Tax Loss Carried Forward	2,677.00	
TOTAL ASSETS		**$ 3,943.20**

LIABILITIES AND STOCKHOLDERS' EQUITY:

LIABILITIES:

Accounts Payable	195.00	
Note Payable to Officer	4,906.69	
Interest Payable to Officer	335.36	
TOTAL LIABILITIES		5,437.05

STOCKHOLDERS' EQUITY:

Common Stock, Par Value $.01/Share; 5,000,000 Shares Authorized; 100,000 Shares Outstanding	1,000.00	
Capital Contributed in Excess of Par	14,025.00	
Retained Earnings	(16,518.85)	
TOTAL STOCKHOLDERS' EQUITY		(1,493.85)
TOTAL LIABILITIES AND STOCKHOLDERS' EQUITY		**$ 3,943.20**

Income Statement
Shorewood Press, Inc.
formerly
General Admissions, Inc.
(Audited)
For Period of December 17, 199- to December 31, 199-

Revenues	$ 84.00
Expenses:	
Cost of Goods Published	$ 57.41
Selling	2,074.57
Administration	16,812.51
Interest	335.36
Income Taxes	(2,677.00)
Total Expenses	$ 16,602.85
Net Loss for Period	$(16,518.85)
Net Loss Per Share	$ (.09)

Notes:

Taxes on Income:
The tax effect of the items in the Statement of Income (Loss), are recognized in the current period. The tax loss in 199- was carried forward to 199- and is therefore reported as taxes receivable.

Property:
The office furniture and equipment was transferred to the Company by Mr. Foster in December, 199-. Depreciation and amortization are computed on a straight line basis as follows:

>Furniture & Equipment — 3 years
>Organizational Fees — 5 years

Net Income (Loss) Per Share:
Net Income (Loss) Per Share is computed by dividing the net income (loss) by the number of common stock shares outstanding and was rounded off.

Notes Payable and Interest Payable:
In 199-, Mr. Foster loaned $4,906.69 to General Admissions, Inc. The annual interest rate charged was 12%.

Stockholders' Equity
Shorewood Press, Inc.
formerly
General Admissions, Inc.
(Audited)

Capital contributions were as follows during the first year of operation:

199-	William C. Foster	-Furniture & Equipment	$ 1,530
		Salaries	9,970
		Rent	3,125
	Jack W. Olson	-Services	400
	Total Capital Contribution in 199-		$ 15,025

SHOREWOOD PRESS, INC.

Proforma Statement of Profit or Loss for the Balance of *199- and the two year period immediately following the Offering:

	*199-	199-	199-
SALES:			
Display Advertising	$ 17,714	258,100	499,200
Classified Advertising	1,371	50,400	72,000
NSJ Subscriptions	930	119,700	259,200
Mailing List Sales	221	15,600	15,600
Other Books & Audio Sales	1,080	58,500	72,000
SPI Publications Sold @ Retail	0	222,000	841,500
SPI Publications Sold @ Wholesale	0	151,875	631,125
TOTAL SALES	$ 25,066	966,175	2,534,625
OPERATING EXPENSES:			
Salaries	$ 13,725	166,200	344,400
Payroll Taxes	1,375	16,620	34,440
Med/Hosp/Life Insurance	1,375	16,620	34,440
Business Insurance	300	1,800	3,600
Depreciation & Amortization	1,100	6,000	12,000
Rent & Utilities	1,250	15,000	27,000
Telephone	1,548	7,200	18,000
Outside Services	500	18,000	36,000
Travel	631	3,600	15,000
Office Supplies	715	3,600	8,400
Subscriptions/Memberships	289	600	1,200
Office Postage	766	4,200	10,800
Leased Equipment	916	4,800	9,000
Royalties Paid	0	56,085	220,905
Cost of Goods Sold	2,105	156,990	472,920
Advertising	4,653	104,100	174,000
NSJ Publishing/Distribution	33,401	295,000	384,000
Repairs & Maintenance	225	1,500	3,600
Bad Debts	0	3,000	7,200
Legal & Audit Fees	50	6,000	12,000
Staff Education	0	2,400	4,800
TOTAL OPERATING EXPENSES	$ 64,924	889,315	1,834,505
PROFIT OR (LOSS) BEFORE TAX	$ (39,858)	76,860	700,120

* The first year of the forecast is for ONE MONTH ONLY after the Offering.

Appendix E
Prospectus For A Large Public Offering — American Pipeline Services, Inc.

Highlights of the Prospectus

1. Summary
2. The Company
3. Special Considerations
4. Risk Factors
5. Business of the Company
6. Assets Purchase Agreement
7. Underwriting
8. Underwriter's Warrants

PROSPECTUS

AMERICAN PIPELINE SERVICES, INC.

5,000,000
SHARES OF COMMON STOCK
(No Par Value)

ALL OF THE SHARES OFFERED HEREBY ARE BEING SOLD BY AMERICAN PIPELINE SERVICES, INC. (THE "COMPANY"), WHICH WAS ORGANIZED FOR THE PURPOSE OF OFFERING PROFESSIONAL CONTRACTING SERVICES TO INSPECT, TEST, REHABILITATE AND MAINTAIN INDUSTRIAL AND MUNICIPAL PIPELINES WORLDWIDE AND TO ACQUIRE CERTAIN FIELD PROVEN EQUIPMENT, PARTS INVENTORY AND PATENTS FROM BALLARD INDUSTRIES, INC. TO FACILITATE ITS CORPORATE GROWTH.

THE SECURITIES OFFERED HEREBY ARE HIGHLY SPECULATIVE, INVOLVE A HIGH DEGREE OF RISK AND SHOULD BE PURCHASED ONLY BY PERSONS WHO CAN AFFORD TO LOSE THEIR ENTIRE INVESTMENT.

	Price to Public	Underwriting Commissions (1) (2)	Proceeds to the Company (3) (4)
Per Share	$ 1.00	$ .10	$ .90
Total Maximum	$ 5,000,000	$ 500,000	$ 4,500,000
Total Minimum	$ 4,000,000	$ 400,000	$ 3,600,000

(see notes on following page)

THE SHARES ARE OFFERED ON A BEST EFFORTS "ALL OR NONE" BASIS AS TO THE FIRST 4,000,000 SHARES, AND THE REMAINING 1,000,000 SHARES ON A BEST EFFORTS BASIS, AND THERE IS NO ASSURANCE THAT ALL OF THE SHARES WILL BE SOLD. THE OFFERING PRICE HAS BEEN ARBITRARILY DETERMINED AND BEARS NO RELATIONSHIP TO THE ASSETS, PRESENT BOOK VALUE OR NET WORTH OF THE COMPANY. THERE IS NO MARKET FOR THE SHARES BEING OFFERED, AND THERE CAN BE NO ASSURANCE THAT SUCH A MARKET WILL DEVELOP IN THE FUTURE.

(Underwriter's Name and Address)

The date of this Prospectus is ....

Notes:

(1) Does not include $ _____ payable by the Company to the Underwriter for reimbursement of its expenses on a non-accountable basis; $ _____ of this amount has been paid. (See "Underwriting").

(2) Does not include substantial additional Underwriting compensation to be received by the Underwriter in the form of warrants to purchase a maximum of 500,000 shares of the Company's Common Stock. The Company and the Underwriter have agreed to indemnify each other for certain civil liabilities, including liabilities under the Securities Act of 1933, as amended. The Underwriter also has preferential rights as to future public offerings of the Company.

(3) The shares are being offered by the Underwriter on a "best efforts" basis. The proceeds from the sale of the first 4,000,000 shares will, upon payment by the purchasers thereof, be placed into a non-interest bearing escrow account entitled **"American Pipeline Services, Inc."** with the _____ Bank, _____. Unless $4,000,000 is so placed on deposit in the escrow account within 90 days from the date of this Prospectus (which may be extended for up to 30 days by mutual agreement between the Company and the Underwriter), the offering will be withdrawn and all funds received will be promptly returned to the purchasers by the Escrow Agent without deduction therefrom or interest thereon. If the minimum escrow deposit is attained, the remaining 1,000,000 shares will be offered on a "best efforts" basis until all of the shares are sold or until ninety days from the date of this Prospectus, unless extended, whichever occurs first. There can be no arrangements for the escrow to refund any amounts paid by the purchasers after the minimum escrow deposit of $4,000,000 is reached. (See "Underwriting").

(4) Before deduction of expenses payable by the Company estimated at $100,000 for filing fees, printing, legal, accounting, the Underwriter's non-accountable expense allowance balance of $ _____ and miscellaneous expenses in connection with this offering.

NO PERSON HAS BEEN AUTHORIZED TO GIVE ANY INFORMATION OR TO MAKE ANY REPRESENTATION NOT CONTAINED IN THIS PROSPECTUS IN CONNECTION WITH THE OFFERING MADE HEREBY, AND IF GIVEN OR MADE, SUCH INFORMATION OR REPRESENTATION MUST NOT BE RELIED UPON AS HAVING BEEN AUTHORIZED BY THE COMPANY OR THE UNDERWRITER. THIS PROSPECTUS DOES NOT CONSTITUTE AN OFFER OF ANY SECURITIES OTHER THAN THE REGISTERED SECURITIES TO WHICH IT RELATES OR AN OFFER TO ANY PERSON IN ANY JURISDICTION WHERE SUCH OFFER WOULD BE UNLAWFUL. THE DELIVERY OF THIS PROSPECTUS AT ANY TIME DOES NOT IMPLY THAT THE INFORMATION HEREIN IS CORRECT AS OF ANY TIME SUBSEQUENT TO ITS DATE.

IN CONNECTION WITH THIS OFFERING, THE UNDERWRITER MAY EFFECT TRANSACTIONS WHICH STABILIZE OR MAINTAIN THE MARKET PRICE OF THE COMMON STOCK OF THE COMPANY AT A LEVEL ABOVE THAT WHICH MIGHT OTHERWISE PREVAIL ON THE OPEN MARKET. SUCH STABILIZATION, IF COMMENCED, MAY BE DISCONTINUED AT ANY TIME. IF STABILIZATION IS ENGAGED IN, THE UNDERWRITER MAY BE A DOMINATING INFLUENCE AND, THEREFORE, A FACTOR OF DECREASING IMPORTANCE IN THE MARKET. UNDER SUCH CIRCUMSTANCES, THE MARKET BID OR ASK PRICES OF THE COMMON STOCK MAY NOT BE PRICES AS DETERMINED SOLELY BY SUPPLY AND DEMAND, BUT MAY BE PRICES IN EXCESS THEREOF, AND AT THE EXPIRATION OF ANY STABILIZATION, SUCH MARKET MAY CEASE TO HAVE THE SUPPORT, IF ANY, THERETOFORE FURNISHED BY THE UNDERWRITER SINCE NO MARKET FOR THE COMPANY'S COMMON STOCK PRESENTLY EXISTS.

UNTIL _____ (90 DAYS AFTER THE DATE OF THIS PROSPECTUS), ALL DEALERS EFFECTING TRANSACTIONS IN THE REGISTERED SECURITIES TO WHICH THIS PROSPECTUS RELATES, WHETHER OR NOT PARTICIPATING IN THIS DISTRIBUTION, MAY BE REQUIRED TO DELIVER A CURRENT PROSPECTUS. THIS IS IN ADDITION TO THE OBLIGATION OF DEALERS TO DELIVER A PROSPECTUS WHEN ACTING AS UNDERWRITERS AND WITH RESPECT TO THEIR UNSOLD ALLOTMENTS OR SUBSCRIPTIONS.

THE SHARES ARE OFFERED BY THE UNDERWRITER AS AGENT FOR THE COMPANY, SUBJECT TO PRIOR SALE, TO ALLOTMENT AND WITHDRAWAL, AND TO CANCELLATION OR MODIFICATION OF THE OFFERING WITHOUT NOTICE. THE UNDERWRITER RESERVES THE RIGHT IN ITS DISCRETION TO REJECT ORDERS, IN WHOLE OR IN PART, FOR THE PURCHASE OF ANY OF THE SHARES OFFERED HEREBY.

Table of Contents

Offering Announcement	1
Notes to Offering Announcement	2
Prospectus Summary	5
The Company	7
Special Considerations	9
Risk Factors	10
Dilution	12
Use of Proceeds	15
Business of the Company	16
Equipment Manufactured by the Company	16
Proprietary Capital Equipment to be Purchased by the Company	19
Services of the Company	20
Marketing	21
Competition	22
Employees	22
Property	22
Intangible Assets (Patents)	23
Management and Controlling Shareholders	24
Background of Management	25
Capitalization	26
Remuneration of Officers and Directors	27
Assets Purchase Agreement With BII	28
Description of Common Stock	29
Underwriting	31
Underwriter's Warrants	32
Determination of the Public Offering Price	33
Legal Opinion	34
Experts	34
Litigation	34
Further Information	34
Auditor's Opinion Letter	---
Audited Financial Statements	---
Exhibit A — Patent Abstracts	---
Exhibit B — Photographs of Equipment to be Purchased from BII	---

Prospectus Summary

The following summary information is qualified by the detailed information and financial statements appearing elsewhere in this Prospectus. Prospective investors should read the Prospectus in its entirety.

The Company

American Pipeline Services, Inc. (the "Company"), will purchase certain field proven pipeline television and sealant systems, parts inventory, electronic diagnostic equipment and patents of the Pipeline Rehabilitation Division of Ballard Industries, Inc. ("BII") for the value of such systems, parts inventory and patents on the date of purchase estimated to be $400,000 — but in no event more than $500,000 depending upon the inventory of BII on the purchase date. Such purchase is planned to be simultaneous with the closing of the sale of the shares of Common Stock being offered pursuant to this Prospectus and will be paid in cash.

The Company will then assemble its own proprietary equipment to be used by its field operations crews to televise, inspect, test, rehabilitate and maintain industrial and municipal wastewater pipelines throughout the world on a contract basis. The Company intends to purchase other proprietary cleaning and maintenance equipment and vehicles to enhance its capabilities to conduct business as a "full service" pipeline maintenance enterprise. This additional equipment, to be purchased ad deemed necessary by management, is expected to cost between $400,000 and $500,000 depending upon the types, models and specifications required to fulfill certain future contracting obligations.

The Company plans to "joint venture" selected pipeline inspection, testing, rehabilitation and maintenance contracts with other reputable national and international contracting companies when joint participation is beneficial to both parties or a requirement of specific contracts to be negotiated with municipalities and/or other specific domestic or foreign governments. Consideration will be given to franchising the Company's technical expertise and systems in assigned territories where business development opportunities may be better served by independent, locally based and financed contractors.

The Company further plans to develop certain technical equipment and field engineering expertise to locate freshwater pipeline leaks for local, state and federal governments requiring such services and engineering consultation, and in order to expand the scope of the Company's "full service" concept, it will allocate funds for the research and development of a non-explosive, multi-environmental closed-circuit television inspection system for video examination of gas, coal/ore slurry and agricultural pipelines.

The Offering

Type of Securities	Common Stock, No Par Value
Shares Offered by the Company	5,000,000 Maximum 4,000,000 Minimum
Shares Outstanding Prior to Offering	1,200,000
Number of Shares to be Outstanding	6,200,000 Maximum 5,200,000 Minimum
Net Proceeds to the Company (before Underwriting and Miscellaneous Expenses)	$4,400,000 Maximum $3,500,000 Minimum
Use of Proceeds	Primarily to purchase certain proprietary equipment; to establish field operations crews; research and development; marketing and for operating capital.

Shares and Percentages held by the Founder, Promoters, Directors and Officers:

Before Offering:	1,200,000	100.00%
After Offering:	1,200,000	19.35% Maximum 23.08% Minimum

The Company

American Pipeline Services, Inc. (the "Company") was incorporated in the State of Colorado on _____, 199- for the purpose of contracting pipeline services to industrial clients, municipalities and other government agencies throughout the world by direct invitation, negotiation or by open bid solicitation. These specialized services will include the remote controlled, closed-circuit television inspection, testing, cleaning, rehabilitation and general maintenance of pipelines as may be required.

To facilitate the Company's technical expertise and ability to assure prompt and satisfactory completion of its contracting obligations, it plans to manufacture and assemble the closed-circuit television and sealant systems to be utilized by its field operations crews. Certain field proven pipeline television and sealant system components, parts inventories and patents will be purchased from the Pipeline Rehabilitation Division of Ballard Industries, Inc., Denver, Colorado ("BII") at a estimated cost of $400,000 but in no event to exceed $500,000 depending upon the inventory BII has on hand on the date of purchase. Such purchase is planned to be simultaneous with the closing of the sale of the shares of Common Stock being offered pursuant to this Prospectus and will be paid for in cash. The Company intends to purchase other proprietary cleaning and maintenance equipment and vehicles to enhance its capabilities to conduct business as a "full service" pipeline rehabilitation and maintenance company. This supplementary capital equipment is expected to cost between $400,000 and $500,000 depending upon the types, models and specifications required to fulfill certain contract agreements.

The Company intends to "joint venture" selected pipeline inspection, testing, cleaning, rehabilitation and general maintenance contracts with other reputable domestic and international contracting companies when joint participation is deemed beneficial and in the best interests of both parties or is a requirement of a specific contract to be awarded by certain governments. Consideration will be given to franchising the Company's technical expertise and systems in assigned territories where business development opportunities may be better served by independent, locally based and financed contractors.

The Company plans to develop certain electronic equipment and field engineering expertise to locate freshwater pipeline leaks for local, state, federal and foreign governments requiring such services and engineering consultation. In addition, and to the expand the scope of the Company's services, it will allocate funds for the research and development of a non-explosive, multi-environmental, closed-circuit television inspection system for remote video examination of gas, coal/ore slurry and agricultural pipelines.

The Company has $600,000 in total assets and has not engaged in operations since its incorporation. Selected key employees will be employed to staff the business whom the Company believes have the necessary backgrounds, talents and expertise to conduct the Company's business activities. (See "Background of Management").

The Company plans to commence operations following the closing of the sale of the shares of Common Stock being offered herein and pursuant to the purchase of the system components, parts inventories and patents from BII. A substantial investment will be made in promoting and advertising the Company's pipeline service capabilities worldwide which will be followed up with a vigorous sales effort to develop the business. Initially, and at the direction of management, the Company will establish a limited number of field operation crews or units. These crews will be trained to operate and repair the closed-circuit television inspection, testing, cleaning, rehabilitation and general maintenance systems and equipment as a "unit" to fulfill the Company's contract obligations in distant and often remote areas of the world. Each crew will be managed by a Project Manager, to be recruited from the industry, who will have the necessary skills and expertise to provide the required management and field leadership. Additional field operation crews will be organized and trained as warranted.

To maintain its vehicles, technical, electronic and mechanical equipment systems, the Company will hire experienced personnel to provide the necessary maintenance services that cannot be expected of the field operation crews.

The Company believes that the proceeds of this offering will satisfy its cash requirements for at least three years of operation.

The Company's executive offices are located at 15010 Edgewood Road, Denver, Colorado 80010 and its telephone number is (303) 555-1200.

Special Considerations

The purchase price to be paid for the BII pipeline television and sealant systems, parts inventory and patents on the date of purchase will be at current market value. Work in process on selected systems will be purchased at current market value plus a reasonable profit based upon the percentages of work completed. Since the Company will be purchasing the entire inventory of the Pipeline Rehabilitation Division of BII and intends to employ a majority of the employees of that division, including those individuals who now provide the technical and electronic maintenance services for those systems, the Company has agreed to assume the warranty service responsibility for systems previously sold by BII which are presently in the field and under BII warranty. This warranty obligation expires two years from the date of closing of the sale of the shares of Common Stock being offered herein, and the simultaneous purchase of systems, parts inventories and patents of BII. The Company will therefore assume the warranty time remaining on these previously sold systems of BII but will only provide such services as BII would have under their sales and warranty agreements. The Company assumes no further liability of BII's systems, parts or equipment other than to fulfill BII's warrant obligations.

Risk Factors

The shares offered hereby are highly speculative, involve a high degree of risk and should be purchased only by persons who can afford to lose their entire investment. Prospective investors should carefully consider the high risks associated with this offering. Each offeree of the shares should, prior to purchase, carefully consider the following risk factors, as well as the other information contained herein.

1. **Lack of Profitability.** There can be no assurance that the Company will be able to commercially market its services or operate profitably in the future.

2. **Absence of Operating History.** The Company was only recently incorporated and does not have a history of operating as a viable business.

3. **Purchase of Systems, Parts and Patents from Ballard Industries, Inc.** The purchase price of the system components, parts inventories and patents from BII would not exceed $500,000 in cash. It should be noted that BII is receiving _____ shares of the Common Stock of the Company for a reduced cost, which shares may have a market value of $_____ based on the public offering price per share. The purchase price was negotiated in an attempt to reflect BII's past research and development expenses relating to the systems and patents which are the products of the Pipeline Rehabilitation Division. John T. Fellow, Chairman of the Board of Directors of BII was responsible for negotiations on behalf of BII, and Andrew C. Anderson, President of the Company, was responsible for negotiations on behalf of the Company, and during such time, was simultaneously an employee of BII. Therefore, the negotiations cannot be considered to have been at arm's length.

4. **Business Dependent Upon Key Employees.** The business of the Company is dependent upon the active participation of the Company's proposed executive officers and managers. Loss of one or two of these executives could adversely affect the conduct of the Company's business.

5. **Additional Financing May Be Required.** Although the Company believes that the funds raised in this offering will be sufficient for its growth needs for the next three years, the conduct of the Company's business may require the raising of additional funds during that time frame.

6. **Reduction of Government Funding.** In the pipeline maintenance of wastewater pipelines, the Company would be dependent upon federal and foreign government aid, grants and other funding allocated to wastewater pipeline maintenance programs. Although several states in the United States and certain municipalities in foreign countries are now allocating funds for this work, there can be no guarantee that funding will continue in the future. The restrictions of U. S. federal revenue awards to individual states and communities may have a materially adverse affect on the demand for the Company's services in regard to wastewater pipelines.

7. **Contractor's Liability.** Although the Company will purchase considerable insurance protection against liability claims, it will be required to post contractor performance bonds on contracted work. As a contractor, its exposure to lawsuits will be continually present.

8. **Warranty Obligation For Previously Sold BII Systems.** The Company has agreed to assume the warranty service responsibility for those systems currently in the field and under BII warranty. This warranty assumption is an added expense to the Company's operating costs.

9. **No Dividends.** No dividends will be paid by the Company in the foreseeable future. Any future dividends will depend upon the earnings of the Company, its financial requirements, and other factors. Investors who anticipate the need for immediate income from their investment in the Company's Common Stock should refrain from the purchase of the shares being offered hereby. (See "Description of Common Stock").

10. **Underwriter's Warrants.** The Company will issue warrants to the Underwriter to purchase up to 500,000 shares of the Company's Common Stock. The Company has agreed that it will register, at its expense, not more than once, under the Securities Act of 1933, as amended, at any time within the five year period commencing on the date of this Prospectus, the shares of Common Stock required upon exercise of warrants on written request of a majority of the then holders of the warrants or shares acquired through exercise of the warrants. This right to call for registration could be a substantial expense to the Company and could prove to be a hindrance to future financing. In addition, holders of Common Stock acquired upon exercise of the warrants have the right, at the expense of the Company, at any time, to join with the Company in any registration statement on a Regulation A or larger filing, to the maximum extent permissible. If the warrants are exercised, the percentage of Common Stock held by the public shareholders will be reduced. (See "Underwriting" and "Underwriter's Warrants").

11. **Lack of Contracts.** The Company does not have any contracts as of the date of this Prospectus.

12. **Non-Arm's Length Transactions.** The number of shares issued to the present shareholders for cash, services and patent rights to be assigned to the Company were arbitrarily determined and may not be considered to be arm's length transactions. (See "Transactions with Management").

13. **Competition.** The Company will be in competition with other businesses with greater financial resources and capabilities in the inspection, maintenance and rehabilitation of pipelines. (See "Competition").

Dilution

The Company has, as of _____, 199-, 1,200,000 shares of its Common Stock outstanding with a net tangible book value (total assets less liabilities and intangible assets) of $600,000 or $.50 per share.

Upon incorporation on _____, 199-, the Company issued 1,200,000 shares to the founder, promoters, directors and officers for $600,000 or $.50 per share. Cumulative voting is not allowed in the selection of directors or officers and the holders of the above shares could be in a position to control the Company.

Upon the sale of the minimum number of shares, the purchasers will own 4,000,000 shares or approximately 76.92% of the Company's outstanding stock, for which they will have paid $1.00 per share or a total of $4,000,000. The Company, in this event, will have 5,200,000 shares outstanding with a net tangible book value (after deducting discounts, commissions and other estimated expenses of $540,000 to sell the minimum number of shares) of $4,060,000 or $.7808 per share. The public shareholders will incur an immediate dilution or reduction in the present value of their investment of approximately $.2192 per share in the net tangible book value of the shares held by them, and the present shareholders will benefit by an increase of approximately $.2808 per share in the net tangible book value of the shares held by them.

In the event the maximum number of shares offered hereby are sold, the purchasers will own 5,000,000 shares, or approximately 80.65% of the Company's outstanding stock, for which they will have paid $1.00 per share or a total of $5,000,000. Assuming the maximum number of shares offered are sold, the Company will have 6,200,000 shares outstanding with a net tangible book value (after deducting discounts, commissions and other estimated expenses of $640,000 to sell the maximum number of shares) of $.80 per share. Accordingly, the public shareholders will incur an immediate dilution or reduction in the present value of their investment of $.20 per share in the net tangible book value of the shares held by them, and the present shareholders will benefit by an increase of approximately $.30 per share in the net tangible book value of the shares held by them.

Per Share Dilution

"Net Tangible Book Value" is the amount that results from subtracting the total liabilities and intangible assets of the Company from its total assets. "Dilution" is the difference between the public offering price and the net tangible book value of the shares immediately after the offering expenses have been deducted.

Percentages of Equity

The following charts illustrate the percentage of equity in the Company purchased by the public investors and the percentage of total capital invested by the public investors compared with the percentage of equity purchased by the founder, promoters, directors and officers, and the percentage of total capital invested by them assuming the minimum and/or the maximum number of shares are sold.

Maximum

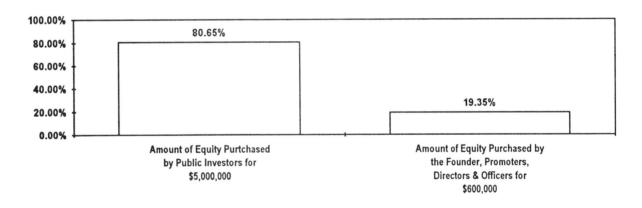

Minimum

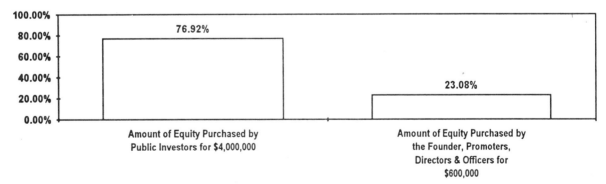

These charts do not give consideration to the warrants for 500,000 shares which will be issued to the Underwriter.

176 *Raising Capital: How To Write A Financing Proposal*

Net Book Values

The following charts illustrate the public offering price paid by public investors, net tangible book value before and after sale and the dilution for new investors and the gain experienced by present shareholders.

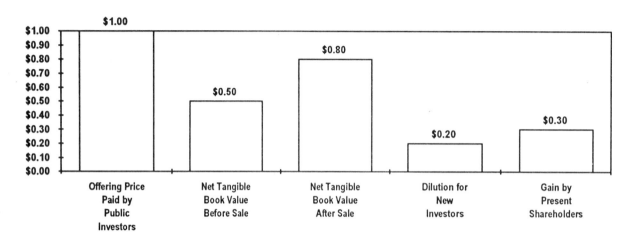

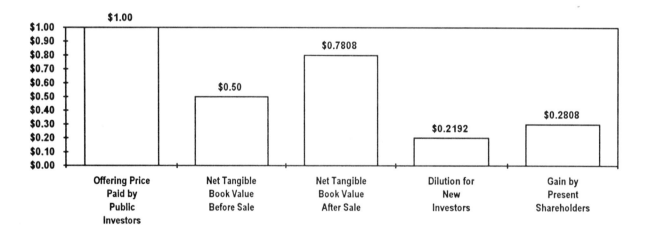

14

Use of Proceeds

The net proceeds to the Company, after deducting underwriting and other expenses connected with this offering will be approximately $4,360,000 assuming all of the 5,000,000 shares offered to the public are sold, which is not assured; and the net proceeds from the sale of 4,000,000 shares, after payment of underwriting and other expenses of this offering will be approximately $3,460,000. The net proceeds will be allocated and applied in the order of their priority as follows:

	Minimum	Maximum
To purchase the television and sealant system components, parts inventories and patents from Ballard Industries, Inc....	$ 400,000	$ 500,000
To purchase other capital proprietary pipeline cleaning and maintenance vehicles and equipment ...	400,000	500,000
To purchase supporting inventory for field operations ...	175,000	175,000
Cost to establish three pipeline field operation crews for selected areas of the United States and foreign countries ...	150,000	150,000
Startup costs to promote, advertise, market and sell the Company's services worldwide ...	275,000	350,000
Research and development of freshwater leak location equipment and Remote Control Video Systems ...	325,000	350,000
Total ...	$ 1,725,000	$ 2,025,000

The balance of the proceeds and other cash assets of the Company will be utilized for general corporate purposes, including working capital and the payment of personnel salaries. The Company will further seek to establish credits lines with banks and other institutions to ensure that sufficient working capital is available. The Company, however, does not have any present intention to borrow funds except as may be necessary for the Company's business development. Accordingly, and because presently unforeseen circumstances may cause some variation in the allocation of the proceeds of this offering, the Company reserves the right to make such variations as the circumstances warrant.

To the extent that the foregoing proceeds and other cash assets of the Company are not immediately used, they will be invested in income producing financial obligations or securities, including certificates of deposit, short-term government securities and/or a money market savings account.

Business of the Company

The Company will be engaged in contracting pipeline services to industrial clients, municipalities and other governmental agencies located throughout the world. These services will include the closed circuit television inspection, testing, cleaning, rehabilitation and general maintenance of pipelines. To insure prompt and satisfactory completion of its contracting obligations, the Company plans to manufacture and assemble its own closed circuit, black and white and color television monitoring systems and chemical sealant systems to be utilized by its field operation crews.

The Company plans to "joint venture" certain pipeline maintenance contracts with other reputable domestic and international contracting companies when joint participation is beneficial and in the best interests of both parties or a requirement of certain municipalities or governments. The Company will also consider franchising its technical expertise and systems in assigned territories where business development opportunities may be better served by independent, locally based and financed contractors.

The Company intends to develop reliable technical equipment and field engineering expertise to locate freshwater pipeline leaks for local, state and federal governmental agencies requiring such services and engineering consultation. To expand the "full service" concept, the Company will allocate funds for the research and development of a non-explosive, multi-environmental, remote controlled, closed circuit television inspection system for the video examination of gas, coal/ore slurry and agricultural pipelines used to transport grain.

Equipment Manufactured by the Company

Systems For Contracting Assignments

For locating leaks in existing wastewater lines and repairing same, the Company will manufacture and assemble (i) the "Remote Controlled Video Inspection System"; (ii) the "Remote Controlled Pipeline Sealing System"; and (iii) the "Remote Controlled Video Inspection and Pipeline Sealing System." These systems have been previously manufactured and marketed under the name "Ballard Industries, Inc.", however, the Company intends to purchase BII's complete inventory and systems to produce its own equipment. Please see the illustrations of these systems on pages ___ and ___.

Remote Controlled Video Inspection System ("REVIS")

The Remote Controlled Video Inspection System, to be manufactured by the Company, consists of specially designed closed circuit television cameras, monitors, coaxial cabling, a power retrieve system, video information input device, video tape recording system and auxiliary components. This system, called the REVIS, is a fully self-contained device used to inspect the interior of underground wastewater pipelines and it can be truck or trailer mounted.

The TV cameras, mounted on a skid, are drawn through pipelines six inches in diameter or larger, transmitting a high resolution TV picture back to the operations console located in the vehicle or trailer above ground. This procedure allows for complete visual inspection and logging of the exact conditions within a pipeline and produces a video tape recording to document the inspection for later use. Color or black and white systems will be built depending upon a project's specific needs and system components will be added as required. The REVIS will range in cost from $20,000 to $50,000 depending upon the components included and whether or not the system is to be mounted in a utility trailer or a step van.

Remote Controlled Pipeline Sealing System ("REPAIRS")

The Remote Controlled Pipeline Sealing System or REPAIRS, to be manufactured by the Company, incorporates an engineered system of pumps, controls, feeder lines and supporting components to allow a specially designed machine to be drawn through a pipeline six inches in diameter or larger. When defects are discovered in an existing line (either through the use of the REVIS or other independent means), the REPAIRS is stopped in the area showing a suspected leak, break or defect and a pressure test is performed. If the test results show the need for rehabilitation of the line (in most cases the defect is a leaking joint or broken gasket), the defect is sealed by using a non-toxic sealant material. The REPAIRS is stopped in the area of the defect (guided by its own miniature TV camera and monitor) and by remote control, can be activated to inject sealant into the defect through a mechanical injecting device. After five minutes, the sealant forms a tight, open cell gasket in the area of the defect or leak and seals it effectively. The entire process, taking only a few minutes, is controlled from a console located above the ground in a van or trailer mounted unit. The REPAIRS will range in cost of $18,000 to $30,000 depending upon the components included in the system and whether it is to be mounted in a utility trailer or step van.

Combination Systems ("REVIS/REPAIRS — 1")

In addition to the independent operations of the REVIS and REPAIRS, both systems can be operated in tandem to provide for the ongoing visual inspection of the process, and employ the sealing system (when needed) for the rehabilitation of the pipeline. This system is called the Remote Controlled Video Inspection and Pipeline Sealing System or "REVIS/REPAIRS — 1." These two systems, when combined, have the ability to visually inspect a leaking pipeline, test the suspected defects, and at the same time, seal the problem area. A combination of these two systems will be built in a self-contained, self-powered step van which is heated and air conditioned for year around work which contains a control studio and equipment room area. This combination of systems — REVIS/REPAIRS —1, will cost up to $80,000 per unit depending upon the components selected.

Portability of Systems

The Company will be able to build the aforementioned systems in several vehicular configurations, to be mounted in various size trailers, trucks and vans as a package. Such configurations include a closed circuit television inspection trailer, or a sealing system trailer, or a combination unit in either a trailer, step or utility type van. This equipment could also be installed in container units suitable for shipping internationally and mounted on a vehicle frame once it arrived at its destination.

Advantages of Company Built Systems

Although the Company is not planning to manufacture its equipment and technical systems for resale, it does believe that there are distinct advantages in manufacturing its own systems. Among the reasons for this are: (1) The Company can produce the systems at cost and as a direct result, place itself in a highly competitive position when bidding contracts for municipalities and other agencies.

(2) When bidding a municipal or government contract, the Company can offer an alternative bid that would include giving a certain system or systems to the community once the Company's contract was completed — thus affording them the system(s) needed for a continuing inspection and/or maintenance program. A profit could be earned by the Company through such an agreement and eliminate the expense of transporting the equipment and/or systems to other contracting sites or the cost of storage pending new contract assignments. (3) The Company would be able to maintain the quality and reliability of its systems destined for projects in remote areas of the world. (4) As a pipeline contractor, the Company would have the flexibility to adapt its equipment and systems, on short notice, to certain contract specifications and in the process, be able to build new generations of equipment that would more efficiently meet the Company's needs in the future.

Proprietary Capital Equipment to be Purchased by the Company

Pneumatic Plugs

Pneumatic plugs are devices inserted into wastewater lines to block or isolate parts of a line enabling it to be tested for the location of leaks or breaks. The plugs are inserted at various intervals in the wastewater line to be tested and are inflated by a hand pump or a compressor to form a seal against the sides of the pipeline at both ends of the test area. Once testing is completed, and the repair is made, the plugs are deflated for removal and can be reused. The Company intends to purchase various types and sizes of these plugs manufactured by several companies worldwide.

Air-Seal System

The Company will from time to time require the Air-Seal System to fulfill certain contracting obligations. This system, manufactured by Ballard Industries, Inc., is trailer mounted and consists of two air-seal balls (two specifically designed pneumatic plugs), an air compressor, hoses, cable, control panel, cable reel and a unwind cable with a metering device. The unit is available in kit form or as a complete trailer mounted system. The Company does have alternative sources for this product.

Chemical Sealants

The Company will use non-toxic, environmentally safe sealants manufactured by the Phelps Manufacturing Company. Should the Company not be able to obtain these sealant products in the future, it would be required to refurbish its equipment and systems to accommodate other suitable chemical sealants available in the marketplace.

High Velocity Jet Cleaner

A high pressure hydraulic cleaning system used to clean pipe sizes from 6 to 15 inches in diameter will be purchased by the Company to clean pipelines with light to medium deposit buildups. A necessary piece of equipment for each field operations crew, the Jet Cleaner cost ranges from $35,000 to $39,000 per unit depending upon the components included.

High Velocity Cleaner Vacuum

Commonly known as a "Sucker", or by the trade name "Vactor", this machine combines high velocity sewer cleaning with the ability to evacuate the accumulated debris to a self contained dump depository in a truck by means of a suction tube. This eliminates the time consuming work of shoveling and lifting debris from a manhole entry to the line being cleaned. This unit is preferable to the High Velocity Jet Cleaner because it can be used for other remedial municipal and industrial applications not necessarily confined to sanitary sewer maintenance. Two well known manufacturers' of this equipment in the United States are Super Products (Camel) Company and Vactor Corporation. The approximate unit cost ranges from $90,000 to $120,000 depending on truck chassis, storage capacity and auxiliary equipment selected.

Services of the Company

The initial operations of the Company will be focused on securing contracts for specialty services needed by communities for their sanitary and storm sewer lines. These services will include testing, television inspection and internal pipeline rehabilitation of new and active wastewater lines, restoration of manhole structures, maintenance of wastewater lines, flow monitoring and interpretation, and to provide field support to selected consulting engineering firms engaged in waste-water system studies.

Although it is probable that most, if not all, initial contracts awarded to the Company will be obtained through the competitive bidding process, it will be the goal of the Company to secure a sizable proportion of its contract work on a negotiated basis. This is expected to occur after the Company has established a history of performance and a reputation for delivering the desired results.

During the first months of operation, the Company will recruit, staff, equip, train and position three Field Operation Crews or Units in assigned territories. The actual geographical locations have not been finalized, however the Company is considering the following areas in the domestic market: (1) the Northeast (New England or Upstate New York); (2) the Mid-Atlantic (Virginia, North Carolina or South Carolina); (3) the Southeast (Alabama or Tennessee); (4) the Central area (Beaumont or Houston, Texas), and (5) West (California or the state of Washington). Territories under consideration for unit placement in the international market are: (1) Europe (Denmark, Germany or France); (2) Far East (Japan); (3) Mid-East (Egypt) and (4) North Atlantic (England).

Expansion in the western hemisphere countries will be a priority of the Company. The Canadian market is presently in a mode closely resembling the United States market of 1970 to 1980. It is anticipated, based upon recently instituted guidelines enacted by the Canadian government, that their wastewater and freshwater programs will closely parallel the Clean Water Enforcement Program of the United States, enacted into law in the 1970s. With relatively few experts capable of providing extensive pipeline testing, inspection and repair in Canada, the Company will offer its services as the opportunities present themselves.

Other ongoing projects that could include joint venture participation for the Company are presently in various stages of development in such countries as Mexico, Panama, Brazil and several other South American countries. Mexico is showing the strongest possibilities since it is now planning to update its entire wastewater system throughout the country.

In recognition of the impending freshwater crisis facing the United States and several other nations, the Company plans to investigate certain electronic leak location equipment that can be utilized above ground to detect subsurface leaks in pressurized water transmission lines. Recently, large financial appropriations in Massachusetts, Pennsylvania, California and other states have been or will be funded for these projects, and the Company foresees an excellent potential for its specialized services in this market during the years ahead.

This same freshwater leak locating equipment could offer an entry into the petrochemical pipeline market by utilizing the electronic listening system for electronic "pig" location (cleaning and monitoring devices) in gas and oil pipelines. Furthermore, the development of a non-explosive, multi-environmental, closed circuit television inspection system would provide the Company with the necessary capability to internally inspect pressurized gas lines as well as coal/ore slurry and agricultural transmissions pipelines.

Marketing

The Company will market its pipeline service capabilities to industrial clients, municipalities and governmental agencies throughout the world and will actively seek contracted work by direct invitation, negotiation and by open bid solicitation. In conjunction with its "joint venture" plans, the Company will actively seek out other reputable domestic and international contracting companies where joint contract participation would be deemed beneficial and in the best interests of both parties. A substantial investment will be made in trade publication advertising, direct mail and personal calls on potential clients to promote and sell the Company's services, and to build the image of a business able and willing to provide service as a international pipeline contractor.

Competition

There are several small firms involved in wastewater pipeline rehabilitation work throughout the United States; however, the consulting engineering community is demanding a higher level of technical expertise and support today when the inspection, sealing and cleaning of underground pipelines is concerned. There are perhaps three major companies presently operating on levels at least partially responsive to the engineering community's needs. One of these competitors offers a variety of contracting disciplines including evacuation of pipelines and underground utility contracting on a limited basis, as well as with limited engineering expertise. Employing approximately 200 persons, this company's sphere of operations is primarily in the Texas, Louisiana and Mississippi areas. They enjoy a good reputation and have grown to a current sales level of $12,000,000 annually.

Although the Company will compete directly with other pipeline rehabilitation firms in all areas of the domestic and international market, it does anticipate joint ventures with certain competitors by offering its field support services of inspection, testing and rehabilitation of pipelines when its competition does not have the expertise or the equipment to complete the work, or when joint participation is a requirement of a specific contract assignment.

Employees

After the closing of the successful sale of shares being offered pursuant to this Prospectus, the Company will immediately employ 26 persons. This employee complement will include 4 executives and managers, 7 individuals to staff three field operations crews, 3 sales persons and 12 administrative and technical persons. The Company is not a party to any union or collective bargaining agreement affecting its employees and believes its relationship with them will be satisfactory.

Property

The Company's executive offices are presently located at 15010 Edgewood Road, Denver, Colorado 80010 and occupy a total of 2,700 square feet. Rental of this space is on a month to month basis at a cost of $1,600 per month from the Crandel Realty Company. In addition, and after the satisfactory completion of this offering, the Company will lease approximately 10,000 square feet of warehouse space, on a month to month basis, located at 15020 Edgewood Road, Denver, Colorado 80010 at a cost of approximately $3,600 per month. Utility costs are included in the rental charges of both the executive offices and warehouse space. The Company's leased properties described above are of modern concrete block and steel construction, are well maintained and are of ample size for its present needs.

Intangible Assets

BII will assign to the Company its patents No. 4,672,381 — expiration date December 11, 2010 (Remote Controlled Pipeline Sealing System) and No. 5,873,210 — expiration date September 17, 2014 (Remote Controlled Television Inspection and Monitoring Apparatus), at no cost or royalty to the Company. Patent abstract descriptions have been included in this Prospectus as Exhibit A and Exhibit B.

The Company will follow a policy of filing patent applications for any new products or improvements it develops in the future. The Company believes that while patent protection is important, it will not be the deciding factor in determining whether or not it will develop a new product or service technique.

186 Raising Capital: How To Write A Financing Proposal

Management and Controlling Shareholders

The names and resident addresses of the directors, officers, promoters and shareholders owning more that 1% of the Common Stock Shares of the Company as of the date of this Prospectus are listed as follows:

Name, Resident Address & Office Held	Shares owned of Record & Beneficially	% of Shares owned prior to Offering	% of Shares owned after Offering	% of time devoted to the Company
Andrew C. Anderson (1) 2700 Hill Road, Arvada, CO 80004 Founder, Promoter, Chairman & CEO	900,000	75.00%	17.31% MIN 15.52% MAX	100%
John T. Fellows 710 Boland Avenue, Denver, CO 80016 Promoter & Director	100,000	8.33%	1.92% MIN 1.61% MAX	1%
James P. Owens 4212 Smith Street, Denver, CO 80012 Promoter, Director & CFO	100,000	8.33%	1.92% MIN 1.61% MAX	100%
Randall O. Thomas 10 W. 7th Avenue Arvada, CO 80004 Promoter, Director & V. Pres.	50,000	4.17%	0.96% MIN 0.81% MAX	100%
Burton P. Dalton 212 Fulton Road Denver, CO 80017 Promoter & Director	25,000	2.08%	0.48% MIN 0.40% MAX	1%
Carl W. Solinik 10140 Noll Drive, Denver, CO 80013 International Sales Manager	25,000	2.08%	0.48% MIN 0.40% MAX	100%

(1) Andrew C. Anderson is the founder of the Company within the meaning of the Securities Act of 1933, as amended, and may be deemed a controlling entity and founding shareholder.

Background of Management

Andrew C. Anderson, age 54, is the founder, chairman of the board, chief executive officer and promoter of the Company. He is presently the executive vice president of Ballard Industries, Inc., and has been associated with that Company for the past 15 years. Prior to joining BII, he was the vice president of marketing for Rotech Corporation, Los Angeles, California from 197- to 198-. Mr. Anderson is a 196- graduate of the University of Southern California and holds a BS degree in Electrical Engineering. He currently serves on the Board of Directors for the Wyman Company, Inc. and the Spring Water Corporation, located in Denver. Mr. Anderson will serve the Company on a full-time basis after the offering has been successfully completed.

James P. Owens, age 48, is a director, chief financial officer and promoter of the Company. Mr. Owens is currently serving as the chief financial officer for the Zeller Company, Inc. in Denver and has been with that firm for over 24 years. He will join the Company on a full-time basis upon the successful completion of this offering. Mr. Owens holds a BS degree in Accounting from the University of Arizona and has been a CPA for the past 10 years. He is a member of the American Institute of CPAs and the Colorado Society of CPAs.

Randall O. Thomas, age 47, is a director, vice president and promoter of the Company. Mr. Randall is currently the general manager of the Pipeline Rehabilitation Division of Ballard Industries, Inc. and has been in their employ for the past 20 years. He will join the Company on a full-time basis upon the successful completion of the offering. Mr. Thomas holds a BS degree in Mechanical Engineering from the University of Oregon, has published several papers on wastewater management, and is considered to be a expert in the industry.

John T. Fellows, age 68, is a director and promoter of the Company. Mr. Fellows is the founder, chairman and chief executive officer of Ballard Industries, Inc. and has directed that company's business activities for the past 30 years.

Burton P. Dalton, age 64, is a director and promoter of the Company. Mr. Dalton is the founder and president of the Dalton Machine Tool Company, Inc. in Denver and has directed that company's business for the past 40 years.

Carl W. Solinik, age 45, is the proposed sales manager of international sales for the Company. Mr. Solinik has 20 years experience in international marketing and sales in the wastewater/freshwater industry. He was born and raised in West Germany, is fluent in four languages and has a working knowledge of three others. He is a graduate of the University of Berlin, Electrical Engineering School and served ten years as the international sales representative (based in West Germany) for the Logan Manufacturing Company located in Seattle, Washington. He was then transferred to the

United States in 197- and became a U. S. citizen in 198-. He joined Ballard Industries, Inc. in 198- as their manager of international sales and will become the international sales manager for the Company upon the successful completion of this offering.

Management will, from time to time, seek to use the securities of the Company as incentives or bonuses for its executives and key employees and plans to invite up to four more individuals to serve on its board of directors.

Capitalization

The Capitalization of the Company on _____, 199- and as adjusted to reflect the sale of shares offered hereby, is set forth in the following table.

Title and Class	Amount Authorized	Amount Outstanding Before Offering	Amount to be Outstanding After Offering	
Stockholders' Equity; Common Stock, No Par Value (1)	10,000,000	1,200,000	6,200,000	MAXIMUM
			5,200,000	MINIMUM
Underwriter's Stock Purchase Warrants (2)	500,000	-0-	500,000	MAX (2)

(1) Does not include up to 500,000 shares for issuance upon exercise of the Underwriter's warrants to purchase stock.

(2) See "Underwriting" and "Underwriter's Warrants."

Transactions with Management

As the founder, chairman, chief executive officer and promoter, Mr. Andrew C. Anderson received 900,000 shares of the Company's Common Stock for which he paid $450,000 in cash; Mr. John T. Fellows received 100,000 shares for which he paid $50,000; Mr. James P. Owens received 100,000 shares for which he paid $50,000; Mr. Randall O. Thomas received 50,000 shares for which he paid $25,000; Mr. Burton P. Dalton received 25,000 shares for which he paid $12,500 and Mr. Carl W. Solinik received 25,000 shares for which he paid $12,500. All purchases of the stock were made by the officers and directors on _____, 199-.

Remuneration of Officers and Directors

The following table sets forth the remuneration to be paid the first year of operation to the executive officers and directors of the Company who will receive annual remuneration in excess of $50,000 and all directors and officers as a group during this period.

Name of Individual and Number of Persons in Group	Salaries, Fees, Directors Fees, Commission and Bonuses (1) (2)	Insurance Benefits and Personal Benefits
Andrew C. Anderson	$ 75,000	$ 4,800
James P. Owens	66,000	4,800
Randall O. Thomas	66,000	4,800
Carl W. Solinik	66,000	4,800
Directors & Officers as a Group of 4 Persons	$ 273,000	$ 19,200

(1) Bonuses may be paid to various officers based on the profits of the Company. No bonus plan has been adopted.

(2) The directors will receive fees of $125 per meeting and will be reimbursed for expenses while attending meetings of the Board of Directors.

ASSETS PURCHASE AGREEMENT WITH BII

The Company plans to enter into a Purchase Agreement with Ballard Industries, Inc. ("BII") whereby BII agrees to sell to the Company all remote controlled, closed circuit television and sealant system components, parts inventory, tools and patents of the Pipeline Rehabilitation Division of BII as follows:

a. All of the inventory of finished goods and work-in-process of the Pipeline Rehabilitation Division and the inventory of systems components relating to the Remote Controlled Video Inspection System and the Remote Controlled Pipeline Sealing System and the combination of the two aforementioned systems.

b. All equipment and tools utilized by BII for the manufacturing of the above systems.

c. The BII Patents No. 4,672,381 — Remote Controlled Pipeline Sealing System and No. 5,873,210 — Remote Television Inspection and Monitoring Apparatus will be assigned to the Company at no additional cost or future royalty expense.

d. BII agrees that it will not engage in the future manufacture or sale of equipment to be sold to the Company as described in the Purchase Agreement.

The purchase price for such assets is estimated to be $400,000, but in no event more than $500,000 subject to adjustment for final inventory figures at the closing of the Purchase Agreement. Payment will be made in cash, and will be transacted simultaneously with the closing of the sale of the Common Stock shares being offered pursuant to this Prospectus.

Description of Common Stock

General

The Company's authorized capital stock consists of 10,000,000 shares of its no par value Common Stock and warrants to purchase 500,000 such shares. See "Underwriter's Warrants."

Dividends

Holders of the Company's Common Stock are entitled to receive dividends when and as declared by the Company's Board of Directors out of funds legally available therefor. Any such dividends may be paid in cash, property or shares of the Company's Common Stock. The Company presently anticipates that all earnings, if any, will be retained for development of the business and that no dividends on its Common Stock will be declared in the foreseeable future. Any future dividends will be subject to the discretion of the Company's Board of Directors, and would depend upon, among other things, future earnings, the operating and financial condition of the Company, its capital requirements and general business conditions. Therefore, there can be no assurance that any dividends on the Company's Common Stock will be paid in the future.

Voting Rights

All shares of the Company's Common Stock have equal voting rights and, when validly issued and outstanding, have one vote per share on all matters to be voted on by the stockholders. Cumulative voting on the election of Directors and Officers is not allowed.

Miscellaneous Rights and Provisions

Shares of the Company's Common Stock have no preemptive or conversion rights, no redemption or sinking fund provisions, and are not liable to further call or assessment. The outstanding shares of the Company's Common Stock are, and any shares sold pursuant to this Offering will be, fully paid and non-assessable. Each share of the Company's Common Stock is entitled to share ratably in any assets available for distribution to holders of its equity securities upon liquidation of the Company.

Incentive Stock Option Plan

On _____, 199-, the shareholders of the Company approved an Incentive Stock Option Plan as defined under Section 83 of the Internal Revenue Code.

Under the Plan, options may be granted to key employees, officers and directors for a maximum of 500,000 shares subject to adjustment in case of stock splits, stock dividends and the market price of shares on the date the option is granted. Options may be granted for terms up to five years and the option price must not be less than the fair market value of the stock at the time the option is granted. The option may only be exercised after one year from the date of grant. Additionally, the Plan requires that the aggregate fair market value of eligible stock, determined at the time of grant of the option for which the employee, officer or director may be granted options, may not exceed $100,000 per calendar year, and the total amount of options granted to any individual for all years cannot exceed $300,000. No options have been granted and there are no options currently outstanding; however, the Underwriter may purchase warrants to purchase shares of the Company's Common Stock in connection with this Offering. See "Underwriter's Warrants."

Escrow of Shares

All of the Common Stock Shares of the Company issued and outstanding prior to the offering made hereby will be held in escrow by the _____ Bank of Denver, Colorado for 13 months from the date of this Prospectus and will be released only upon written advice after 13 months from the date of this Prospectus Circular. The Company and the shareholders represent that none of the interests of the shares have been transferred or otherwise disposed of.

Report to Shareholders

The Company intends to furnish annual reports to its shareholders containing financial statements reported upon by independent certified public accountants, and may also issue unaudited quarterly or other interim reports to its shareholders as it deems appropriate.

Transfer Agent

_____, Denver, Colorado is the transfer agent for the Company's no par value Common Stock.

Underwriting

Summary of Underwriting

The Company has entered into an Underwriting Agreement with _____ _____.

Under the Agreement, the Company has employed the Underwriter as its exclusive agent to sell up to 5,000,000 shares of the Company's no par value Common Stock at a price to the public of $1.00 per share. The first 4,000,000 shares will be offered by the Underwriter on a "best efforts, all-or-none basis." Therefore, if 4,000,000 shares are not sold within 90 days from the date of this Prospectus, unless extended for an additional period of 30 days by mutual agreement between the Company and the Underwriter, all monies received will be refunded without any deduction for commissions or expenses and without any interest thereon. All proceeds from the sale of the first 4,000,000 shares will be promptly transmitted to an escrow account at the _____ Bank ("Escrow Agent"), at _____.
After 4,000,000 shares have been sold, the offering will continue on a "best efforts" basis, but without any escrow or refund provision, until all 5,000,000 shares offered are sold, or until 90 days after the date of this Prospectus (unless extended per above), whichever event first occurs.

Subject to the same of the minimum of 4,000,000 shares prior to the termination of this offering, the Company has agreed to pay the Underwriter a sales commission of 10% ($.10 per share). The Company has also agreed to pay the Underwriter a non-accountable expense allowance of $_____ of which $_____ has been paid as of the date of this Prospectus. If at least the minimum of 4,000,000 shares are sold, the $_____ balance of the non-accountable expense allowance will be paid. The Underwriter's non-accountable expense in excess of $_____ will be borne by the Underwriter. The $_____ non-accountable expense allowance may be deemed to be additional underwriting compensation to the Underwriter. If the minimum of 4,000,000 shares are not sold before termination of this offering, the Underwriter will only be reimbursed for its accountable expenses up to a maximum of $_____. If the Underwriter's accountable expenses are less than $_____, the balance must be returned to the Company.

The Underwriter has the right to purchase from the Company stock purchase warrants to acquire up to 500,000 shares of the Company's Common Stock. Such warrants and shares may be considered additional compensation to the Underwriter. See "Underwriter's Warrants."

The Company has agreed that, if it makes any future public offering of its securities within five years from the date hereof, the Underwriter will have the right of first refusal to underwrite such offering.

The Underwriter intends to offer a portion of the shares offered hereby through selected licensed securities dealers who are members of the National Association of Securities Dealers, Inc. and may allow such dealers a portion of the 10% commission as the Underwriter may determine. The Underwriter intends to enter into written Selected Dealer Agreements with other securities dealers regarding this public offering.

The Company has agreed to indemnify the Underwriter against any costs or liabilities incurred by the Underwriter by reason of misstatements or omissions to state material facts in connection with the statements made in the Registration Statement and Prospectus. The Underwriter has in turn agreed to indemnify the Company against any liabilities by reason of misstatements or omissions to state material facts in connection with the statements made in the Registration Statement and Prospectus based on information relating to and furnished by the Underwriter.

The foregoing does not purport to be a complete statement of the terms and conditions of the Underwriting Agreement which are on file at the offices of the Underwriter, the Company and the Securities and Exchange Commission, Washington, DC and the Colorado Office of the Commission, _____, Denver, CO 80012.

Underwriter's Warrants

Subject to the sale of the minimum of 4,000,000 shares prior to the termination of this offering, the Company has agreed to sell to the Underwriter, for a total of $_____, warrants to purchase one share of the Company's Common Stock for each 10 shares sold in the offering. If the entire offering of 5,000,000 shares is sold, the Underwriter will be entitled to purchase for $_____ warrants to purchase 500,000 shares of the Company's Common Stock. The warrants are not salable, exercisable, transferable or assignable for a period of thirteen months following the date of this Prospectus, except to and among the officers, directors, shareholders or employees of the Underwriter. The warrants will be exercisable, assignable and transferable commencing thirteen months after the date of this Prospectus and ending upon the expiration of the warrants four years thereafter. The transfer or assignment of the warrants by the Underwriter to its officers and directors, must be made in accordance with the provisions of the Securities Act of 1933, as amended.

If the holders of at least a majority of the warrants and/or the underlying shares wish to make a public offering of such warrants or shares during the period commencing thirteen months after the date of this Prospectus and ending four years after such date, the Company has agreed to register or qualify such shares, one time only, upon the request of the holder(s) of at least a majority of such warrants and/or underlying shares. If at any time during the period commencing thirteen months after the date of this Prospectus and ending four years after such date, the Company registers any of its securities, the holders of the warrants and/or underlying shares shall have the right to register all or any part of such warrants and/or shares in conjunction with the Company's registration. In either event, the Company will bear the full expense of such registration or qualification, which will be of substantial cost to the Company.

Holders of the warrants are protected against dilution of the equity interest represented by the underlying shares of Common Stock upon the occurrence of certain events including, but not limited to, stock dividends. If the Company merges or reorganizes in such a way as to terminate the warrants, the warrants may be exercised immediately prior to such action. In the event of liquidation, dissolution or winding up of the Company, warrant holders are not entitled to participate in the Company's assets or the distribution thereof.

It may be expected that the warrants will be exercised only if it is advantageous to the holders of the warrants. It may also be expected that if the warrants are exercised, the value of the Company's Common Stock held by the public investors will be diluted if the value of such stock immediately prior to the exercise of the warrants exceeds the exercise price, with the extent of such dilution depending upon such excess. Therefore, for the life of the warrants, the holders thereof are given, at a nominal cost, the opportunity to profit from a rise in the market price of the Company's Common Stock. The terms upon which the Company could obtain additional capital during such period may be adversely affected. The holders of such warrants might be expected to exercise them at a time when the Company would, in all likelihood, be able to obtain additional needed capital on terms more favorable than those provided by the warrants. Any gain realized by the Underwriter on any resale of the warrants and/or underlying shares may be deemed as additional underwriting compensation.

Determination of the Public Offering Price

The initial offering price of the shares offered hereby has been established by negotiation between the Company and the Underwriter. The primary factors involved in determining the offering price were the amount of funds necessary for the Company to undertake the activities referred to herein and the percentage of the total equity of the Company that management believes should be publicly offered pursuant to this offering. The value that the public offering price purports to place on the Company's securities may bear no relationship to the assets or other criteria of value applicable to the Company. See "Dilution."

Legal Opinion

Legal matters in connection with the Company's securities will be passed upon for the Company by _____, _____, counsel to the Company and legal matters in connection with this offering will be passed upon by _____, _____, counsel to the Underwriter.

Experts

The financial statements included in this Prospectus have been examined by _____, independent certified public accountants, to the extent set forth in their report included in this Prospectus and have been so included in reliance upon the authority of that firm as experts in accounting and auditing.

Litigation

No legal proceedings to which the Company is a party or to which any of its property is the subject is pending, known or contemplated, and the Company knows of no legal proceedings pending or threatened, or judgements entered against any director or officer in his or her capacity as such.

Further Information

The Company has filed with the Securities and Exchange Commission, A Registration Statement (and such terms shall encompass any amendments thereto) under the Securities Act of 1933, as amended, with respect to the securities offered hereby. This Prospectus does not contain all of the information set forth in the Registration Statement. For further information with respect to the Company and such securities, reference is made to the Registration Statement and to exhibits filed therewith.

Each statement made in this Prospectus referring to a document filed as an exhibit to the Registration Statement and such exhibits can be inspected at the office of the Commission 150 "L" Street, NW, Washington, DC. Copies of such material can be obtained at prescribed rates by writing to the Commission's Public Reference Section, Securities and Exchange Commission, 575 N. Capital Street, NW, Washington, DC 20550. Copies are also on file with the Regional Office of the Commission.

Notice to Reader

This concludes the example of a rough draft prospectus for a large public offering. To complete it, the following items would have to be included:

1. The Auditor's Opinion Letter.

2. An audited Balance Sheet.

3. An audited Statement of Operations.

4. A Statement of Stockholders' Equity — (prepared by the auditor).

5. The auditor's notes to the financial statements.

6. The patent abstracts.

7. Pictures of the equipment the Company plans to purchase from Ballard Industries, Inc.

Appendix F
Bank Or Private Loan Proposal — The Birchwood Logging Company, Inc.

Highlights of the Proposal

1. Business of the Company

2. Products and Pricing

3. Markets

4. Management

5. Proforma Financials

6. Support Letters

FINANCING PROPOSAL
FOR
THE BIRCHWOOD LOGGING COMPANY, INC.

Submitted By:

Robert M. & Mary T. Jones
RR#1, Box 750
Virginia, Minnesota 55201
Telephone: (218) 455-3133

Table of Contents

Purpose of Loan Request	3
The Company	4
Business of the Company	6
Marketing	7
Competition	7
Birch As A Firewood	7
Management	8
Property	8
Exhibit A — Personal Financial Statement — Robert M. and Mary T. Jones	9
Exhibit B — Proforma P & L — First Year of Operation	10
Proforma P & L — Second Year of Operation	11
Proforma P & L — Third Year of Operation	12
Exhibit C — Proforma Cash Flow Statement — First Year of Operation	13
Proforma Cash Flow Statement — Second Year of Operation	14
Proforma Cash Flow Statement — Third Year of Operation	·15
Exhibit D — Proforma Balance Sheets for First, Second & Third Year	16
Exhibit E — Letters of Commitment to Purchase Firewood	17
Exhibit F — Letter from the USDA — Forest Service	18
Exhibit G — Letter from Terrance Brothers Logging Company	19
Personal Tax Returns of Robert M. and Mary T. Jones	
The Jones Resort Tax Returns	

Purpose of Loan Request

The Birchwood Logging Company, Inc. (the "Company") is seeking a loan of $150,000 in order to contract for the logging of 5,000 cords of birch timber that will be felled, split and stacked into salable firewood and subsequently sold to retail firewood operations located in Minnesota, North Dakota, South Dakota, Iowa and Nebraska.

The sum of $150,000 — in addition to an initial investment of $90,000 by Robert and Mary Jones plus additional personal loans from Mr. and Mrs. Jones totaling $135,000 is expected to be sufficient to finance the business of the Company to the point where it will be able to operate as a profitable enterprise.

At this time, the Company is a non-operating entity with the exception that Mr. Jones has secured (1) A letter of permission from the U. S. Department of Agriculture - Forest Service to annually log up to 220,000 cords of birch trees located in northern Minnesota; (2) A letter of intent from Terrance Brothers Logging Company, Virginia, Minnesota to contract with the Company to perform the actual logging, splitting, transporting and stacking of the firewood on the Company's property; and, (3) Reference to ten letters of commitment from retail firewood dealers who will purchase a total of 5,000 cords of birch firewood from the Company in August and September, 199- for resale to their customers

Mr. and Mrs. Jones will pledge personal assets to secure the loan of $150,000 and they will make personal loans to the Company as required in years #2 and #3 (Please see the Proforma Cash Flow Statements in this proposal). They prefer to arrange repayment of the $150,000 loan over a three year period at a favorable interest rate.

The Company

Background

Recently, Mr. Robert M. Jones and his wife Mary T. Jones investigated the possibility of logging birch trees in northern Minnesota that could be sold to large firewood retailers in Minnesota, North and South Dakota, Iowa and Nebraska.

They found that permissions could be obtained to harvest up to 50,000 cords per year in Minnesota's federal state and private forest lands. The supply of birch for firewood presently exceeds 10,000,000 (ten million) cords in one small area of federally controlled forest land near Orr, Minnesota alone. See "Exhibit F — Letter from the U. S. Department of Agriculture — Forest Service."

Until the recent development of paper board plants, birch trees were not harvested to any great degree in federal or state forests. There were instead cut and burned or crushed on the forest floor to make room for planting various species of lumber-producing pine trees. It is also known that the life of a birch tree generally does not exceed 40 years and most die long before full maturity. Therefore, the federal and state governments would like these trees harvested in order to produce new stands of pine and to better manage their forest resources for future generations.

In their investigation, Mr. and Mrs. Jones also found that many private owners of large forested tracts in northern Minnesota would welcome the harvest of their birch stands because they would prefer to raise timber producing stands.

Stumpage Charges

The USDA Forest Service charges a "Stumpage Fee" to harvest the birch trees. This Stumpage or Cutting Fee amounts to $1.00 per cord (a cord of wood is 4' wide x 4' high x 8' long). Mr. Jones was also advised by the Forest Service that if he planned to harvest birch, his logging contractors could set up their splitting operations on government land at no charge.

In this event, the birch trees would be felled at selected sites by the Company's logging contractor; cut into 8 foot bolts; skidded out of the forest to an assembly area; stacked temporarily; then cut into firewood lengths of 16 inches and split. The split firewood would then be transported by the contractor to the Company's woodlot located 20 miles north of Virginia, Minnesota — where it would be stacked for drying and eventual sale to retail firewood dealers.

Logging Contractors

Mr. Jones then contacted several logging contractors in northern Minnesota and invited them to bid on harvesting at least 5,000 cords of birch per year for a proposed Company to be called The Birchwood Logging Company, Inc. Several bids were received; however, the most competitive bid was from the Terrance Brothers Logging Company, Virginia, Minnesota. They would fell, cut, split and transport 5,000 cords of birch to the Company's woodlot at a cost of $35 per cord or a total cost of $175,000 and would guarantee this price for up to three years. Please see Exhibit G — "Letter of Intent from Terrance Brothers Logging Company."

Retail Firewood Outlets

Mr. and Mrs. Jones then contacted several large firewood retailers in the aforementioned states to determine their interest in purchasing birch firewood at a wholesale price of $66 per cord FOB the Company's woodlot. Within a few weeks, over fifty letters were received from interested dealers. Forty of these businesses expressed interest in buying but did not make a firm commitment as to the amount they might purchase. Ten firewood retailers did make a commitment totaling 5,000 cords at the "pick-up price" of $66/per cord. See Exhibit E — "Letters of Commitment to Purchase Firewood Inventories." The payment for all purchases would be made at the time of pick-up and would be paid in the form of a cashier's check payable to the Company. The buyers would be responsible for loading the firewood on their trucks, but the Company would provide a portable conveyor system to expedite the loading process.

Organization of the Company

After completing the feasibility study, Mr. and Mrs. Jones decided to organize the Company and incorporated it on August 21, 199- as a Subchapter "S" Corporation in the State of Minnesota. The business was capitalized with 5,000,000 shares of common stock authorized and has 100,000 shares outstanding for which Mr. and Mrs. Jones paid $90,000 in cash as their equity investment.

Proposed Loan

Now that the Company has been organized, a business loan in the amount of $150,000 is required to retain the services of the logging contractor to fell, bolt, split and transport 5,000 cords of birch firewood to the Company's woodlot for drying and subsequent sale.

It is proposed that the loan be made for a period of three years at a favorable interest rate and Mr. and Mrs. Jones are willing to pledge personal assets as collateral security. Please see "Exhibit A — Personal Financial Statement of Robert and Mary Jones", and refer to the proforma balance sheet, profit or loss statements and cash flow forecasts presented with this proposal.

Business of the Company

The Company will not engage in the actual logging, cutting, splitting, stacking, transporting or loading of the firewood to be sold, but will contract this work with logging contractors and operate primarily as a firewood marketing business.

In this event, the logging contractor(s) retained by the Company will be responsible for his/their own operating expenses, insurance, payroll, payroll taxes and employee benefits. The Company, acting as the primary contractor will pay the "Stumpage Fees", when required, in behalf of its subcontractors.

The logging contractor(s) would be paid weekly for the actual firewood felled, cut into bolts, split, transported and stacked at the Company's woodlot. It is anticipated that a single contractor and his crew could produce approximately 1,000 cords of split and stacked firewood per month during the winter season (December through April). However, should it become necessary, logging operations can be conducted year-around.

Once the loan proceeds are received, the Company plans to enter into a contract with Terrance Brothers Logging Company and the tentative date they would begin operations is December 1, 199-. Firewood sales would be conducted during the following August and September (the split firewood would be thoroughly dry and ready for sale). Subsequent sales would be made to the Company's dealers at the same time each year since this is when most dealers require their inventories for the wood burning season.

The Company plans to expand its sales during the first three years of operation as follows:

Year	Cords Harvested	Sales
1st	5,000	$330,000
2nd	6,000	$396,000
3rd	7,000	$462,000

The business will employ Mr. and Mrs. Jones and one part-time woodlot manager during its first year of operation. All accounting services will be contracted with an independent accountant. Business activities will be directed from the Company's offices located at: RR#1, Box 750, Virginia, Minnesota 55201 and its telephone number is (218) 455-3133. The offices are attached to the home of Mr. and Mrs. Jones at their farm located 20 miles north of Virginia. This farm is also the site of the Company's woodlot. See "Property."

Marketing

Since the Company has received written commitments for 5,000 cords of firewood for August/September, 199-, no marketing expenses will be incurred during the first year of operation. Future marketing will consist of contacting large firewood dealers located in the states of Minnesota, North and South Dakota, Iowa and Nebraska. Commitments to purchase firewood are preferred prior to commencing logging operations each year, but the Company may elect to log up to 1,000 additional cords for those retailers who are unwilling to make a purchase commitment prior to the sales season.

The Company has found that the best way to market its firewood is by personal letter and telephone. Since the dealers are generally large firewood retail outlets that purchase hundreds of cords each per year, the Company does not anticipate its marketing expenses to exceed $3,000 a year, even if its production were to increase to 10,000 cords per season.

Competition

Although there are a few logging companies in northern Minnesota that cut trees and resell them as firewood, the Company has found very little competition when it comes to offering birch firewood to large firewood retailers. The Company has been told by its dealers that birch firewood is the most highly prized by their customers and that until the Company contacted them, they were having difficulty in obtaining it in any volume. As the letters in "Exhibit — E" indicate, the Company's dealers are willing to commit to purchasing several hundred cords each and are happy to have a reliable source available.

Birch As A Firewood

According to the *Farmer's Almanac*, the best burning firewoods are birch, oak, maple and cherry. Birch, as most other woods, should be cut during the late fall and winter months, but can be harvested year around. Curing or drying takes about five to six months if the wood is split.

Considered an excellent hardwood, birch is heavy, averaging 43 pounds per cubic foot when green or freshly cut. It has a specific gravity averaging 0.55. Since it is an extremely strong wood that can withstand severe shock, it is used to manufacture veneer, furniture, cross ties, crates and general millwork. It is by far the most popular firewood in America and Canada.

When thoroughly dried, birch requires very little kindling to ignite it because of its paper-like bark. It burns evenly hot and produces a colorful and pleasant smelling fire. If the fire is set properly in a fireplace, very little birch is necessary for a long lasting fire and if the coals are covered with ashes before retiring, they will stay hot throughout the night.

Management

Robert M. Jones, age 52, is the chief executive officer, chief financial officer and a director for the Company and holds 75,000 shares of its Common Stock. Mr. Jones is the owner of The Jones Resort — located on Clear Lake near Virginia, Minnesota and has managed this resort operation since 196-. He also owns a 1,200 acre farm located 20 miles north of Virginia, Minnesota of which 600 acres are share-cropped with another farm family to produce 200,000 Christmas Trees annually. Mr. Jones is a 196- graduate of the University of Minnesota and holds a BA degree in Accounting. He is also the Chairman of the Clear Lake Resort Owner's Association.

Mary T. Jones, age 51, is the secretary and a director for the Company and holds 25,000 shares of its Common Stock. Mrs. Jones has co-managed The Jones Resort for the past ten years and was previously employed from 196- to 198- as a Vice President of the First Savings Bank in Virginia. She is a graduate of the University of Wisconsin at Milwaukee and holds a BS degree in Business Administration.

Both Mr. and Mrs. Jones will devote their full-time efforts to managing the Company and have hired a manager to supervise The Jones Resort and Christmas Tree operations.

The Company intends to hire a part-time manager to supervise the woodlot operation of the business. This person will be employed approximately 20 hours per week throughout the year.

Property

The Company will lease approximately 30 acres of land for its woodlot operation to be located on the farm owned by Mr. and Mrs. Jones. The lease will run for five years (renewable) at a cost of $1,200 per year. The Company's offices are also located on the farm and will be leased from year to year at a cost of $600 per year which includes utilities.

EXHIBIT A
PERSONAL FINANCIAL STATEMENT
OF
ROBERT M. AND MARY T. JONES
AS OF
AUGUST 31, 199-

ASSETS:
Current:
Cash on Hand and in Savings	$ 38,600	
Securities (Savings Bonds)	295,300	
Securities (Stock Equity in The Birchwood Logging Company, Inc.)	90,000	
TOTAL CURRENT ASSETS		$ 423,900

Other Assets:
1,200 Acre Farm (land only — appraised)	290,000	
4 Bedroom Home, 2 Car Garage, Barn, Shed on Farm — appraised)	229,000	
The Jones Resort (appraised)	425,000	
Farm Equipment (fair market value)	31,000	
199- Chev. 4X4 Pickup Truck	19,800	
199- Ford Tempo Sedan	13,200	
199- Chev. Suburban Truck	17,400	
TOTAL OTHER ASSETS		$1,025,400
TOTAL ALL ASSETS		$1,449,300

LIABILITIES:
Current:
Credit Cards	1,300	
Long Term Debt:		
Improvement Loan for The Jones Resort (3 years remaining on 8 year note) First Bank of Virginia, Virginia, MN	52,000	
TOTAL LIABILITIES		$ 53,300
NET WORTH		$1,396,000

ANNUAL GROSS INCOME:
Before Tax Income from The Jones Resort (after Mrs. Jones Salary as Manager)	$ 165,000
Before Tax Income from share-crop of Christmas Trees (Farm Income)	50,000
Mrs. Jones Salary as Manager of The Jones Resort	36,000
TOTAL ANNUAL GROSS INCOME (Tax Returns Attached — 3 Years)	$ 251,000

EXHIBIT B
THE BIRCHWOOD LOGGING COMPANY, INC.
Proforma Profit or (Loss) Statement - FIRST YEAR OF OPERATION - Beginning December 1, 199-

Month	DEC	JAN	FEB	MAR	APR	MAY	JUN	JUL	AUG	SEP	OCT	NOV	TOTAL
Sales	0	0	0	0	0	0	0	0	165000	165000	0	0	330000
Operating Exp's:													
Stumpage Fees	1000	1000	1000	1000	1000	0	0	0	0	0	0	0	5000
Logging Services	35000	35000	35000	35000	35000	0	0	0	0	0	0	0	175000
Rent	150	150	150	150	150	150	150	150	150	150	150	150	1800
Telephone	125	125	125	125	125	125	125	125	125	125	125	125	1500
Office Supplies	150	50	50	50	50	50	50	50	50	50	50	50	700
Office Postage	20	20	20	20	20	20	20	20	20	20	20	20	240
Business Ins.	2000	0	0	0	0	0	0	0	0	0	0	0	2000
Office Printing	1000	0	0	0	0	0	0	0	0	0	0	0	1000
Equip Maint	125	125	125	125	125	125	125	125	125	125	125	125	1500
Payroll	3000	3000	3000	3000	3000	3000	3000	3000	3000	3000	3000	3000	36000
Payroll Taxes	300	300	300	300	300	300	300	300	300	300	300	300	3600
Benefits	300	300	300	300	300	300	300	300	300	300	300	300	3600
Marketing	0	0	0	0	0	0	0	0	0	0	0	0	0
Legal	200	0	0	0	0	0	0	0	0	0	0	0	200
Acctg Service	550	100	100	100	100	100	100	100	100	100	100	100	1650
*Loan Interest	0	1500	1500	1500	1500	1500	1500	1500	1500	1500	1500	1500	16500
Loan Principal	0	0	0	0	0	0	0	0	0	0	0	50000	50000
T. OP EXP's	43920	41670	41670	41670	41670	5670	5670	5670	5670	5670	5670	55670	300290
Profit or (Loss)	-43920	-41670	-41670	-41670	-41670	-5670	-5670	-5670	159330	159330	-5670	-55670	29710
Loan Balance	150000	150000	150000	150000	150000	150000	150000	150000	150000	150000	150000	100000	100000

Notes:
* Loan Interest Estimated at 12.00%
The P & L includes a Loan Principal Payment of $50,000 at the end of the first year.

EXHIBIT B
THE BIRCHWOOD LOGGING COMPANY, INC.
Proforma Profit or (Loss) Statement - SECOND YEAR OF OPERATION

Month	DEC	JAN	FEB	MAR	APR	MAY	JUN	JUL	AUG	SEP	OCT	NOV	TOTAL
Sales	0	0	0	0	0	0	0	0	198000	198000	0	0	396000
Operating Exp's:													
Stumpage Fees	1200	1200	1200	1200	1200	0	0	0	0	0	0	0	6000
Logging Services	42000	42000	42000	42000	42000	0	0	0	0	0	0	0	210000
Rent	150	150	150	150	150	150	150	150	150	150	150	150	1800
Telephone	125	125	125	125	125	125	125	125	125	125	125	125	1500
Office Supplies	150	50	50	50	50	50	50	50	50	50	50	50	700
Office Postage	20	20	20	20	20	20	20	20	20	20	20	20	240
Business Ins.	2500	0	0	0	0	0	0	0	0	0	0	0	2500
Office Printing	0	0	0	0	0	0	0	0	0	0	0	0	0
Equip Maint	0	0	0	0	0	0	0	0	0	0	0	0	0
Payroll	4200	4200	4200	4200	4200	4200	4200	4200	4200	4200	4200	4200	50400
Payroll Taxes	420	420	420	420	420	420	420	420	420	420	420	420	5040
Benefits	350	350	350	350	350	350	350	350	350	350	350	350	4200
Marketing	500	500	500	500	500	0	0	0	0	0	0	0	2500
Legal	0	0	0	0	0	0	0	0	0	0	0	0	0
Acctg Service	100	100	100	100	100	100	100	100	100	100	100	100	1200
*Loan Interest	1000	1000	1000	1000	1000	1000	1000	1000	1000	1000	1000	1000	12000
Loan Principal	0	0	0	0	0	0	0	0	0	0	0	50000	50000
T. OP EXP's	52715	50115	50115	50115	50115	6415	6415	6415	6415	6415	6415	56415	348080
Profit or (Loss)	-52715	-50115	-50115	-50115	-50115	-6415	-6415	-6415	191585	191585	-6415	-56415	47920
Loan Balance	100000	100000	100000	100000	100000	100000	100000	100000	100000	100000	100000	50000	50000

Notes:
* Loan Interest Estimated at 12.00%
The P & L includes a Loan Principal Payment of $50,000 at the end of the second year.

EXHIBIT B
THE BIRCHWOOD LOGGING COMPANY, INC.
Proforma Profit or (Loss) Statement - THIRD YEAR OF OPERATION

Month	DEC	JAN	FEB	MAR	APR	MAY	JUN	JUL	AUG	SEP	OCT	NOV	TOTAL
Sales	0	0	0	0	0	0	0	0	231000	231000	0	0	462000
Operating Exp's:													
Stumpage Fees	1400	1400	1400	1400	1400	0	0	0	0	0	0	0	7000
Logging Services	49000	49000	49000	49000	49000	0	0	0	0	0	0	0	245000
Rent	150	150	150	150	150	150	150	150	150	150	150	150	1800
Telephone	125	125	125	125	125	125	125	125	125	125	125	125	1500
Office Supplies	150	50	50	50	50	50	50	50	50	50	50	50	700
Office Postage	20	20	20	20	20	20	20	20	20	20	20	20	240
Business Ins.	2750	0	0	0	0	0	0	0	0	0	0	0	2750
Office Printing	0	0	0	0	0	0	0	0	0	0	0	0	0
Equip Maint	0	0	0	0	0	0	0	0	0	0	0	0	0
Payroll	4350	4350	4350	4350	4350	4350	4350	4350	4350	4350	4350	4350	52200
Payroll Taxes	435	435	435	435	435	435	435	435	435	435	435	435	5220
Benefits	375	375	375	375	375	375	375	375	375	375	375	375	4500
Marketing	500	500	500	500	500	500	0	0	0	0	0	0	3000
Legal	0	0	0	0	0	0	0	0	0	0	0	0	0
Acctg Service	100	100	100	100	100	100	100	100	100	100	100	100	1200
*Loan Interest	500	500	500	500	500	500	500	500	500	500	500	0	5500
Loan Principal	0	0	0	0	0	0	0	0	0	0	50000	0	50000
T. OP EXP's	59855	57005	57005	57005	57005	6605	6105	6105	6105	6105	56105	5605	380610
Profit or (Loss)	-59855	-57005	-57005	-57005	-57005	-6605	-6105	-6105	224895	224895	-56105	-5605	81390
Loan Balance	50000	50000	50000	50000	50000	50000	50000	50000	50000	50000	0	0	0

Notes:
* Loan Interest Estimated at 12.00%
The P & L includes the final Loan Principal Payment of $50,000 in the 11th month of the third year.

EXHIBIT C
THE BIRCHWOOD LOGGING COMPANY, INC.
Proforma Cash Flow Statement - FIRST YEAR OF OPERATION - Beginning December 1, 199-

Month	DEC	JAN	FEB	MAR	APR	MAY	JUN	JUL	AUG	SEP	OCT	NOV
CASH BAL FWD	90000	196080	154410	112740	71070	29400	23730	18060	12390	171720	331050	325380
Loan	150000	0	0	0	0	0	0	0	0	0	0	0
Sales	0	0	0	0	0	0	0	0	165000	165000	0	0
CASH AVAIL	240000	196080	154410	112740	71070	29400	23730	18060	177390	336720	331050	325380
LESS EXP'S:												
Operations	43920	41670	41670	41670	41670	5670	5670	5670	5670	5670	5670	55670
Earnings Distrib.	0	0	0	0	0	0	0	0	0	0	0	0
T. EXPENSES	43920	41670	41670	41670	41670	5670	5670	5670	5670	5670	5670	55670
CASH BAL	196080	154410	112740	71070	29400	23730	18060	12390	171720	331050	325380	269710

Note: Loan Interest and Principal Payment are included in Operating Expenses. See Profit or (Loss) Statements.

EXHIBIT C
THE BIRCHWOOD LOGGING COMPANY, INC.
Proforma Cash Flow Statement - SECOND YEAR OF OPERATION

Month	DEC	JAN	FEB	MAR	APR	MAY	JUN	JUL	AUG	SEP	OCT	NOV
CASH BAL FWD	269710	187125	137010	86895	36780	36665	30250	23835	17420	209005	350590	344175
Jones Loan	0	0	0	0	50000	0	0	0	0	-50000	0	0
Sales	0	0	0	0	0	0	0	0	198000	198000	0	0
CASH AVAIL	269710	187125	137010	86895	86780	36665	30250	23835	215420	357005	350590	344175
LESS EXP'S:												
Operations	52715	50115	50115	50115	50115	6415	6415	6415	6415	6415	6415	56415
Earnings Distrib.	29870	0	0	0	0	0	0	0	0	0	0	0
T. EXPENSES	82585	50115	50115	50115	50115	6415	6415	6415	6415	6415	6415	56415
CASH BAL	187125	137010	86895	36780	36665	30250	23835	17420	209005	350590	344175	287760

Note: Loan Interest and Principal Payment are included in Operating Expenses. See Profit or (Loss) Statements. A short term loan will be made to the Company by Mr. Jones and be repaid in September.

EXHIBIT C
THE BIRCHWOOD LOGGING COMPANY, INC.
Proforma Cash Flow Statement - THIRD YEAR OF OPERATION

Month	DEC	JAN	FEB	MAR	APR	MAY	JUN	JUL	AUG	SEP	OCT	NOV
CASH BAL FWD	287760	180105	123100	66095	94090	37085	30480	24375	18270	158165	383060	326955
Jones Loan	0	0	0	85000	0	0	0	0	-85000	0	0	0
Sales	0	0	0	0	0	0	0	0	231000	231000	0	0
CASH AVAIL	287760	180105	123100	151095	94090	37085	30480	24375	164270	389165	383060	326955
LESS EXP'S:												
Operations	59855	57005	57005	57005	57005	6605	6105	6105	6105	6105	56105	5605
Earnings Distrib.	47800	0	0	0	0	0	0	0	0	0	0	0
T. EXPENSES	107655	57005	57005	57005	57005	6605	6105	6105	6105	6105	56105	5605
CASH BAL	180105	123100	66095	94090	37085	30480	24375	18270	158165	383060	326955	321350

Note: Loan Interest and Principal Payment are included in Operating Expenses. See Profit or (Loss) Statements. A short term loan will be made to the Company by Mr. Jones and repaid in August.

EXHIBIT D
THE BIRCHWOOD LOGGING COMPANY, INC.
PROFORMA BALANCE SHEETS
THREE YEAR PERIOD

YEAR ENDING	ONE	TWO	THREE
CURRENT ASSETS:			
Cash on Hand	$ 269,710	$ 287,760	$ 321,350
OTHER ASSETS:			
Organizational Expenses	200	200	200
Less Depreciation (5 Yrs.)	(40)	(80)	(120)
TOTAL ASSETS	$ 269,870	$ 287,880	$ 321,430
LIABILITIES AND STOCKHOLDERS' EQUITY:			
LIABILITIES:			
Note Payable to Bank (Balance)	$ 100,000	$ 50,000	$ 0
TOTAL LIABILITIES	$ 100,000	$ 50,000	$ 0
STOCKHOLDERS' EQUITY:			
Common Stock, No Par Value, 5,000,000 Shares Authorized, 100,000 Shares Issued for	$ 90,000	$ 90,000	$ 90,000
Additional Capital Paid In	50,000	100,000	150,000
Earnings Distributed Sub "S" **	29,870	47,800	81,430
TOTAL STOCKHOLDERS' EQUITY	$ 169,870	$ 237,880	$ 321,430
TOTAL LIABILITIES AND STOCKHOLDERS' EQUITY	$ 269,870	$ 287,880	$ 321,430

** Earnings distributed are before taxes.

Appendix F — Bank Or Private Loan Proposal — The Birchwood Logging Company, Inc. 217

EXHIBIT E
LETTERS OF COMMITMENT TO PURCHASE FIREWOOD INVENTORIES

The following dealers have sent the Company letters of commitment and have indicated the quantities of firewood they are willing to purchase in August and September, 199-. All letters are on file at the Company and will be presented to a prospective lender for varification.

CUSTOMER	ADDRESS	QUANTITY ORDERED
FUEL & GO SERVICE STATIONS - MINNESOTA	Minneapolis, MN	750 Cords
WYLER'S FIREWOOD, INC.	Minneapolis, MN	600 Cords
BALES SUPERMARKETS	Minneapolis, MN	500 Cords
CRANDEL WOOD SERVICE	Fargo, ND	500 Cords
FLOYD'S FIREPLACE COMPANY	Sioux Falls, SD	500 Cords
DELMONT FOOD'S INC.	Des Moines, IA	500 Cords
THOMPSON FIREWOOD COMPANY	Omaha, NE	500 Cords
HARRISON BUILDING MATERIALS, INC.	Sioux City, IA	500 Cords
MILLER FIREPLACE COMPANY	St. Paul, MN	350 Cords
BUTLER WOOD PRODUCTS, INC.	Dubuque, IA	300 Cords
TOTAL		5,000 Cords

NOTE: The Company has also received letters from 40 other companies expressing a interest in purchasing birch firewood during the early fall months of next year.

EXHIBIT F
LETTER FROM THE U. S. DEPARTMENT OF AGRICULTURE FOREST SERVICE

July 6, 199-

Mr. Robert M. Jones
RR#1, Box 750
Virginia, MN 55201

Dear Mr. Jones:

In response to our recent conversations regarding the availability of paper birch trees in this area for harvest, the figures shown are for the National Forest land. A very considerable volume is also available from the State Forests and Private Owners in this area of Minnesota.

Our timber management plan data indicates that the following volumes would be available on an annual basis to your proposed company.

District	Pure Birch Stand Sites	Est. Total Volume in Cords
LaCroix	10	25,000 Cords
Aurora	2	60,000 Cords
Virginia	6	100,000 Cords
Isabella	3	35,000 Cords

Please let me know if we can be of further assistance. Our current demand for birch is almost non-existent. The development of a new market for this resource would greatly facilitate forest management in this area. The stumpage charge is $1.00 per cord harvested and we would allow your logger to set up his firewood spliting equipment at the sites.

Sincerely,

David O. McFarland
District Ranger
LaCroix Ranger District

Appendix F — Bank Or Private Loan Proposal — The Birchwood Logging Company, Inc.

EXHIBIT G
LETTER FROM TERRANCE BROTHERS LOGGING COMPANY

July 15, 199-

Mr. Robert M. Jones
RR#1, Box 750
Virginia, MN 55201

Dear Mr. Jones:

Our Company would be happy to furnish your new company with birch firewood and propose the following:

For $35.00 Per Cord — Price Guaranteed for Three Years — Payment on Delivery, we will:

1. Fell the birch trees on parcels of land where you have paid the stumpage fees.

2. Cut the logs into bolts of 8 feet and skid them out of the logging site.

3. Cut the bolts into 16 inch lengths and split the pieces that are 4 inches in diameter or over.

4. Load the split wood on our trucks and transport it to your property near Virginia.

5. Unload the wood and stack it in continuous cords for drying.

We see no problems in logging 5,000 to 10,000 cords each year and could easily increase this volume upon request and at the same price. We would appreciate it if you would secure the proper permissions from the Forest Service for us to set up our equipment at the sites. Once we are finished at a site, we will clean up the area to expedite the Forest Service's planting of pine trees. We could start logging operations, at the sites you select, by December 1, 199-. Please contact me if you have any questions or wish to arrange another meeting.

Sincerely,

Bruce Terrance
General Partner
Terrance Brothers Logging Company
Virginia, Minnesota 55202

Index

Accountant .... viii, 2-3, 11-12
Accounting firm 3
Assets vii
Attorney .... vii-viii, 2-3, 7, 11-12
Audit 3
Auditor 7
Auditor's opinion letter 3, 5, 12

Balance sheet 5, 12
Bank 5
Bank or Private Loan Proposal ... 199-219
Bankruptcy 2
Borrower 2
Business loan .... vii, 11
Business plan 13-14
    Components of 13-14

Cash flow forecast 5
Certified Public Accountant (CPA) firms
.... 3, 12
Collateral .... vii, 2
Consultant 11-12
Co-signer 3

Directors 2

Employees 2
Equity .... vii, 1, 5

Financial statements 2, 5-7, 14
Financing proposal .... vii-viii, 1, 5, 11, 13
    Contents of 5
    Format of 11
Financing sources .... viii, 11

Income statement 5
Initial Public Offering (IPO) 7
Internal status reports 14
Investment capital .... vii, 1, 8, 11
Investor .... vii-viii, 1-3, 5, 8, 11, 13

Lender .... viii, 1, 3, 11
Limited partnership .... vii, 1
Limited Partnership Circular
.... vii, 2, 8, 89-126
    Contents of 8-9
Limited Partnership Offering 1
Loan .... vii, 1

Management 2, 14

Net worth 1

Owners 2, 11

Partnership .... vii, 8
Private Placement Circular
.... vii, viii, 1, 2, 5, 12, 15-51, 127-160
Private Placement Memorandum
    (see Private Placement Circular)
Private Placement Offering
    (see Private Placement Circular)
Proceeds 1
Profit and loss statement 5
Proforma financial statements 5
Public Offering Circular 1, 2, 6, 7, 12
    Contents of 7-8
Public Offering Prospectus
.... vii-viii, 11-12, 53-87, 161-197

Registration statement 6-7
Regulations
    Federal vii
    State vii
Risk 1-2

S corporation 3
Sales forecast 5
Securities and Exchange Commission
(SEC) 1, 6-7, 12

Securities commission/department, state ....vii, 2, 6
Shareholders..2
Sole proprietorship 3
Stock.. vii, 1-2, 5-8
Successful Business Plan, The (book) 14

Tax returns.. 3, 5
The Money Connection: Where and How to Apply for Business Loans and Venture Capital (book)..................................viii, 11

Underwriter (brokerage house) .... viii, 1-3, 6-7, 11
Up-front expenses 7
    Auditing fees 7
    Filing fees 7
    Legal fees..7
    Printing costs 7
    Underwriter's expenses 7

Venture capital ....vii, 1, 11

Notes

Notes

The book that will change for good the way you think about creating a business plan

We were impressed! In our world of business publishing, we sometimes see the unusual. A book so well conceived and well written that it gives you, the reader, value in ways you would never expect.

The Successful Business Plan by Rhonda M. Abrams is a great example. Frankly, it has more of what it *now* takes to get your idea or venture on paper in a way that sells.

More on marketing & sales. Better probe of target market. Tighter industry analysis. A new look at operations. Even a sharp new way for you to get the P&L and balance sheets on paper quickly. So simple it will bring sighs of relief. And there is something else here to make those reading your final plan sit up and take notice. It's the *look* of your plan. The logic of it. The way it presents itself clearly. *The Successful Business Plan* is strong on giving you ways to show your venture at its best. Proven ways. A needed aspect of business planning we found lacking until this book was written.

– *The Editors at Oasis Press, PSI Research*

1 You get expert help
Listen in, as Rhonda M. Abrams interviews some of today's most savvy business owners and venture financers. Bill Walsh, Nancy E. Glaser, Eugene Kleiner and a dozen more. 159 tips from 15 experts reveal what works in business plans, and what doesn't. What they have to say will help you write a plan that responds best to what people are looking for now. Straight talk by those who read business plans — about what should be in yours.

2 Worksheets to make it easy
You know plenty about your business. What you want now is your facts gathered and organized. You want the plan done fast, but complete, decisive. Get all that with the 72 worksheets in this book. They are packed with questions designed to draw out and organize all you know about your venture. The questions cover all the 11 critical plan sections and are clear on what to get and where it goes. You'll have the whole picture in front of you before you start writing the plan itself. No time wasted.

3 Sample plan to guide you
The sample plan is so interesting, you might forget it's there to guide you. Written in the actual wording and style used in plans already read and accepted. Section by section, the sample shows you how to put your facts & figures into a readable, compelling story. The story of your idea. To help present your idea there are specifics on retail, manufacturing, service and in-house corporate plans.

4 Get the binder and software combination
Give your plan a finished look. Use the 12 tabbed dividers to organize your final presentation. Also, a two-page planning checklist keeps you from missing even the smallest point. Extra copies of 28 critical worksheets give you plenty of room to work out details. IBM software includes a text editor program and prompts, as well as information taken directly from the book.

About Rhonda M. Abrams
Educated at both UCLA and Harvard, Ms. Abrams heads a west coast management consulting firm. Her common-sense approach to problem solving has made *The Successful Business Plan* as readable as it is powerful. Over 11 months of writing, two hundred hours of interviews, and Ms. Abrams' years of experience make this new book the best for business planning today.

Her comment? *"No other work propels you as far forward in your enterprise as building your plan of action."*

© 1992 Publishing Services Inc.

YES! Send me: ☐ BINDER ONLY $49.95 OR ☐ BINDER & IBM- COMPATIBLE SOFTWARE $125.95

Name _____ Title _____
Company _____ Phone _____
Street Address _____
City/State/Zip _____

☐ Check payable to PSI Research (With a check, UPS ground shipping is free within the Continental USA)
☐ Charge to My: ☐ VISA ☐ MASTERCARD ☐ AMEX ☐ DISCOVER   RR 4 09 3

Card Number: _____ Expires _____
Name on card: _____ Signature: _____

PSI Research 300 N. Valley Dr. Grants Pass, OR 97526   800-228-2275 FAX: 503-476-1479

Related Resources

Proven tools and ideas to expand your business.
Marketing & Public Relations

Power Marketing

Book

A wealth of basic, how-to marketing information that easily takes a new or experienced business owner through the essentials of marketing and sales strategies, customer database marketing, advertising, public relations, budgeting, and follow-up marketing systems. Written in a friendly tone by a marketing educator, the book features worksheets with step-by-step instructions, a glossary of marketing terms, and a sample marketing plan.

How To Develop & Market Creative Business Ideas

Book

Step-by-step manual guides the inventor through all stages of new product development. Discusses patenting your invention, trademarks, copyrights, and how to construct your prototype. Gives information on financing, distribution, test marketing, and finding licensees. Plus, lists many useful sources for prototype resources, trade shows, funding, and more.

Marketing Your Products and Services Successfully

Book

Helps small businesses understand marketing concepts, then plan and follow through with the actions that will result in increased sales. Covers all aspects from identifying the target market, through market research, establishing pricing, creating a marketing plan, evaluating media alternatives, to launching a campaign. Discusses customer maintenance techniques and international marketing.

Customer Profile and Retrieval (CPR)
Software for IBM-PC & compatibles

Stores details of past activities plus future reminders on customers, clients, contacts, vendors, and employees, then gives instant access to that information when needed. "Tickler" fields keep reminders of dates for recontacts. "Type" fields categorize names for sorting as the user defines. "Other data" fields store information such as purchase and credit history, telephone call records, or interests.

Has massive storage capabilities. Holds up to 255 lines of comments for each name, plus unlimited time and date stamped notes. Features perpetual calendar, and automatic telephone dialing. Built-in word processing and merge gives the ability to pull in the information already keyed into the fields into form or individual letters. Prints mail labels, rotary file cards, and phone directories. *Requires a hard disk, 640K RAM and 80 column display. (Autodial feature requires modem.)*

Cost-Effective Market Analysis

Book

Workbook explains how a small business can conduct its own market research. Shows how to set objectives, determine which techniques to use, create a schedule, and then monitor expenses. Encompasses primary research (trade shows, telephone interviews, mail surveys), plus secondary research (using available information in print).

International Business

Export Now

Book

Prepares a business to enter the export market. Clearly explains the basics, then articulates specific requirements for export licensing, preparation of documents, payment methods, packaging, and shipping. Includes advice on evaluating foreign representatives, planning international marketing strategies, and discovering official U.S. policy for various countries and regions. Lists sources.

EXECARDS®
International Communication Cards

EXECARDS offer unique cards you can send to businesspeople of many nationalities to help build and maintain lasting relationships. One distinguished EXECARD choice is a richly textured and embossed white card of substantial quality that expresses thank you in thirteen languages; Japanese, Russian, French, Chinese, Arabic, German, Swahili, Italian, Polish, Spanish, Hebrew, and Swedish, as well as English. Another handsome option is an ivory card with thank you embossed in Russian and English. To each, you can add a personal note or order a custom printed message. *Please call for more information.*

Now – Find Out How Your Business Can Profit By Being Environmentally Aware

The Business Environmental Handbook

Book

Save your business while you are saving the planet. Here's your chance to learn about the hundreds of ways any business can help secure its future by starting to conserve resources now. This book reveals little-understood but simple techniques for recycling, precycling, and conservation that can save your business money now, and help preserve resources. Also gives tips on "green marketing" to customers.

Give yourself & your business every chance to succeed. Order the business tools you need today. Call 800-228-2275.

Related Resources

Unique cards get you noticed. Books & software save you time.

Business Communications

Proposal Development: How to Respond and Win the Bid

Book

Orchestrates a successful proposal from preliminary planning to clinching the deal. Shows by explanation and example how to: determine what to include; create text, illustrations, tables, exhibits, and appendices; how to format (using either traditional methods or desktop publishing); meet the special requirements of government proposals; set up and follow a schedule.

Write Your Own Business Contracts

Book

Explains the "do's" and "don'ts" of contract writing so any person in business can do the preparatory work in drafting contracts before hiring an attorney for final review. Gives a working knowledge of the various types of business agreements, plus tips on how to prepare for the unexpected.

Complete Book of Business Forms

Book

Over 200 reproducible forms for all types of business needs: personnel, employment, finance, production flow, operations, sales, marketing, order entry, and general administration. Time-saving, uniform, coordinated way to record and locate important business information.

EXECARDS®
Communication Tools

EXECARDS, business-to-business message cards, are an effective vehicle for maintaining personal contacts in this era of rushed, highly-technical communications. A card takes only seconds and a few cents to send, but can memorably tell customers, clients, prospects, or co-workers that their relationship is valued. Many styles and messages to choose from for thanking, acknowledging, inviting, reminding, prospecting, following up, etc. *Please call for complete catalog.*

PlanningTools™
Paper pads, 3-hole punched

Handsome PlanningTools help organize thoughts and record notes, actions, plans, and deadlines, so important information and responsibilities do not get lost or forgotten. Specific PlanningTools organize different needs, such as Calendar Notes, Progress/Activity Record, Project Plan/Record, Week's Priority Planner, Make-A-Month Calendar, and Milestone Chart. *Please call for catalog.*

Customer Profile & Retrieval (CPR)
Software for IBM-PC & compatibles

Easy computer database management program streamlines the process of communicating with clients, customers, vendors, contacts, and employees. While talking to your contact on the phone (or at any time), all notes of past activities and conversations can be viewed instantly, and new notes can be added at that time. *Please see description under "Marketing & Public Relations" section on previous page.*

Business Relocation

Company Relocation Handbook: Making the Right Move

Book

Comprehensive guide to moving a business. Begins with defining objectives for moving and evaluating whether relocating will actually solve more problems than it creates. Worksheets compare prospective locations, using rating scales for physical plant, equipment, personnel, and geographic considerations. Sets up a schedule for dealing with logistics.

Retirement Planning

Retirement & Estate Planning Handbook

Book

Do-it-yourself workbook for setting up a retirement plan that can easily be maintained and followed. Covers establishing net worth, retirement goals, budgets, and a plan for asset acquisition, preservation, and growth. Discusses realistic expectations for Social Security, Medicare, and health care alternatives. Features special sections for business owners.

Mail Order

Mail Order Legal Guide

Book

For companies that use the mail to market their products or services, as well as for mail order businesses, this book clarifies complex regulations so penalties can be avoided. Gives state-by-state legal requirements, plus information on Federal Trade Commission guidelines and rules covering delivery dates, advertising, sales taxes, unfair trade practices, and consumer protection.

Need it tomorrow? In most cases that's possible if you order before noon, PST. Just give us a call at 800-228-2275.

RR 4 09 3

Related Resources

Step-by-step techniques for generating more profit.
Financial Management

Financial Management Techniques for Small Business

Book and software for IBM

Clearly reveals the essential ingredients of sound financial management in detail. By monitoring trends in your financial activities, you will be able to uncover potential problems before they become crises. You'll understand why you can be making a profit and still not have the cash to meet expenses, and you'll learn the steps to change your business' cash behavior to get more return for your effort. Software makes your business' financial picture graphically clear, and lets you look at "what if" scenarios.

Risk Analysis: How to Reduce Insurance Costs

Book

Straightforward advice on shopping for insurance, understanding types of coverage, comparing proposals and premium rates. Worksheets help identify and weigh the risks a particular business is likely to face, then determine if any of those might be safely self-insured or eliminated. Request for proposal form helps businesses avoid over-paying for protection.

Debt Collection: Strategies for the Small Business

Book

Practical tips on how to turn receivables into cash. Worksheets and checklists help businesses establish credit policies, track accounts, and flag when it is necessary to bring in a collection agency, attorney, or go to court. This book advises how to deal with disputes, negotiate settlements, win in small claims court, and collect on judgments. Gives examples of telephone collection techniques and collection letters.

Negotiating the Purchase or Sale of a Business

Book

Prepares a business buyer or seller for negotiations that will achieve win-win results. Shows how to determine the real worth of a business, including intangible assets such as "goodwill." Over 36 checklists and worksheets on topics such as tax impact on buyers and sellers, escrow checklist, cash flow projections, evaluating potential buyers, financing options, and many others.

Business Owner's Guide to Accounting & Bookkeeping

Book

Makes understanding the economics of business simple. Explains the basic accounting principles that relate to any business. Step-by-step instructions for generating accounting statements and interpreting them, spotting errors, and recognizing warning signs. Discusses how banks and other creditors view financial statements.

Controlling Your Company's Freight Costs

Book

Shows how to increase company profits by trimming freight costs. Provides tips for comparing alternative methods and shippers, then negotiating contracts to receive the most favorable discounts. Tells how to package shipments for safe transport. Discusses freight insurance and dealing with claims for loss or damage. Appendices include directory of U.S. ports, shipper's guide, and sample bill of lading.

Accounting Software Analysis

Book

Presents successful step-by-step procedure for choosing the most appropriate software to handle the accounting for your business. Evaluation forms and worksheets create a custom software "shopping list" to match against features of various products, so facts, not sales hype, can determine the best fit for your company.

Financial Templates
Software for IBM-PC & Macintosh

Calculates and graphs many business "what-if" scenarios and financial reports. Forty financial templates such as income statements, cash flow, and balance sheet comparisons, break-even analyses, product contribution comparisons, market share, net present value, sales model, *pro formas*, loan payment projections, etc. Requires 512K RAM hard disk or two floppy drives, plus Lotus 1-2-3 or compatible spreadsheet program.

Yes, we accept credit cards — VISA, MasterCard, American Express, Discover, or your personal or business check.

Related Resources

Get business tips from over 157 seasoned experts.

Business Formation and Planning

The Successful Business Plan: Secrets & Strategies

Book and optional kit

Start-to-finish guide to creating a successful business plan. Includes tips from venture capitalists, bankers, and successful CEOs. Features worksheets for ease in planning and budgeting with the Abrams Method of Flow-Through Financials. Gives a sample business plan, plus specialized help for retailers, service companies, manufacturers, and in-house corporate plans. Also tells how to find funding sources.

Starting and Operating a Business in... series
Book available for each state in the United States, plus District of Columbia

One-stop resource to current federal and state laws and regulations that affect businesses. Clear "human language" explanations of complex issues, plus samples of government forms, and sources for additional help or information. Helps seasoned business owners keep up with changing legislation, and guides new entrepreneurs step-by-step to start and run the business. Includes many checklists and worksheets to organize ideas, create action plans, and project financial scenarios.

Starting and Operating a Business: U.S. Edition
Set of eleven binders

The complete encyclopedia of how to do business in the U.S. Describes laws and regulations for each state, plus Washington, D.C., as well as the federal government. Includes lists of sources of help, plus post cards for requesting materials from government agencies. This set is valuable for businesses with locations or marketing activities in several states, plus franchisors, attorneys, and other consultants.

The Essential Corporation Handbook

Book

This comprehensive reference for small business corporations in all 50 states and Washington, D.C. explains the legal requirements for maintaining a corporation in good standing. Features many sample corporate documents which are annotated by the author to show what to look for and what to look out for. Tells how to avoid personal liability as an officer, director, or shareholder.

Surviving and Prospering in a Business Partnership

Book

From evaluation of potential partners, through the drafting of agreements, to day-to-day management of working relationships, this book helps avoid classic partnership catastrophes. Discusses how to set up the partnership to reduce the financial and emotional consequences of unanticipated disputes, dishonesty, divorce, disability, or death of a partner.

California Corporation Formation Package and Minute Book

Book and software for IBM & Mac

Provides forms required for incorporating and maintaining closely held corporations, including: articles of incorporation; bylaws; stock certificates, stock transfer record sheets, bill of sale agreement; minutes form; plus many others. Addresses questions on fees, timing, notices, regulations, election of directors and other critical factors. Software has minutes, bylaws, and articles of incorporation already for you to edit and customize (using your own word processor).

Franchise Bible: A Comprehensive Guide

Book

Complete guide to franchising for prospective franchisees or for business owners considering franchising their business. Includes actual sample documents, such as a complete offering circular, plus worksheets for evaluating franchise companies, locations, and organizing information before seeing an attorney. This book is helpful for lawyers as well as their clients.

Home Business Made Easy

Book

Thinking of starting a business at home? This book is the easiest road to starting a home business. Shows you how to select and start a home business that fits your interests, lifestyle, and pocketbook. Walks you through 153 different businesses you could operate from home full or part time. Author David Hanania has boiled the process down to simple steps so you can get started now to realize your dreams.

The Small Business Expert
Software for IBM-PC & compatibles

Generates comprehensive custom checklist of the state and federal laws and regulations based on your type and size of business. Allows comparison of doing business in each of the 50 states. Built-in worksheets create outlines for personnel policies, marketing feasibility studies, and a business plan draft. *Requires 256K RAM and hard disk.*

To order these business tools, use the enclosed order form, FAX 503-476-1479 or call us toll-free at 800-228-2275

Related Resources

Gain the power of increased knowledge — Oasis is your source.

Acquiring Outside Capital

Financing Your Small Business

Book

Essential techniques to successfully identify, approach, attract, and manage sources of financing. Shows how to gain the full benefits of debt financing while minimizing its risks. Outlines all types of financing and walks you step by step through the process, from evaluating short-term credit options, through negotiating a long-term loan, to deciding whether to go public.

The Loan Package

Book

Preparatory package for a business loan proposal. Worksheets help analyze cash needs and articulate business focus. Includes sample forms for balance sheets, income statements, projections, and budget reports. Screening sheets rank potential lenders to shorten the time involved in getting the loan.

The Successful Business Plan: Secrets & Strategies
Book and software for IBM-PC

Now you can find out what venture capitalists and bankers really want to see before they will fund a company. This book gives you their personal tips and insights. The Abrams Method of Flow-Through Financials breaks down the chore into easy to manage steps, so you can end up with a fundable proposal. Requires a hard drive.

Financial Templates
Software for IBM-PC & Macintosh

Software speeds business calculations including those in PSI's workbooks, *The Loan Package, Venture Capital Proposal Package, Negotiating the Purchase or Sale of a Business, The Successful Business Plan: Secrets & Strategies*. Includes 40 financial templates including various projections, statements, ratios, histories, amortizations, and cash flows. *Requires Lotus 1-2-3, Microsoft Excel 2.0 or higher*

Business Planning System
Software for IBM-PC

Complete your business plan quickly and easily using this StandAlone program. Enjoy the flexibility of writing segments of the plan as you collect the information or as time allows. Examples of wording are included. Questions lead you through the development process.

Managing Employees

A Company Policy and Personnel Workbook

Book

Saves costly consultant or staff hours in creating company personnel policies. Provides model policies on topics such as employee safety, leave of absence, flextime, smoking, substance abuse, sexual harassment, performance improvement, grievance procedure. For each subject, practical and legal ramifications are explained, then a choice of alternate policies presented.

A Company Policy and Personnel Workbook
Software for IBM-PC & Macintosh

The policies in *A Company Policy and Personnel Workbook* are on disk so the company's name, specific information, and any desired changes or rewrites can be incorporated using your own word processor to tailor the model policies to suit your company's specific needs before printing out a complete manual for distribution to employees. *Requires a word processor and hard disk and floppy drive.*

Managing People: A Practical Guide

Book

Focuses on developing the art of working with people to maximize the productivity and satisfaction of both manager and employees. Discussions, exercises, and self-tests boost skills in communicating, delegating, motivating, developing teams, goal-setting, adapting to change, and coping with stress.

Safety Law Compliance Manual for California Businesses

Book

Now every California employer must have an Injury and Illness Prevention Program that meets the specific requirements of Senate Bill 198. Already, thousands of citations have been issued to companies who did not comply with all seven components of the complicated new law. Avoid fines by using this guide to set up a program that will meet Cal/OSHA standards. Includes forms.

Plus optional binder for your company's safety program
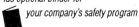

Also available — Company Injury and Illness Prevention Program Binder — Pre-organized and ready-to-use with forms, tabs, logs and sample documents. Saves your company time, work, and worry.

People Investment

Book

Written for the business owner or manager who is not a personnel specialist. Explains what you must know to make your hiring decisions pay off for everyone. Learn more about the Americans With Disabilities Act (ADA), Medical and Family Leave, and more.

Why hesitate? If any product you order doesn't meet your needs, just return it for full refund or credit. 800-228-2275.

PSI Successful Business Library / Tools for Business Success Order Form (Please fill out other side also)

BOOKS FROM THE OASIS PRESS® Please check the edition (binder or paperback) of your choice

TITLE	BINDER	PAPERBACK	QUANTITY	COST
The Business Environmental Handbook		☐ $19.95		
Business Owner's Guide to Accounting & Bookkeeping		☐ $19.95		
California Corporation Formation Package and Minute Book	☐ $39.95	☐ $29.95		
A Company Policy and Personnel Workbook	☐ $49.95	☐ $29.95		
Company Relocation Handbook	☐ $49.95	☐ $19.95		
Complete Book of Business Forms	☐ $49.95	☐ $19.95		
Controlling Your Company's Freight Costs	☐ $39.95			
Cost-Effective Market Analysis	☐ $39.95			
Debt Collection: Strategies for the Small Business	☐ $39.95	☐ $17.95		
The Essential Corporation Handbook		☐ $19.95		
Export Now	☐ $39.95	☐ $19.95		
Financial Management Techniques For Small Business	☐ $39.95	☐ $19.95		
Financing Your Small Business		☐ $19.95		
Franchise Bible: A Comprehensive Guide	☐ $49.95	☐ $19.95		
Home Business Made Easy		☐ $19.95		
How to Develop & Market Creative Business Ideas		☐ $14.95		
The Loan Package	☐ $39.95			
Mail Order Legal Guide	☐ $45.00	☐ $29.95		
Managing People: A Practical Guide	☐ $49.95	☐ $19.95		
Marketing Your Products and Services Successfully	☐ $39.95	☐ $18.95		
People Investment	☐ $39.95	☐ $19.95		
Power Marketing for Small Business	☐ $39.95	☐ $19.95		
Proposal Development: How to Respond and Win the Bid (HARDBACK BOOK)	☐ $39.95	☐ $19.95		
Retirement & Estate Planning Handbook	☐ $49.95	☐ $19.95		
Safety Law Compliance Manual for California Businesses		☐ $24.95		
Company Illness & Injury Prevention Program Binder (OR GET KIT WITH BOOK AND BINDER $49.95)	☐ $34.95	☐ $49.95		
Starting and Operating A Business in... BOOK INCLUDES FEDERAL SECTION PLUS ONE STATE SECTION —	☐ $29.95	☐ $21.95		
PLEASE SPECIFY WHICH STATE(S) YOU WANT:				
STATE SECTION ONLY (BINDER NOT INCLUDED) — SPECIFY STATES:	☐ $ 8.95		BOOK & BINDER KIT	
U.S. EDITION (FEDERAL SECTION — 50 STATES AND WASHINGTON, D.C. IN 11-BINDER SET)	☐ $295.00			
Successful Business Plan: Secrets & Strategies (GET THE BINDER...IT'S A BUSINESS PLAN KIT)	☐ $49.95	☐ $21.95		
Surviving and Prospering in a Business Partnership	☐ $39.95	☐ $19.95		
Write Your Own Business Contracts (HARDBACK BOOK)	☐ $39.95	☐ $19.95		

BOOK TOTAL (Please enter on other side also for grand total)

SOFTWARE Please check whether you use Macintosh or 5-1/4" or 3-1/2" Disk for IBM-PC & Compatibles

TITLE	5-1/4" IBM Disk	3-1/2" IBM Disk	MAC	PRICE	QUANTITY	COST
Business Planning System	☐	☐		☐ $129.95		
California Corporation Formation Package Software	☐	☐	☐	☐ $ 39.95		
★ California Corporation Formation Binderbook & Software	☐	☐	☐	☐ $ 69.95		
Company Policy & Personnel Software (Text Files)	☐	☐	☐	☐ $ 49.95		
★ Company Policy & Personnel Binderbook & Software (Text Files)	☐	☐	☐	☐ $ 89.95		
Customer Profile & Retrieval: Professional	☐	☐		☐ $119.95		
Financial Management Techniques		☐		☐ $ 99.95		
★ Financial Management Techniques Binderbook & Software		☐		☐ $129.95		
Financial Templates	☐	☐	☐	☐ $ 69.95		
The Small Business Expert	☐	☐		☐ $ 34.95		
Successful Business Plan (Full Standalone)	☐	☐		☐ $ 99.95		
★ Successful Business Plan Binderbook & Software (Full Standalone)	☐	☐		☐ $125.95		

SOFTWARE TOTAL (Please enter on other side also for grand total)

Please add above totals on other side to complete your order. Thanks!

Order Form Code: RR 4 09 3

PSI Successful Business Library / Tools for Business Success Order Form (please see other side also)
Call, Mail or Fax to: PSI Research, 300 North Valley Drive, Grants Pass, OR 97526 USA
Order Phone USA (800) 228-2275   Inquiries and International Orders (503) 479-9464   FAX (503) 476-1479

Sold to: PLEASE GIVE STREET ADDRESS NOT P.O. BOX FOR SHIPPING

Name _____ Title: _____

Company _____ Daytime Telephone: _____

Street Address _____

City/State/Zip _____

❑ **YES, I want to receive the PREMIERE ISSUE of the PSI 1993 NEWSLETTER.**
   Be sure to include: Name, address, and telephone number above.

Ship to: (if different)   PLEASE GIVE STREET ADDRESS NOT P.O. BOX FOR SHIPPING

Name _____

Title _____

Company _____

Street Address _____

City/State/Zip _____

Daytime Telephone _____

Payment Information:

☐ Check enclosed payable to PSI Research (When you enclose a check, UPS ground shipping is free within the Continental U.S.A.)

Charge - ☐ VISA ☐ MASTERCARD ☐ AMEX ☐ DISCOVER   Card Number: _____ Expires ____

Signature: _____   Name on card: _____

EXECARDS — The Proven & Chosen Method of Personal Business Communications

ITEM	PRICE EACH	QUANTITY	COST
EXECARDS Thank You Assortment (12 assorted thank you cards)	$ 12.95		
EXECARDS Recognition Assortment (12 assorted appreciation cards)	$ 12.95		
EXECARDS Marketing Assortment (12 assorted marketing cards)	$ 12.95		
EXECARDS TOTAL (Please enter below also for grand total)			$

Many additional options available, including custom imprinting of your company's name, logo or message. Please request a complete catalog.

PLANNING TOOLS — Action Tracking Note Pads

ITEM		NUMBER OF PADS
Calendar Note Pad	☐ 1993	
	☐ 93/94	
	☐ 1994	
Total number of pads		
Multiply by unit price:		x
PLANNING TOOLS TOTAL		$

UNIT PRICE FOR ANY COMBINATION OF PLANNING TOOLS
1-9 pads $3.95 each
10-49 pads $3.49 each
50 or more pads $2.98 each

SAFETY PROGRAM FORMS

ITEM	PRICE EACH	QUANTITY
Employee Warning Notification (Package of 20)	$4.95	
Request for Safety Orientation (Package of 20)	$4.95	
Report of Potential Hazard (Package of 20)	$4.95	
SAFETY PROGRAM FORMS TOTAL	$	

YOUR GRAND TOTAL

BOOK TOTAL (from other side)	$
SOFTWARE TOTAL (from other side)	$
EXECARDS TOTAL	$
PLANNING TOOLS TOTAL	$
SAFETY PROGRAM FORMS TOTAL	$
TOTAL ORDER	$

Rush service is available. Please call us for details.

Please send me:

_____ **EXECARDS Catalog**

_____ **Oasis Press Software Information**

_____ **Oasis Press Book Information**

Order Form Code: RR 4 09 3

Use this form to register for advance notification of updates, new books and software releases, plus special customer discounts!

Please answer these questions to let us know how our products are working for you, and what we could do to serve you better.

Title of book or software purchased from us: _____

It is a:
- ☐ Binder book
- ☐ Paperback book
- ☐ Book/software combination
- ☐ Software only

Rate this product's overall quality of information:
- ☐ Excellent
- ☐ Good
- ☐ Fair
- ☐ Poor

Rate the quality of printed materials:
- ☐ Excellent
- ☐ Good
- ☐ Fair
- ☐ Poor

Rate the format:
- ☐ Excellent
- ☐ Good
- ☐ Fair
- ☐ Poor

Did the product provide what you needed?
- ☐ Yes ☐ No

If not, what should be added? _____
_____
_____
_____

This product is:
- ☐ Clear and easy to follow
- ☐ Too complicated
- ☐ Too elementary

Were the worksheets (if any) easy to use?
- ☐ Yes ☐ No ☐ N/A

Should we include:
- ☐ More worksheets
- ☐ Fewer worksheets
- ☐ No worksheets

How do you feel about the price?
- ☐ Lower than expected
- ☐ About right
- ☐ Too expensive

How many employees are in your company?
- ☐ Under 10 employees
- ☐ 10 – 50 employees
- ☐ 51 – 99 employees
- ☐ 100 – 250 employees
- ☐ Over 250 employees

How many people in the city your company is in?
- ☐ 50,000 – 100,000
- ☐ 100,000 – 500,000
- ☐ 500,000 – 1,000,000
- ☐ Over 1,000,000
- ☐ Rural (under 50,000)

What is your type of business?
- ☐ Retail
- ☐ Service
- ☐ Government
- ☐ Manufacturing
- ☐ Distributor
- ☐ Education

What types of products or services do you sell?
_____
_____
_____

What is your position in the company?
(please check one)
- ☐ Owner
- ☐ Administration
- ☐ Sales/marketing
- ☐ Finance
- ☐ Human resources
- ☐ Production
- ☐ Operations
- ☐ Computer/MIS

How did you learn about this product?
- ☐ Recommended by a friend
- ☐ Used in a seminar or class
- ☐ Have used other PSI products
- ☐ Received a mailing
- ☐ Saw in bookstore
- ☐ Saw in library
- ☐ Saw review in:
  - ☐ Newspaper
  - ☐ Magazine
  - ☐ TV/Radio

Where did you buy this product?
- ☐ Catalog
- ☐ Bookstore
- ☐ Office supply
- ☐ Consultant
- ☐ Other _____

Would you purchase other business tools from us?
- ☐ Yes ☐ No

If so, which products interest you?
- ☐ EXECARDS® Communication Tools
- ☐ Books for business
- ☐ Software

Would you recommend this product to a friend?
- ☐ Yes ☐ No

If you'd like us to send associates or friends a catalog, just list names and addresses on back.

Do you use a personal computer for business?
- ☐ Yes ☐ No

If yes, which?
- ☐ IBM/compatible
- ☐ Macintosh

Check all the ways you use computers:
- ☐ Word processing
- ☐ Accounting
- ☐ Spreadsheet
- ☐ Inventory
- ☐ Order processing
- ☐ Design/graphics
- ☐ General data base
- ☐ Customer information
- ☐ Scheduling

May we call you to follow up on your comments?
- ☐ Yes ☐ No

May we add your name to our mailing list?
- ☐ Yes ☐ No

If there is anything you think we should do to improve this product, please describe: _____
_____
_____
_____

Thank you for your patience in answering the above questions.
Just fill in your name and address here, fold (see back) and mail.

Name _____
Title _____
Company _____
Phone _____
Address _____
City/State/Zip _____

PSI Research creates this family of fine products to help you more easily and effectively manage your business activities:

The Oasis Press®
PSI Successful Business Library
PSI Successful Business Software
EXECARDS® Communication Tools

If you have friends or associates who might appreciate receiving our catalogs, please list here. Thanks!

Name_____ Name_____
Title_____ Title_____
Company_____ Company_____
Phone_____ Phone_____
Address_____ Address_____
City/State/Zip_____ City/State/Zip_____

FOLD HERE FIRST

BUSINESS REPLY MAIL
FIRST CLASS MAIL PERMIT NO. 002 MERLIN, OREGON

POSTAGE WILL BE PAID BY ADDRESSEE

PSI Research
PO BOX 1414
Merlin OR 97532-9900

NO POSTAGE
NECESSARY
IF MAILED
IN THE
UNITED STATES

FOLD HERE SECOND, THEN TAPE TOGETHER

✂
Please cut
along this
vertical line,
fold twice,
tape together
and mail.
Thanks!